MW00639986

George Washington's
LONG ISLAND SPY RING

George Washington's
LONG ISLAND SPY RING

A History and Tour Guide

BILL BLEYER

Photographs by Audrey C. Tiernan

THE
History
PRESS

Published by The History Press
Charleston, SC
www.historypress.com

Copyright © 2021 by Bill Bleyer
All rights reserved

Front cover, top: "Evacuation day and Washington's triumphal entry in New York City, Nov. 25th, 1783" by lithographer Edmund P. Restein. Library of Congress. *Bottom*: Robert Townsend, the chief Culper spy in New York City, in a painting by Long Island historical artist Mort Künstler. Courtesy of Künstler Enterprises, Ltd., from the original painting *The Culper Spy* by Mort Künstler © 2013 Mort Künstler Inc., www.mkunstler.com.

First published 2021

Manufactured in the United States

ISBN 9781467143479

Library of Congress Control Number: 2021931181

Notice: The information in this book is true and complete to the best of our knowledge. It is offered without guarantee on the part of the author or The History Press. The author and The History Press disclaim all liability in connection with the use of this book.

All rights reserved. No part of this book may be reproduced or transmitted in any form whatsoever without prior written permission from the publisher except in the case of brief quotations embodied in critical articles and reviews.

To Beverly Tyler and Claire Bellerjeau, dedicated local historians without whose help and expertise on the Culper Spy Ring this book would have been impossible.

CONTENTS

CONTENTS

ACKNOWLEDGMENTS

Beverly Tyler of the Three Village Historical Society; Claire Bellerjeau and Harriet Gerard Clark of the Raynham Hall Museum; Natalie Naylor; former North Hempstead town historian Howard Kroplick; Southold town historian Amy Folk; Gloria Rocchio and Marie Gilberti of the Ward Melville Heritage Organization; former Cutchogue–New Suffolk Historical Council director Zach Studenroth; Islip town historian George Munkenbeck; Brookhaven town historian Barbara Russell; Huntington town historian Robert Hughes; Southampton town historian Julie Greene; Babylon town historian Mary Cascone; Maryanne Douglas, Millie Zimmerman and Suzanne Johnson of the Davis Town Meeting House Society; Mike Fricchione; Richard Wines; Suffolk County director of historic services Richard C. Martin; Sagtikos Manor Historical Society president Christeen Gottsch; 1 in 9 at Hewlett House director Geri Barish; Matthew Blum at Rock Hall Museum; Kim Barteau, Barbara Compono and Karen Liotta at the Bayville Public Library; Mort and Jane Künstler; artist Mark Maritato; Bert Seides of the Ketcham Inn Foundation; Richard Welch; Oyster Bay town historian John Hammond; and John Staudt.

Audrey C. Tiernan for her superb photographs of surviving sites.

My volunteer editor/proofreaders for the entire manuscript—Claire Bellerjeau, Joe Catalano (who read it twice), Joan Bleyer Lazarus, Beverly Tyler, Richard Welch, and especially Natalie Naylor—or for select chapters, John Hammond and John Staudt.

ACKNOWLEDGMENTS

My editors at The History Press: Banks Smither and Abigail Fleming.
And special thanks to former Congressman Steve Israel for suggesting I do a book about Long Island's George Washington Spy Trail.

INTRODUCTION

A courier meets clandestinely with a merchant in Manhattan. He's given a report on British troop dispositions written in invisible ink. He hides the document in his saddle, takes a ferry across the East River and then speeds fifty-five miles east to Setauket. There the letter is handed off to a farmer who passes it to a whaleboat captain waiting in a secluded cove. The document is rowed across Long Island Sound and carried by a relay of dispatch riders to General George Washington's headquarters north of New York City, where it guides the Continental Army's commander in chief in planning his moves.

That ongoing Revolutionary War scenario may not be as famous or compelling as the one-time ride of Paul Revere and his two Boston compatriots to warn their fellow Patriots of the coming of the redcoats to Lexington and Concord. But it is one of the most critical activities of the American Revolution because the efforts of what has become known as the Culper Spy Ring played an important role in winning independence from Great Britain.

The Patriot commander knew that gaining intelligence of British military actions through a spy network was critical if his underdog army was to have a chance of successfully fighting the largest military power in the world for the colonies' independence. So when the British gained control of New York City and Long Island after the Battle of Long Island in 1776, Washington began a long and difficult process of creating an espionage operation in the region.

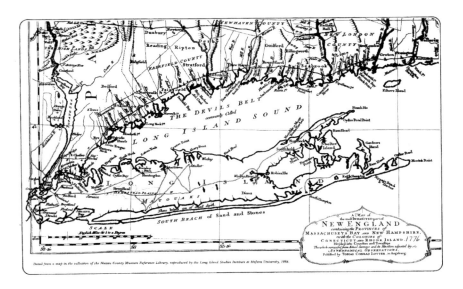

A 1776 map of Long Island. *Long Island Studies Institute at Hofstra University.*

Historians have long been fascinated by the intelligence efforts undertaken by the patriotic and enthusiastic amateurs. In more than a dozen books, researchers have tried to sort out who was involved and exactly what their roles were. The biggest mystery was the identity of Culper Junior, the chief spy in Manhattan in the later years of the war. Most of the spy ring operatives identified themselves or were identified after the war, but not Culper Junior. So when Suffolk County historian Morton Pennypacker revealed him to have been Robert Townsend of Oyster Bay in 1930 and then proved it with document analysis nine years later, it generated considerable attention.

Interest in the Patriots' intelligence network soared when the AMC television series *Turn: Washington's Spies* aired for four seasons between 2014 and 2017. Unfortunately, it took great liberties with the facts. These included having the ring created in 1776 rather than two years later, depicting Setauket as a neighborhood of stately stone homes rather than wooden structures, having the hamlet occupied by regular army redcoats rather than Loyalist troops wearing green, portraying Abraham Woodhull's minister father as a Tory socializing with the occupiers rather than showing the reality of him being a Patriot sympathizer badly beaten by soldiers trying to find and arrest his son and, most ludicrously, having Woodhull and the happily married and older Anna Strong engage in a secret affair. But the series did get people reading and talking about espionage during the war.

As with *Turn*, Pennypacker and many of the authors who have written about the Culper Ring subsequently have strayed from the truth. Pennypacker's books, which lack footnotes, transformed some anecdotal information and legends into fact. And later writers have often repeated that material without researching or even questioning it. And while they may have sought information from Long Island historians who have spent decades studying the subject, they didn't always listen to them.

The most prominent writer in that category would be Fox News co-host Brian Kilmeade, who lives on Long Island. In preparing his 2013 bestseller with coauthor Don Yaeger and other writers, he convened gatherings of local historians from Culper-connected locations such as Setauket and Oyster Bay. They provided him with much information, some of which he ignored when it didn't fit into his narrative. He also strayed into historical fiction by filling the book with invented dialogue without indicating that the words were never spoken by the participants.

Kilmeade's work is also filled with supposed statements of fact that can be disputed. These start with the title and subtitle of the book: *George Washington's Secret Six: The Spy Ring That Saved the American Revolution.* In a volume lacking footnotes and offering only a smattering of sources, the authors state that the spy ring consisted of exactly six individuals. Many more than that played roles in the operation, including couriers and boat captain Caleb Brewster. He played a critical role in carrying the messages across Long Island Sound to get them to George Washington's headquarters. Without Brewster there is no Culper Spy Ring. They have Robert Townsend playing the central role. While he was certainly important and the main source of information from New York City in the later years, the chief spy who coordinated the espionage throughout the war was Abraham Woodhull of Setauket. Without him, the spy ring never would have been created.

Furthermore, Kilmeade and Yeager include two individuals among their chosen six who are questionable: James Rivington and a mysterious woman named as only "Agent 355." Local historians have concluded that Rivington, publisher of a Loyalist newspaper in Manhattan, is unlikely to have served as a spy and was definitely not part of the Culper Ring. They, and other historians, believe there was no Agent 355, as discussed in chapter 5. And while other historians generally agree the Culper network played an important role, no one else goes as far as to say that it "saved the

American Revolution." Their contention that the spy ring "broke the back of the British military" is hyperbole.[1]

This volume attempts to synthesize the known information on the spy ring while sorting fact from historical fiction, which makes it unique. I'm hoping readers will care about the nuances of where and how Nathan Hale was captured, for example. I wanted to create the definitive account of the spy ring with the help of the local experts who are often overlooked or ignored and set the record straight on stories such as Anna Strong using her clothesline to signal where Caleb Brewster would be coming to pick up and drop off letters as a service to researchers and history buffs.

Now it will be up to the readers to make up their own minds.

Those readers will notice in the following chapters variant spellings of some words, especially place names, in quotations from the letters. In the late eighteenth century, spelling was not yet standardized. In all of the Culper letters cited, irregular spellings have not been corrected, and no editorial [*sic*] has been added for misspelled words. Only when abbreviations or misspellings make it difficult to understand what is written will the corrected spelling be inserted in brackets. Capitalization and punctuation also follow the original cited source.

PART I

THE CULPER SPY RING

THE BATTLE OF LONG ISLAND

In early June 1776, several British warships appeared off Sandy Hook at the entrance of New York Harbor. General George Washington and his officers suspected an attack on New York was imminent. But they never did anything to fortify either side of the Narrows between Brooklyn and Staten Island to keep the British out of the Upper Bay and away from Manhattan.

As a result, when the rest of the British fleet began to arrive on June 29, there was nothing to stop them. And by the following day, the entire fleet had arrived from Halifax, Nova Scotia, and was gathered in the Lower Bay south of the Narrows. One observer wrote that it looked like "something resembling a wood of pine trees."[2]

On July 2—the day that the delegates at the Continental Congress in Philadelphia would vote to declare independence—the British ships began sailing up through the Narrows. By 9:00 p.m., the redcoats had landed unopposed on Staten Island, where they were welcomed by the mostly Loyalist residents and the local militia.[3]

More reinforcements would follow until General William Howe had 24,000 soldiers—including 7,800 mercenaries from Hesse (Hessians)—at his command, along with nearly 400 transport ships and smaller landing craft built on Staten Island to move the troops to Long Island. The warships, manned by 10,000 sailors, were commanded by General Howe's brother, Lord Richard Howe. It was not only the largest and best-equipped expeditionary force ever mounted by the British but also the largest invasion force ever assembled anywhere before D-Day in 1944. "The whole Bay was full of the shipping as ever it could be," wrote Continental Army private Daniel McCartin.[4]

Howe's initial plan was to trap and destroy the Continental Army in a single decisive battle. But the general changed his mind, deciding to force Washington and his troops out of western Long Island and New York City so he could easily take control of the whole region. Subordinates Henry Clinton and William Tryon urged Howe to land north of the city on Manhattan Island to cut off the Patriots from the mainland, but Howe decided to land on Long Island instead.[5]

Howe changed his strategy because western Long Island was Loyalist territory that could supply his army with provisions and timber instead of having to rely on a supply chain that spanned the ocean. The commanding general also reasoned that attacking Manhattan while ignoring Brooklyn could leave his troops subject to fire from batteries in Brooklyn Heights.[6]

New York was clearly undefendable without huge forts at its gateways or overwhelming sea power, and the Patriots had neither. But giving up the city without a fight was politically impossible and would have struck a serious blow to colonists' morale. Congress strongly instructed the army commander to defend New York. So Washington established a line of fortifications across northwest Brooklyn. At Brooklyn Heights, a line of forts, redoubts and trenches ran one and a half miles from Wallabout Bay—now the site of the Brooklyn Navy Yard—on the north to Gowanus Bay on the south. Several miles southeast of Brooklyn Heights, at the current site of Green-Wood Cemetery, the Continental Army occupied a thickly forested ridge—the terminal moraine left behind by glaciers as high as 190 feet above sea level and called the Heights of Guan, or Gowanus.[7]

The Patriots' fortifications in Brooklyn Heights were initially oriented to protect against an attack from the East River. But eventually, Washington and his generals realized they were vulnerable to attack from the south as well, from the interior of Kings County. Southeast of Brooklyn Heights, newly promoted Major General Nathanael Greene ordered his four thousand men to work on a new chain of forts and trenches that would extend a mile and a half to protect the rear or southern side of the Brooklyn Heights fortifications. Each of the five redoubts was surrounded by a wide ditch, and the breastworks that connected them were also fronted by a ditch.[8]

Washington knew that for the British to attack from interior Brooklyn, they would have to get through one of four passes where roads cut through the Heights of Guan. From west to east the passes were known as Martense Lane, Flatbush, Bedford and Jamaica. The distance between the westernmost and

A detail from "Plan of the attack on the provincial army on Long Island, August 27th 1776. With the draughts of New York Island, Staten Island, and the adjacent part of the continent" by John Bowles, 1776. *Library of Congress.*

easternmost passes was six and a half miles. General John Sullivan had his men cut down trees for roadblocks and breastworks for artillery at the three westernmost passes and planned to station eight hundred men at each. He did nothing to protect Jamaica Pass, four miles from the Brooklyn Heights fortifications, apparently thinking it was too far east for the British to utilize. To defend New York, Washington had nineteen thousand troops, Continental regulars and militiamen.[9]

Washington desperately needed to know Howe's troop strength and intentions. But early in the war, the Continental Army had no well-organized intelligence network. There was one operative living on Staten Island, probably John Mersereau, son of a patriotic merchant who was already supplying intelligence to Washington. But for days, Washington had trouble finding someone who could reach Mersereau. It was only on August 20 that a courier named Lawrence Mascoll was able to rendezvous with the agent and return to headquarters by the twenty-second with an accurate description of the British forces. Unfortunately, that was the day the British began moving troops from Staten Island to Long Island.[10]

As former Central Intelligence Agency senior case officer Kenneth Daigler wrote, "[F]or intelligence to be useful it must also be timely, and in this case, because of the lack of a functioning clandestine communication system, it arrived too late to assist Washington and his defensive preparations." The only information Washington had on the attacking force came from his scouts. "And because of the fact that these localized reports could only describe the British presence each scouting party saw, Continental Army commanders had the impression that the attacking forces were only about half the actual British strength."[11]

As the battle was looming, Patriot Brigadier General Nathaniel Woodhull was given an important task. Woodhull was born into a wealthy landholding family in Mastic in 1722 and later married his neighbor Ruth Floyd, sister of William Floyd, a signer of the Declaration of Independence. At age thirty-six, Woodhull enlisted with the New York provincial militia as a major to fight for the British in the French and Indian War and rose to the rank of colonel. Woodhull had been appointed commander of the combined militias of Suffolk and Queens Counties by the New York Provincial Congress, which he served as president. He had connections with both Loyalist and Patriot factions, and he did not sign the state's endorsement of the Declaration of Independence because he thought it was too radical a move.[12]

Woodhull was ordered to take 190 militiamen to herd cattle spread across Long Island and drive the livestock east to keep it out of British hands. Although more than half of his men had deserted by late on August 27, five days after the British began their assault in Brooklyn, Woodhull's troops had driven 1,400 cattle out onto the Hempstead Plains and had 300 more ready to move. The next day, he wrote his final letter to the state convention from Jamaica, stating that "my men and horses are worn out with fatigue."[13]

During a severe thunderstorm, the general took refuge for the night in a tavern run by Increase Carpenter about two miles east of Jamaica. After a British cavalry patrol surrounded the tavern, Woodhull was captured and mortally wounded in the head and arm. Various accounts have him caught and wounded while trying to escape over a fence—the official British version—or Woodhull standing his ground and offering his sword in surrender before being slashed by an officer's saber, or slashed after refusing to surrender his sidearms. According to legend, a British major ordered Woodhull to say "God save the king!" The Mastic resident instead defiantly proclaimed, "God save us all!" before being wounded. While it's unlikely Woodhull uttered those words, he became a martyr and Long Island's most prominent military casualty of the war.[14]

There are also conflicting accounts of what happened to Woodhull after he was wounded. Most authors have him treated by a British surgeon in Jamaica, then sent aboard a prison hulk in New York Harbor and later taken to a hospital in Brooklyn, where his gangrenous arm was amputated before he died. Alexander Rose, author of *Washington's Spies*, has Woodhull transported to the Church of New Utrecht in Brooklyn, where he was deprived of medical care and food. All the accounts agree that Woodhull died on September 20 at age fifty-four and was buried at his Mastic home.[15]

As Woodhull and the rest of the Patriot commanders prepared for the coming attack, General Howe was ready to move his forces from Staten Island to Brooklyn on August 18. But stormy weather delayed the transfer. It took several days to load fifteen thousand troops onto transports. On the twenty-second, the advance guard of four thousand troops under Clinton and Lord Charles Cornwallis waded ashore from Gravesend Bay north to

The fatal wounding of General Nathaniel Woodhull during his capture while trying to keep livestock out of the hands of the British on Long Island in August 1776. *Long Island Studies Institute at Hofstra University.*

Denyse's Ferry—now Fort Hamilton—with more troops to follow as the landing craft were reloaded. With the bay filled with more than four hundred vessels, the Continental Army made no attempt to interfere with the landing, and the British operation moved smoothly. Most of the troops landed in only three hours, from 9:00 a.m. until noon. Landing craft built on Staten Island with ramps that could be lowered at the bow allowed the British to bring forty pieces of artillery with them.[16]

Skirmishing broke out the next day, the twenty-third. Washington, unsure of where the major British blow would land and concerned that the Brooklyn landing was a feint, remained in Manhattan receiving dispatches. He crossed the East River on the twenty-sixth and spoke to the troops in Brooklyn. The commander in chief warned them that he had given orders that any soldier who attempted "to skulk, lay down, or retreat without Orders" would be "instantly shot down as an example." He added that "the enemy have now landed on Long Island, and the hour is fast approaching on which the Honor and Success of this army and the safety of our bleeding Country depend."[17]

With almost twenty thousand redcoats and Hessian mercenaries in Brooklyn facing a Continental Army of fewer than nine thousand, the Battle of Long Island—also known as the Battle of Brooklyn—began about 2:00 a.m. on August 27. It would be the largest engagement of the American Revolution.

The fighting started on the western end of the Continental Army line at the intersection of the Gowanus Road and the Martense Lane Pass. British General James Grant had been ordered to make the feint that Washington had feared to distract the Patriots by attacking their right flank. About three hundred redcoats made the initial assault, surprising the defenders who fled up the Gowanus Road. The colonials' commander, Major James Burd, was captured with some of his men, but not before he managed to dispatch a messenger to General Israel Putnam in Brooklyn Heights.

Putman ordered his soldiers into the fortifications and used signal lights to alert Washington to come from Manhattan. Putman directed General William Alexander, also known as Lord Stirling, to respond to the British attack. He gathered almost two thousand men, including troops from Delaware and Pennsylvania and Colonel William Smallwood's elite First Maryland Regiment, for a counterattack. It was the first time that the two armies confronted each other in regular battle formation in open terrain. The Continental Army surprised the British by holding its ground against repeated attacks until the true intentions of the redcoats were revealed to the east.[18]

General Howe had begrudgingly accepted the suggestion of his chief subordinate, Henry Clinton, to turn the enemy's left or eastern flank and get behind the bulk of the Continental Army on the higher ground by capturing and marching through the Jamaica Pass. It would require a column to march six miles at night. About 8:00 p.m. on the twenty-sixth, the advance element of about four thousand troops with fourteen cannons stepped out from Flatlands. Clinton covered the movement by leaving a regiment to maintain campfires and make campground sounds. Anyone encountered along the way was taken prisoner to prevent the spreading of an alarm.[19]

The first Patriots to learn where the primary attack would strike were five officers on guard just south of the Jamaica Pass about 3:00 a.m. They were taken from behind by the British, who had left the Jamaica Road, which the Patriots were watching, and traveled across fields to the critical spot. Clinton seized the passage at dawn and two hours later was joined by General Howe, who had left Flatlands at midnight at the head of an additional six thousand troops.[20]

By 8:00 a.m., the British column of 10,000 troops had turned westward and was now behind the 2,500 Patriots defending the three other passes. At 9:00 a.m., Howe had two cannons fired as a signal to the rest of the troops south of the ridge that he was in position. Colonel Samuel Miles, whose 500 Patriot troops had been guarding the area east of the Bedford Pass, had learned about the British movement along the Jamaica Road about 7:00 a.m. and marched his men east through the woods. He ended up intersecting the British after most of them had already passed him on the road west. Miles sent word back to Putnam before he was captured with about half of his men. The others fled back to the forts on Brooklyn Heights.[21]

After reaching the crossroads at Bedford, Cornwallis sent troops to cut off the retreat northward to the Continental Army forts. These Patriots joined fellow troops retreating from Flatbush Pass. They crossed Gowanus Creek with British grenadiers on their heels. Some, including General John Sullivan, who had stayed behind to help with the retreat, were captured and others bayoneted by the Hessians, who refused to let them surrender.

By 11:00 a.m., the British had crushed the center of the defenses. The militiamen from Queens and Kings Counties, who had been assigned to picket duty guarding the Bedford Pass, were scared off by the British even before the major battle began and ran to the safety of the Patriot lines. Part of the Suffolk regiment surrendered to a large Hessian force.

With the collapse of most of the resistance, all that remained for the British was to deal with Lord Stirling's Patriot forces on the Gowanus Road. Squandering a strong chance of immediate and overwhelming victory, Howe exercised caution and ordered his subordinates not to attack the forts to limit casualties among his troops, who had marched all night and fought half the day. Instead, he planned to lay siege to the Patriots he believed were trapped in their works.[22]

From 7:00 a.m. to 11:00 a.m., Lord Stirling's men held a strong position in the woods near the Gowanus Road on the far right of the Continental Army line against artillery fire from Grant's column. But then, with two other British columns threatening to surround him, Stirling ordered a withdrawal. He told his men to escape through a marsh and wade or swim across Gowanus Creek, eighty yards wide with a swift current from the incoming tide. Seven soldiers drowned in the attempt. Stirling saved most of the soldiers of the right wing by leading between 250 and 400 highly disciplined Maryland troops in six attacks against Cornwallis's men despite overwhelming odds while the rest of the troops crossed the creek. Finally overwhelmed, Stirling surrendered to Hessian General Philip von Heister. Only ten men from the rearguard force made it back to the Continental Army lines; more than half were killed and the rest wounded and/or captured.[23]

Washington crossed over from Manhattan midmorning after determining that adverse northerly winds would keep the British fleet from simultaneously attacking Manhattan. He watched the disintegration of his army with his subordinates from a fort at Cobble Hill. Legend has it that he remarked, "Good God! What brave fellows I must this day lose!"[24]

Howe didn't lose many of his "brave fellows" that day. He reported just 63 killed, 293 wounded and 31 captured or missing. The British lost more men from disease—about 8 percent of their force—crossing the Atlantic than they did in the battle. Washington put Continental Army losses at about 800, with more than 75 percent of them captured. Modern historians have put the Patriot loss at about 200 killed or wounded and close to 900 prisoners, including three generals.[25]

However, the situation could have been far worse for the Continental Army had it not been for Howe's caution in halting his offensive—over the objections of his subordinates—to regroup and pursue a peace settlement. In addition, Howe's decision to fire signal guns to let the British forces in front of the outer lines know his men were ready to turn Washington's eastern flank also alerted his enemy of the danger. This allowed the bulk of the Continental Army to retreat intact to the rear line on Brooklyn Heights.[26]

Rather than withdraw his surviving troops from Brooklyn in the face of the continuing threat from the British, early on Wednesday, August 28, Washington transferred reinforcements across the river from Manhattan. That brought the total number of troops in Brooklyn to about 9,500. It was a risky move. The soldiers there were "exposed every moment to an attack from a vastly superior force in front, and to be cut off from the possibility of retreat to New York by the fleet, which might enter the East River," wrote Benjamin Tallmadge, a twenty-two-year-old Setauket native serving as a lieutenant with a Connecticut regiment and who would later become Washington's spy chief. Fortunately for the Continental Army, the wind continued to blow out of the north, preventing British ships from sailing up the East River.[27]

Also fortuitously for Washington, two regiments of Continental troops arrived that morning from Massachusetts. Led by Colonels John Glover and Israel Hutchinson, they consisted mostly of fishermen and sailors from coastal towns. The highly disciplined units helped steady the nerves of the troops trapped in Brooklyn. But spirits sagged when a storm late in the day drenched the men, who had no shelter.[28]

That night, Howe's engineers staked out a system of siege trenches so the British could approach the enemy forces without being exposed to gunfire. By the morning of Thursday, August 29, they had completed a three-hundred-yard ditch parallel to the Patriot lines and only six hundred yards distant. They had already started a zigzagging trench toward Fort

"Washington's Retreat at Long Island/Wageman/J.C. Armytage." *Library of Congress.*

Putnam, which jutted out from the defensive lines on high ground. They were probably a day away from digging their way to musket range, but Washington had no intention of waiting for that to happen. He made plans to evacuate his men to Manhattan.[29]

Even if the wind continued to hold the British fleet at bay, the evacuation would be extremely risky. The East River was a mile wide with strong tidal currents. Washington had only ten flatboats at his disposal, and they were needed to transport horses, cannons and other supplies. In order to move about ten thousand soldiers in a single night with all their equipment, he requisitioned "every flat bottomed boat and other craft...fit for transporting troops" available in the area. Aware of the need for absolute secrecy, Washington did not inform most of his generals of his plans.[30]

The Massachusetts units were in position at the Brooklyn ferry landing by 7:00 p.m. The evacuation began an hour later. It started smoothly, but then, with the winds very light, the current shifted and threatened to carry any sail-powered boats down into the bay where the British fleet was waiting. So only rowboats, with their oars wrapped in cloth to muffle the sound, were used at that time. About 11:00 p.m., the wind shifted to blow from the southwest, allowing the mariners to use sails. It would also have allowed the British fleet to sail up into the East River to cut off the Continental Army,

"Retreat from Long Island [N.Y.], Aug. 29, 1776." *Library of Congress.*

but the warships did not budge, in part because the retreat was screened by Governors Island.[31]

The withdrawal was continuing as dawn approached with several regiments still manning the Continental Army lines. Discipline began to break down as soldiers rushed for the ferry landing, where Washington had to personally intervene to keep boats from being overloaded. Luckily, the weather again helped the Patriot cause. Fog described by Tallmadge as "so dense an atmosphere that I could scarcely discern a man at six yards distance" rolled in and continued to shroud the army's movements.[32]

About 7:00 a.m., the fog began to lift as the last Patriots left their posts on Governors Island. About that time, the British probed the fortifications on Brooklyn Heights and found them empty. Washington had escaped with almost all of his men and supplies other than a few cannons that the redcoats turned to fire unsuccessfully at the last of the fleeing enemy.

Benjamin Tallmadge, who was in action for the first time in bloody fighting at Bedford Pass, was part of the rearguard and "stepped into one of the last boats" leaving Brooklyn. But once he got to Manhattan, he regretted leaving his favorite horse tied to a post:

The fog continuing as thick as ever, I began to think of my favorite horse, and requested leave to return and bring him off. Having obtained permission, I called for a crew of volunteers to go with me, and guiding the boat myself, I obtained my horse and got off some distance into the river before the enemy appeared in Brooklyn. As soon as they reached the ferry we were saluted merrily from their musketry, and finally by their field pieces; but we returned in safety.[33]

Only four Continental soldiers were wounded during the evacuation, and three stragglers, who apparently remained behind for looting, were captured.[34]

Washington knew that British control of the waterways could soon leave him trapped on Manhattan. But he needed the consent of Congress and agreement of his chief officers before abandoning the island. By the time he received that consent and agreement, the British had crossed the river from Long Island to Kips Bay on Manhattan. The September 15 attack quickly scattered the militia units defending the shoreline and began a rout of much of the Continental Army. Washington and most of his troops barely escaped as they rushed north up the island, just out of reach to the west of the redcoats.[35]

This was another example where the Patriots' lack of an intelligence network almost proved fatal to the army. "Once again, Washington had no useful intelligence regarding the British move," Daigler wrote. "His army scouts reported that the landing would take place farther north."[36]

In the Battle of Fort Washington at the northern tip of Manhattan on November 16, the British would drive the Continental Army entirely off that island. However, over time, Washington would improve his intelligence capabilities. But first, the victors rapidly occupied the rest of Long Island, beginning seven years of subjugation for its residents.

2

THE BRITISH OCCUPATION

Aafter pushing the Continental Army out of Manhattan in the fall of 1776, the British were free to move east into Suffolk County to complete their control of Long Island. "It is arguable that Long Island suffered more than anywhere—certainly longer, with the occupation lasting seven years and three months," historian Natalie A. Naylor wrote.[37]

The English, Hessian and Loyalist troops faced the challenge of trying to try to achieve a delicate balance between maintaining control and not alienating the pro-British residents while obtaining needed supplies. The occupiers did fairly well on maintaining control and obtaining supplies but were less successful in not antagonizing the inhabitants, regardless of their political leanings.

Long Island quickly became a major source of food, forage, timber and other supplies needed by the British. "For the thousands of troops in New York City, Long Island is the breadbasket," historian Barnet Schecter said. In addition to food, "wagon loads of firewood are coming into the city from Long Island throughout the war to keep them from freezing in winter."[38]

To secure their new supply base, the British constructed forts to deter, with limited success, the Patriots from making raids from Connecticut. A curfew was imposed to curtail movement. Those who violated it were punished severely and publicly, such as when John Weeks was tied to a locust tree in front of Samuel Townsend's prominent home in Oyster Bay and whipped by a Hessian patrol. Homes were occupied. Forests and fences were leveled for firewood, and grain and cattle requisitioned. Inhabitants who favored independence and had not already fled were driven out or terrorized.[39]

In 1771, the population of Suffolk County was 13,100. At the time of the Revolution, most of its residents were Whigs, or Patriots. Queens County, which included what would become Nassau County, was home to nearly 11,000 people. Queens was divided politically leading up to and through the Revolution to the extent that in September 1777, Patriots in northern Hempstead seceded from the rest of the more Loyalist town of Hempstead. That split was made official by New York State after the war in 1784. Oyster Bay was heavily Loyalist. In 1771, 17 percent of Long Islanders were African Americans, most of them enslaved.[40]

With stronger sentiment in most of Queens in favor of the Crown than independence, the Provincial Congress and the Continental Congress stationed soldiers there and sent out scouting parties to apprehend Loyalists. Before the British arrived to attack New York in the summer of 1776, George Washington suspected that Loyalist residents of Queens would rally to the British forces once they landed. Consequently, he authorized General Charles Lee to disarm the Loyalists, an action that alienated the Tories even further.[41]

As part of the effort to seize the arms of "disaffected" Loyalists, in January 1775 a New Jersey Patriot militia unit came to Long Island and arrested

Prominent Loyalist Josiah Martin built Rock Hall in present-day Lawrence in 1767. His family had to endure occupation by Patriot soldiers in the early days of the American Revolution. *Photo by Audrey C. Tiernan, copyright 2020.*

several prominent Tories. They included Dr. Samuel Martin, son of the owner of Rock Hall, a mansion built in Lawrence in 1767. Patriot troops occupied the house, where the doctor's father, Josiah, and seven women from three generations were living. The women were "exposed to the most mortifying insults of the ruling mob" and endured the "mortification of being obliged to entertain all the ragamuffins."[42]

In January 1776, seven months before the Battle of Long Island, the Provincial Congress sent more than one thousand pounds of gunpowder to the Huntington patriotic committee and other supplies to additional communities. In July, three companies of Continental troops were sent to supplement local militia and help protect the East End from British raids. At that point, there were approximately two thousand men, more than 70 percent of those in the eligible age bracket, in militia companies. Many of them, including more than five hundred Suffolk troops commanded by Colonel Josiah Smith of Brookhaven, would participate in the great battle in August.[43]

After surviving that debacle, some Suffolk militia units marched home and disbanded on the advice of their officers. Others crossed the East River to join Washington in Manhattan or crossed Long Island Sound to enlist in New England regiments. But some militia units created to fight for American independence were persuaded to take an oath of loyalty to the Crown after being threatened with loss of their property or confinement on prison ships in New York Harbor. Hundreds of men joined newly formed Loyalist units after the British promised they would only have to serve on Long Island.[44]

Most of the Long Island militia units that agreed to serve the British were relegated to guard duty along the North Shore in an attempt to thwart raids from Patriots in Connecticut and Rhode Island while also restricting the activity of smugglers and spies. Some Loyalist units were recruited into the regular British army, however. Grouped into what became known as the Provincial Corps, they were commanded by Oliver De Lancey, a member of a distinguished New York family. Appointed brigadier general in September 1776, he served on Long Island for the duration of the war, commanding a brigade of more than seven hundred men. Detachments from the brigade spent the winter of 1776–77 in Oyster Bay, Huntington and Brookhaven.[45]

More than 40 British, Hessian and Loyalist units were stationed on Long Island during the war. They included British regulars in their red coats, Scottish highlanders wearing kilts and Loyalist units outfitted in green uniforms. Redcoats were based in Sag Harbor and the towns of Southampton and East Hampton. In February 1779, there were 700 soldiers stationed in Southampton, 150 men from Ludlow's Battalion on Lloyd Neck, 350 members of Simcoe's Queens Rangers in the Oyster Bay–Huntington area and 300 members of the Seventeenth Dragoons around Hempstead. Hessian mercenaries occupied Norwich (today's East Norwich), Jericho, Westbury and Musketo Cove (today's Glen Cove) for most of the war.[46]

The number of British, Hessian and Loyalist troops garrisoning Queens and Suffolk varied widely over the seven years. In 1779, with an expected attack from French and Patriot troops, the British sent 2,500 reinforcements to the island for a total of about 8,500 troops, not including local militia units. They were supported, as they were for the entire war, by British warships blockading and patrolling Long Island Sound. But at other times, there might be only one or two companies of men patrolling each town. And toward the end of the war, when the strategic emphasis on both sides had shifted to the South leading up to the crucial final battle at Yorktown, the British virtually ignored Long Island and left few soldiers there.[47]

The British and Loyalist troops built a network of forts around the island to protect the soldiers and Tories living nearby. These were located in Oyster Bay, Jericho, Lloyd Neck, Huntington, Fort Salonga, Setauket, Shirley, Hampton Bays, Southampton and Sag Harbor. Patriot raiders from Connecticut attacked some of these fortifications, including Fort Franklin on Lloyd Neck, named after William Franklin, Benjamin's son and the last royal governor of New Jersey; Fort Slongo in what became Fort Salonga, named for a British officer; and Fort St. George, named for the colonial manor on which it stood in Shirley on the South Shore. George Washington's future spymaster Benjamin Tallmadge personally led raids on Fort Franklin in 1779 and Fort St. George in 1780.[48]

Because so many eastern Long Island residents had strongly supported independence, the New York Convention, the state's wartime governing body, recommended after the Battle of Long Island that the men living in that area send their women, children, slaves and livestock to Connecticut for safety before the British consolidated their control over the entire island. About five thousand people became "refugees of Long Island." The majority were from Suffolk, where about 30 percent of the population left for Connecticut.[49]

Declaration of Independence signer William Floyd was one of those whose family fled across the Sound. His wife, Hannah, and their three children left Mastic by ship for Middletown, Connecticut, in September while Floyd was in Philadelphia with Congress. Hannah Floyd often brought the children to stay with her husband in Philadelphia before she died in 1781. While Floyd's family was safe, British troops occupied his house for part of the war, and local Tories confiscated the livestock, furniture, bedding and farming implements. At the end of the conflict in 1783, Floyd returned to Mastic. Despite the British occupation and his prominent role in the Revolution, Floyd found little damage to the house or property, despite legends to the contrary. Some women whose husbands were away fighting remained on Long Island to manage farms.[50]

Caleb Brewster, who would play a prominent role in the Culper Spy Ring, was one of the Long Island refugees who fled north and then returned periodically in whaleboats to raid British outposts. Brewster, born in 1747 on a Setauket farm, shipped out on a Nantucket whaling vessel at age nineteen. In December 1775, he signed up with the Brookhaven company of the Suffolk County Militia after the first shots of the war were fired at Lexington and Concord the previous April, rising to the rank of second and then first lieutenant. When that unit disbanded after the Battle of Long Island, its members who wished to continue fighting regrouped in New Haven, Connecticut. Brewster was among them and joined the Fourth Continental Line Regiment as a lieutenant. In October 1776, he began participating in a series of whaleboat battles and raids on and across Long Island Sound. The following month, Brewster volunteered as an ensign in the Second Company of the Fourth Battalion of the Fourth New York Regiment and was quickly promoted back to lieutenant. Three months later, in early 1777, he transferred to an artillery unit but remained mostly on detached duty to fight the British on the Sound and carry dispatches between Setauket and Connecticut under the direction of his friend Benjamin Tallmadge when the spy ring began operating in 1778.[51]

The concept of whaleboat raids across the Sound was introduced by the British on April 26, 1777, when 1,850 men commanded by Major General William Tryon attacked and destroyed much of Danbury, Connecticut. The strategy was adopted by the Patriots with some success. Initially, the aim of the raiders from both sides was to grab prisoners who could be exchanged for military or civilian captives. In 1779, Loyalist judge Thomas Jones was kidnapped from his home in today's Massapequa to be exchanged for a Patriot militia general, Gold Selleck Silliman. The judge later wrote that the Patriots "robbed Mrs. Jones of her wearing apparel and took that of two young ladies in the house," leaving them only with "the clothes upon their backs."[52]

But many of the whaleboat raiders soon began stealing from residents regardless of their political affiliation. "It took little time for many of the raiders to degenerate into pirates and robbers, lacking even the pretense of

Marauding whaleboat raiders from Connecticut demand valuables from a Long Island home in an 1881 magazine illustration. *Courtesy of Richard F. Welch.*

confining their plundering to their putative foes, robbing Revolutionary and Tory alike, and selling their booty wherever they could get the best price," Tallmadge biographer Richard F. Welch wrote. "Sporadic attempts by Washington and state authorities to curtail such abuses proved ineffectual."[53]

On Long Island, the inhabitants who didn't flee north had to endure a British occupation that in Suffolk County became known as the "State of Wretchedness." The British needed places for their officers and men to live in both Suffolk and Queens, especially during winters when there was little fighting. Usually, they established lodging in taverns, inns or private houses.[54]

The private home that has received the most attention from historians for housing British officers was that of Samuel Townsend in Oyster Bay. The Townsends were one of Long Island's oldest families, dating to 1645, when John Townsend was one of the patentees of Flushing. Samuel Townsend was a successful merchant who imported flax, sugar, molasses, tea, coffee, fabrics, rum and other commodities.[55]

Samuel Townsend's house, which would be named Raynham Hall during the Victorian era (see chapter 14), was occupied for most of the war by a succession of commanders from five regiments. Claire Bellerjeau, historian at the Raynham Hall Museum, said:

> *There were multiple brigades that came to Oyster Bay and stayed for a period of time, which was true of every major town. Any time there was a regiment in Oyster Bay, the Townsend house was the headquarters. It's a nice house with a lot of provisions on hand because of his merchant's business, it was centrally located near the fort (built by one of the occupying officers, Lieutenant Colonel John Graves Simcoe), and they were keeping an eye on Samuel, who was pretty well known for his Patriot activities.*

TOWNSEND'S

An 1830s sketch of the Oyster Bay home of Culper spy Robert Townsend and his family, later named Raynham Hall. *Courtesy of the Friends of Raynham Hall.*

The most frequently mentioned uninvited British houseguest was Simcoe, commander of the Queen's Rangers. That Loyalist unit generally occupied the Oyster Bay–Huntington area when it was not off fighting in New Jersey, the Carolinas and other locations. Simcoe stayed at the house three times: from November 1778 to May 1779, mid-August to mid-September 1779 and for a month in the fall of 1780. Simcoe built the fort nearby on high ground overlooking the town and harbor, destroying the family's orchard in the process.

The Townsend home also became the headquarters for Major Joseph Greene, a Long Island resident who served with DeLancey's Brigade, from the fall of 1776 until the spring of 1777; Major James Grant and possibly his superior Colonel Edmund Fanning of the King's American Rangers in the summer of 1777; Major Charles Cochran of Tarleton's Legion; and Hessian officers in late 1782 through May 1783. "There is a record of Samuel in his account book enumerating items Cochran has taken from him including a mahogany table, silver soup spoon, mustard pot and copper 'pye' pan, dated May 29, 1780," according to Bellerjeau.[56]

Even before the British commandeered his home, Samuel Townsend had no love for that country's officials and military officers. After writing a letter on behalf of neutral French citizens and prisoners of war during the French and Indian War, he was jailed for several days in 1758 until he apologized. An ardent Patriot, he served in the Provincial Congress from May 1775 through the summer of 1776 and also was a member of the Committee of Safety, a Patriot organization. He then served on

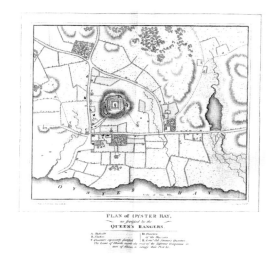

PLAN of OYSTER BAY,
as fortified by the
QUEEN'S RANGERS.

A drawing by British Lieutenant Colonel John Graves Simcoe of a fort he built in Oyster Bay from his "A Journal of the Operations of the Queen's Rangers from the End of 1777 until the Conclusion of the Revolutionary War," published in 1787. *Courtesy of Claire Bellerjeau.*

committees helping Brigadier General Nathaniel Woodhull's efforts to keep Long Island livestock out of the hands of the British before the Battle of Brooklyn.[57]

Townsend's troubles with British authorities did not end with his 1758 arrest. He was taken into custody again in early September 1776 within days of the Battle of Long Island. Soldiers from DeLancey's Brigade first arrested two other Oyster Bay men: George Townsend, a distant cousin of Samuel and leader of a local Patriot group, and John Kirk, another local Patriot organizer. The soldiers brought them to Samuel Townsend's house and knocked on the door, calling out to him that he was under arrest. He was led away with one change of clothing. As the prisoners were being taken up the hill on the southern edge of the hamlet, they encountered a party of residents coming into town. It was led by Thomas Buchanan, who was married to a daughter of Jacob Townsend, Samuel's brother, business partner and next-door neighbor. Buchanan, a wealthy merchant and shipowner who tried to remain on good terms with both the Patriots and the British, rode to his house to get some money and then caught up to the soldiers taking away Townsend. "He flat out bribed them with cash," Bellerjeau said. Townsend was allowed to go home but forced to sign an oath of allegiance to King George III. George Townsend and John Kirk were sent to the prison hulk *Jersey* in New York Harbor and were there for nine weeks before being released at the urging of fellow Quakers. Kirk had contracted smallpox, and his wife and one of their children died of the disease.[58]

During the war, four teenage Townsends lived in the house with Samuel and his wife, Sarah: David and his sisters Audrey, Sally and Phebe. Robert, the spy, and his younger brother William were living in New York, although Robert visited the house frequently based on his writing appearing in Samuel's account books. Robert's older brother Solomon was out at sea as a captain of a trading vessel owned by Thomas Buchanan.

Sally Townsend gained fame because Simcoe presented her with what is said to be the first Valentine composed in America on Valentine's Day 1779. The twenty-six-line poem includes the phrase "choose me for your Valentine." The poem has given rise to speculation that there was a romance between seventeen-year-old Sally and the officer—a notion Bellerjeau dismissed. "Simcoe loved to write; he wrote reams of poems during his life," said the historian, who has read many of them in the Simcoe archives in Ontario, where he settled after the war. "He wrote poems to other girls during the Revolutionary War, and they were all very similar in their style with classical illusions and highly romantic and complimentary. He came back in August of that year and didn't write her another poem and came back a year later and there was no relationship again."

The poetry shows a different side of Simcoe, who is often portrayed as a villain. In the AMC series *Turn*, he is depicted "as a murdering psychopath, and he certainly wasn't that," Bellerjeau said. "He did do violent things because it was a war. He did rough up [chief Culper spy Abraham] Woodhull's father, which is well documented in the Culper letters. But he had a sense of honor." He trained his soldiers so well that the British considered the Queen's Rangers the top provincial unit in America.

Sally has also been the subject of a second widely shared—and inaccurate—account included in numerous books about the Culper Spy Ring. The story, which originated without documentation in Morton Pennypacker's groundbreaking 1939 book *George Washington's Spies on Long Island and New York*, is that Sally played a part in the undoing of Major John André, the chief British spy in America. Sally supposedly overheard a conversation in the house between André and another officer and then discovered an incriminating letter detailing the plan by traitorous Patriot General Benedict Arnold to surrender West Point to the British. The anecdote places this activity shortly before the spy was captured in Tarrytown in Westchester with incriminating documents and then hanged on October 2, 1780. In Pennypacker's oft-repeated version, André visited the house several times, and Sally, who frequently provided her brother and chief Culper spy Robert in Manhattan with important information, wrote a note to him and arranged for a family friend to deliver it to the city. The next morning, it was on its way to Setauket, crossed Long Island Sound overnight and was in spymaster Benjamin Tallmadge's hands soon after.

"It's totally made up," Bellerjeau insisted. Letters that the British officer wrote to his commander, Sir Henry Clinton, document André's only known visit to the house lasting several weeks in March 1779—not the fall of 1780.

When houses like Samuel Townsend's and other structures were not available, the occupying soldiers lived in tents or built huts or barracks in pastures or meadows. Henry Onderdonk Jr. wrote in *Documents and Letters Intended to Illustrate the Revolutionary Incidents of Queens County* in 1846 that the soldiers lived outdoors in tents in the summer and in the winter either in huts or in farmers' kitchens. "Each family was allowed one fire-place, and the officers fixed the number of soldiers to be billeted in each house, which was usually from 10 to 20. They had three tiers of hammocks, one above the other, ranged round the room, and made of boards stripped from some fence or outbuilding."[59]

To help feed its soldiers, the British command issued an order in September 1776, a month after the Battle of Long Island, to drive "all the fat cattle and sheep in Suffolk Company…down to Jamaica…for the refreshment of the King's Troops." The farmers were also instructed to turn over grain, straw and all of their hay. Horses, saddles and wagons were also requisitioned. The British commissary of forage, John Morrison, who needed to feed twenty thousand soldiers in and around Manhattan, printed a blank order form that could be filled in by soldiers confronting Suffolk residents. It stated: "You are hereby ordered to preserve for the King's use ____ loads of hay, bushels of wheat, ____ of oats, ____ of rye, ____ of barley, ____ of Indian corn, and all of your wheat and rye straw; and not to dispose of the same, but to my order in writing as you will answer the contrary at your peril." If the inhabitants refused to supply the British, their commander in the county, General William Erskine, threatened to "lay waste the property of the disobedient as persons unworthy of His Majesty's clemency."

When the occupiers demanded provisions, sometimes an officer would provide a receipt. But mostly the soldiers just took what they wanted. At times, Simcoe ordered the confiscation of goods from Huntington residents without providing receipts "on account of their rebellious principles, and absolute disobedience of the general orders." Even when receipts were issued, they were basically worthless; those who received them rarely were compensated.[60]

British occupation requisition order on display at Sagtikos Manor in West Bay Shore. *Photo by Audrey C. Tiernan, copyright 2019.*

With the arrival of occupying troops, the pro-independence views of many of the residents who remained behind began to shift—or least they tried to give that appearance. In October, 614 Suffolk residents signed a petition pledging their allegiance and sent it to Howe, and 1,182 men from Queens did the same in November.[61]

After the British commander suggested that the residents demonstrate their loyalty by sending two hundred wagons to help move the army's baggage from Brooklyn to Queens, they sent three hundred. Seeking further proof of the allegiance of Long Island residents to the Crown, in 1776 and again two years later, the British tried to compel all men between the ages of sixteen and sixty who were capable of fighting to take a loyalty oath. Those who refused were threatened with banishment and confiscation of property.[62]

Along with food and forage for animals, wood was in much demand for building fortifications and making fires. The Loyalist troops of Colonel Benjamin Thompson, a Tory from New Hampshire who commanded the King's American Dragoons, who occupied Huntington in the winter of 1782–83, burned more than 5,830 wooden rails, 14 loads of timber and 390 feet of boards in that community in less than a year. When the available trees had been cut, the soldiers disassembled fences and even houses of worship of denominations, such as Presbyterian and Quaker, considered unsympathetic to the Crown. As late in the conflict as 1782, a Quaker school was torn down because the occupying troops objected to the Friends' principles of nonviolence and neutrality. (Many Patriot soldiers also objected to the Quakers' neutrality and stole their possessions).[63]

Even if they weren't stripped of their wood, the houses of worship from denominations not favored by the British suffered badly. The Presbyterian church in Babylon was occupied and then burned by the British before they left. The Hempstead Presbyterian church was used as a barracks, then a prison and finally, with the floor ripped out, as a riding school for the cavalry. In Huntington, Presbyterian minister Ebenezer Prime, who was critical of Simcoe, had his house taken over by the army, the furniture broken and many of his books destroyed. His church was also so badly vandalized that it was unfit for use before Prime died in 1779.

As Anglican churches in the American colonies were affiliated with the Church of England, they were generally respected because they were considered Loyalist bastions. Occupying troops regularly attended services at those churches, including Saint George's in Hempstead, which offered pro-British sermons. But even Anglican churches were commandeered as barracks or for other uses, often leading them to be so heavily damaged that they had to be demolished at the end of the war. The churches in Oyster Bay, for example, were occupied as barracks, and several, including Christ Church, an Anglican house of worship, were heavily damaged by their heavy use.[64]

A musket ball fired by a British soldier at Isaac Thompson, owner of Sagtikos Manor, during the Revolution. *Photo by Audrey C. Tiernan, copyright 2019.*

An occupying army rarely makes friends, and by the end of the war, most Queens residents supported the Patriot cause. The troops and their officers could not effectively tell friend from foe in the civilian population and inevitably treated almost everyone as the enemy. British officers took out their frustration over their inability to stamp out the rebellion by venting their frustration on civilians. Coming from the English upper class, they viewed the disloyal Americans as inferior and greedy. They imposed degrading rules such as requiring civilians to dismount their horses and remove their hats when passing the house where an army commander was headquartered. Other abusive actions by British officers could have fatal consequences. A miller named Paul Amberman sold flour to Major Richard Stockton, and when the miller asked for payment, Stockton was offended. The next day, another officer used a horse whip on Amberman and then Stockton killed the miller with his sword. Stockton was court-martialed, found guilty and then released.[65]

At the peak of the occupation, about one in six people living on Long Island was a British or Hessian soldier. With many of the troops quartered in private houses, lives were disrupted. The soldiers could transmit smallpox and other diseases to the people who housed them.

Having so many enemy soldiers around when men were often away fighting fostered fear of rape and venereal disease. The Continental Congress investigated and concluded sexual assaults occurred "on a large scale." Long Island historian John Staudt wrote, "British soldiers attacked pregnant women, the elderly, and girls as young as thirteen years old, and sometimes gang raped their victims over the course of several days."[66]

Some women did have consensual relationships with the foreigners, and a number of weddings have been documented. One of the more prominent was the 1780 marriage of Major Joseph Greene of DeLancey's Brigade, which spent time occupying Oyster Bay, to Hannah Townsend, first cousin and next-door neighbor of Culper spy Robert Townsend. The couple was forced into exile after the war, settling in Ireland.[67]

Under the protection of the occupying forces, Tories were no longer persecuted by their neighbors. Wearing red cockades in their hats or red ribbons running down their backs, they offered refreshments to the British liberators and turned on their Patriot tormentors who had not fled.[68]

But even some Loyalists grumbled about their possessions being confiscated by the army. The Hessians made a more favorable impression than the British because they were more sociable and often made little baskets and other toys for the children or taught them German.[69]

Portrait of British Admiral Richard Howe that hangs in Sagtikos Manor, where English officers stayed during the war. *Photo by Audrey C. Tiernan, copyright 2019.*

It became increasingly difficult for the British to obtain food and other supplies after the first year of occupation. As a result, the commanders in Manhattan dispatched up to five thousand troops to Long Island and New Jersey to seek supplies and did not restrict the soldiers from foraging on their own, which encouraged abuses of the population. "The result was that Long Island towns became largely Patriot, or at least anti-British army, before the end of the war," Setauket historian Beverly Tyler said.[70]

The deprivations did not cease for the Patriots even when the war neared its end. Colonel Thompson ignored the signing of a preliminary peace treaty to order construction of Fort Golgotha atop Huntington's Presbyterian church burial grounds. To gain the materials for the fort, the dragoons tore down the church, stripped barns of siding, demolished rail fences and cut down local orchards.[71]

When the British evacuated, Smithtown innkeeper Epenetus Smith was left with receipts from the occupiers totaling almost £600 for food, livestock, grain, blankets and other goods and services. Smith was one of fifty-four town residents whose claims came close to £4,000 as recorded in a town account book. In larger neighboring Huntington, town ledgers listed claims in excess of £21,000. After the peace, Huntington residents filed claims for reimbursement with New York authorities, but nothing came of it.[72]

NATHAN HALE AND WASHINGTON'S EARLY INTELLIGENCE OPERATIONS

George Washington had firsthand knowledge of the value of military intelligence and what could go wrong with a lack of it. In 1755, during the French and Indian War, Washington was serving as an aide to British Major General Edward Braddock when a force of Redcoats and Virginia militia heading west into the wilderness was ambushed and nearly annihilated in a surprise attack. "Washington carried away from Braddock's defeat recognition of the importance of intelligence as a vital element in military planning," former Central Intelligence Agency senior case officer Kenneth Daigler wrote.[73]

When the American Revolution began, Washington knew the enemy had a sophisticated espionage system. In 1776, with the rebellion at a low point, the general wrote that "there is one evil I dread, and that is, their spies."[74] After operating with little useful intelligence before and after the Battle of Long Island in late August 1776, Washington took action to fill his intelligence vacuum in the fall. While still based in Manhattan, he instructed Colonel Thomas Knowlton, who had served valuably at Bunker Hill and other battles, to select a group of men to undertake reconnaissance missions. The unit became known as Knowlton's Rangers. Its most famous member, Nathan Hale, would be glorified as a hero despite his failure.[75]

Hale was born in Connecticut, where he attended Yale. "He was a lousy spy," Daigler commented. "His selection, training (or lack thereof), and how he conducted his mission were horrible by both intelligence and commonsense standards....Both his family background and his educational

Statue of American spy Nathan Hale in City Hall Park in Manhattan. *Library of Congress.*

experience ingrained in him a strong sense of personal integrity that made it difficult for him to lie effectively."[76]

After his graduation from college, Hale became a teacher. He joined the local militia and was elected first sergeant. But after armed conflict erupted at Lexington and Concord in April 1775, he did not accompany his unit to Boston. A letter dated July 4 from his close friend and Yale classmate Benjamin Tallmadge, a native of Setauket and George Washington's future spymaster, changed his thinking. After traveling to Cambridge to observe the standoff between the Patriot forces and the British, Tallmadge urged Hale to join the Continental Army: "Our holy Religion, the honour of our God, a glorious country, & a happy Constitution is what we have to defend."[77] Hale signed up with the Seventh Connecticut Regiment as a first lieutenant, and within weeks, he was on his way to Boston. In an army reorganization in January 1776, Hale was commissioned a captain in the newly formed Nineteenth Connecticut Regiment, which in the spring moved to New York. In September, when Knowlton's Rangers were established, Hale was invited to join.[78]

Trapped in Manhattan by British ships and troops, George Washington was craving intelligence. He wrote to General William Heath on September

5, urging him and General James Clinton "to exert yourselves to accomplish this most desirable end. Leave no stone unturned, nor do stick at expense, to bring this to pass, as I was never more uneasy than on account of my want of knowledge."[79]

Washington received some reports from his subordinates in Manhattan and New York governor George Clinton. But the general needed more and instructed Knowlton to send a spy behind British lines. When Knowlton's first choice refused the mission, he assembled his officers at their camp near today's Fiftieth Street in Manhattan and asked one to volunteer for what was considered dishonorable duty at that time. No one stepped forward.[80]

Nathan Hale missed the meeting because he had the flu. But frustrated by never having fired a shot at the enemy, he volunteered soon thereafter. Several of his fellow officers tried to persuade him to change his mind because they considered it a suicide mission and something no gentleman would undertake. Hale refused. He discussed the mission with a Yale classmate, Captain William Hull, who told his friend that his personality was not suited for the role. "His nature was too frank and open to deceit and disguise, and he was incapable of acting a part equally foreign to his feelings and habits," Hull wrote. "I ended by saying that should he undertake the enterprise, his short, bright career, would close with an ignominious death." Hull said Hale replied,

> *I am fully sensible of the consequences of discovery and capture....But for a year I have been attached to the army, and have not rendered any material service, while receiving a compensation, for which I make no return. I am not influenced by the expectation of promotion or pecuniary reward, I wish to be useful, and every kind of service, necessary to the public good, becomes honorable by being necessary.*[81]

Daigler wrote that Hale "had great trust in the honesty of his fellow man. Unfortunately for him, Robert Rogers, the commander of Rogers' Rangers during the French and Indian War, was very good at not telling the truth."[82]

When the Revolution broke out, Rogers, deeply in debt, offered his services to George Washington. The Continental Army commander rebuffed him and then had him arrested as a possible spy because he was still receiving half pay from the British Army. Rogers escaped and obtained a commission as a lieutenant colonel from British General William Howe to raise a battalion, the Queen's American Rangers. Unfortunately for Hale, Rogers's recruiting and intelligence-gathering efforts brought him to Long Island at the same time as the inexperienced spy.[83]

While some historians of previous generations state definitively that Washington personally briefed Hale on his role, there is no evidence to support the claim.[84] The mission was compromised even before it began because so many people in the Continental Army camp knew of the plans. Hale also had spent five months in Manhattan, where he could have been recognized by Loyalist residents. In addition, Hale had powder burns on his face from firing a musket. The burns were a telltale giveaway that any soldier would recognize, and they were unlikely to be seen on a teacher, the occupation Hale decided to portray.[85]

Hale left camp sometime between September 12 and 15—about a week after volunteering. Posing as a Dutch schoolmaster, he traveled on foot to avoid suspicion. He was accompanied by a friend, Sergeant Stephen Hempstead, to Norwalk, Connecticut, the first place east of the city where Hale thought he could find a vessel to carry him across Long Island Sound without being intercepted by a British warship.[86]

In Norwalk, Hale encountered Charles Pond, a captain who had served with Hale in the Nineteenth Connecticut. Pond agreed to ferry him to Long Island on his four-gun sloop *Schuyler* that night. Before boarding the privateering vessel authorized by Congress, Hale donned a plain brown suit with a round broad-brim hat made for him by his sister Elizabeth

Nathan Hale Rock monument in Halesite. *Photo by Audrey C. Tiernan, copyright 2020.*

Rose to better portray a teacher. He removed the silver buckles from his shoes, telling Hempstead that "these will not comport with my character of a schoolmaster," and then handed his friend his uniform, the buckles and personal papers, "retaining nothing but his college diploma," Hempstead wrote later.[87] Keeping the diploma was certainly poor spy craft for someone trying to assume a different identity.

Historians offer two conflicting accounts of Hempstead's movements at this point. Some have him bidding farewell to Hale in Norwalk and returning to the Continental Army the way he came; others have him crossing the Sound with Hale. In the latter version, near daylight on September 16, Hale gave Hempstead his watch and landed on a quiet beach in Huntington. His plan was to travel along the North Shore of Long Island to Brooklyn to gather information on British troop activities. Depending on the version, Hale was to proceed to Manhattan to report his findings to Washington or return the way he came.[88]

Rogers, meanwhile, in pursuing his mission to carry out raids against Patriot supply points and troops, had set up a network of informants on both sides of the Sound. He also had a ship for patrolling those waters. On the night that Hale crossed, Rogers was patrolling aboard HMS *Halifax*, a brig of 16 guns commanded by Captain William Quarme. The captain, whose ship was off Huntington, received word about two rebel privateer vessels—*Schuyler* and *Montgomery*—observed in the area the day before. A Tory informant in Norwalk also reported the presence of the *Schuyler* and two Continental Army soldiers in that town, adding that one of them boarded the vessel before it sailed.

Rogers was suspicious and decided to investigate. Knowing it was too late to catch the *Schuyler* and its suspicious passengers on the Sound or in the Huntington area, Rogers suspected the spy or spies would be heading along the northern shore of Long Island gathering information on the way toward Continental Army headquarters in Manhattan, or at least where it had been before Washington had to evacuate lower Manhattan. Hale was never ordered to go to Manhattan. Alexander Rose, author of *Washington's Spies*, the most respected book on the general's espionage network, wrote that the plan was for Hale to reconnoiter on Long Island, return to Huntington and sail back across the Sound.

Historians are divided about the movements of Hale and Rogers leading up to the spy's capture. In the most often-repeated chronology, on the morning of September 18, Rogers landed at Sands Point to pick up the trail. In early 2021, Raynham Hall Museum historian Claire Bellerjeau obtained a copy of the log of the *Halifax* from England, and it indicates Rogers landed two days later than that.

Rogers quickly learned that a stranger was asking suspicious questions about British troops and the loyalty of local citizens.[89] Within two days, the British officer had caught up to Hale and was watching him from afar. When Hale took a room at a tavern—location unknown—and sat down for dinner, Rogers joined him. After some small talk and drinking, he told Hale he was a Continental soldier gathering information on the enemy. Hale then revealed his own identity and secret mission. Rogers wanted Hale to confess in front of witnesses and suggested they meet for breakfast the next morning where Rogers was staying. Hale agreed. Rogers was accompanied by several of his rangers, who the commander said were also fellow rebels. Other soldiers from his unit surrounded the tavern while Hale talked about his mission. When he had heard enough, Rogers stunned Hale by arresting him. As he was dragged out of the building, several Tory refugee onlookers identified him. Rogers took Hale to Flushing, where the British officer maintained a recruiting office, and then transported him to Manhattan on his private sloop.[90]

Most historians have the spy being apprehended on his way *to* Brooklyn. But Hale biographers M. William Phelps and Virginia DeJohn Anderson each embrace a different scenario: that Hale was captured on his way *back to* Huntington.[91] "To his dismay, by the time Hale reached Long Island much of the British Army had relocated to Manhattan," Anderson wrote. "Unwilling to abandon his mission and disappoint his superiors, he decided to follow the redcoats across the East River, prolonging his risky subterfuge."[92]

Citing a Rogers biography, Phelps concluded that Hale made it to Brooklyn by September 18 and took a ferry into Manhattan. He stated that Hale was supposed to rendezvous with Captain Pond near Huntington on September 21 or 22. Phelps placed Hale and Rogers in the same vicinity on September 20, somewhere between Great Neck and East Norwich. Then Hale returned to Huntington, where he asked residents whether they supported the cause of independence while he waited to be picked up the next day by the *Schuyler*. Phelps speculated that Hale stayed overnight in a tavern and Rogers learned of his presence from one of his informants. Then the spy catcher arrived at the tavern and entrapped Hale. When Hale came to meet Rogers for breakfast the next morning, September 21, at the British officer's lodging, he was arrested and taken into the city by the *Halifax*, according to the Phelps account.[93] The *Halifax* log, however, shows the ship sailed as far west as Whitestone, without Rogers, and not to Manhattan before heading east.

The Nathan Hale commemorative column on Main Street in Huntington. *Photo by Audrey C. Tiernan, copyright 2020.*

By all accounts, Rogers brought Hale to General Howe's headquarters in the Beekman Mansion in Manhattan, located at the intersection of today's First Avenue and Fifty-First Street. It was late when they arrived, and the general had to be awakened. In addition to wearing civilian clothes, Hale had been caught with intelligence notes secreted in the soles of his shoes. Howe quickly signed a death warrant based on testimony from Rogers and his men. After the general denied Hale's requests for a Bible and a chaplain at his execution, the spy was held in a greenhouse on the estate under the supervision of Provost Marshal William Cunningham.[94]

After breakfast on Sunday, September 22, a sunny, hot morning, Hale was marched by Cunningham and his men to his place of execution. Over his plain brown suit, he wore a coarse white gown trimmed with black that was to serve as his burial shroud. Soldiers with unloaded muskets and fixed bayonets walked in front of and behind the prisoner, whose hands were tied behind his back. They were followed by a cart loaded with pine boards for fashioning his coffin. Most historians place the execution in an artillery park located at today's intersection of Third Avenue and Sixty-Sixth Street. Phelps puts it at an apple orchard. Some witnesses at the time said the hanging occurred in an orchard about four miles south of the Beekman Mansion near today's Duane and Vesey Streets by present-day city hall, but it seems unlikely that sixty-year-old Cunningham would want to march his prisoner that far.[95]

Whatever the location, the provost marshal chose a tree, and a rope was thrown over a branch about fifteen feet above the ground. Cunningham, a man known for his cruelty, mocked Hale and refused to mail the letters he had written. The condemned man climbed a ladder with the noose around his neck. "Any last dying speech and confession?" Cunningham asked. The unlucky spy asked to be shot rather than hanged—a request Cunningham quickly denied—and then stood proudly with his head tilted upward.

Although author Brian Kilmeade states it as a fact, there is no record of him actually saying "I only regret that I have but one life to lose for my country." Most historians dismiss it as apocryphal and trace the quote to a popular play of its time, *Cato*, by Joseph Addison. Phelps gives Hale's final words as "I am so satisfied with the cause in which I have engaged that my only regret is that I have not more lives than one to offer in its service." Cunningham, who kept Hale's Yale diploma as a souvenir, uttered a final command: "Swing the rebel off!"[96]

Frederick MacKenzie, a British captain stationed in New York City but not present for the hanging, reported in his diary on September 22 what witnesses told him about Hale: "He behaved with great composure and resolution, saying he thought it was the duty of every good Officer, to obey any orders given by his Commander-in-Chief."[97] Later that day, one of Howe's aides wrote in the orderly book: "A spy from the enemy (by his own full confession) apprehended last night, was today executed at 11 oClock in front of the Artillery Park."[98]

Cunningham—who would also be hanged, in London for forgery in 1791—left Hale's body hanging and decomposing in the heat for three days as Loyalists mocked the dead spy and spat on his corpse. A slave finally cut down the body and buried it, reportedly naked. The unmarked grave is believed to be somewhere near today's Third Avenue between Forty-Sixth and Sixty-Sixth Streets.[99]

Continental Army officers learned of Hale's fate on the evening of September 22 when Captain John Montressor, a British engineer, approached the Patriot lines on the Harlem Plains under a flag of truce. An aide to Howe, he carried a letter for the Continental Army commander about the exchange of prisoners. But when he was greeted by Washington's adjutant general, Joseph Reed, General Israel Putnam and Captain Alexander Hamilton, he informed them that Hale had been executed that morning as a spy.

Washington never spoke or wrote about Hale's death. To maintain morale, no announcement was made to the troops. It was officially recorded tersely without detail in the Continental Army records: "Nathan Hale–Capt–killed–22d September." Despite his silence, Washington is said to have been so upset that he hoped to capture a British spy and have him executed in retaliation. He would get his chance four years later with Major John André.[100]

Even if he had survived, Hale's intelligence would have been uselessly out of date because of the rapid advance of the British that forced Washington to abandon lower Manhattan. The inauspicious early attempt at espionage eventually resulted in the creation of the much more effective Culper Spy Ring. "But as yet…no better method was devised than to entrust some officer to get what was needed, either by the capture of prisoners or by sending a trusted man into the enemy's camp," wrote Morton Pennypacker, the historian best known for uncovering details of the intelligence network. Alexander Rose concluded that "by every measure, the Hale mission was a fiasco….The bad decisions and poor planning that led to his death reflect Washington's own confusion as to what his spy's purpose was. Washington, however, would learn from his mistakes."[101]

4

CREATION OF THE SPY RING

A fter the failure of Nathan Hale's ill-conceived solo spy mission, in 1777 George Washington tried to establish a spy network in and around New York City. The Continental Army commander in chief began by signing a contract with Nathaniel Sackett of Fishkill, who was a merchant in New York City, to gather intelligence. Washington authorized paying him $50 per month along with a fund of $500 from which Sackett could pay agents and informants.[102]

BENJAMIN TALLMADGE

Washington selected Benjamin Tallmadge to serve as Sackett's military contact. The general was always on the lookout for talented and resourceful young officers to place on his staff or in key positions elsewhere. The army commander took note of Tallmadge for his initiative and courage in battles around New York and Philadelphia. Washington met the young major during fighting at White Plains after the army had abandoned Manhattan and then directed him to try to stem a route at Germantown outside Philadelphia. Tallmadge likely impressed Washington with his after-battle and reconnaissance reports.[103]

Tallmadge was "dark-eyed, pale, delicately featured, with a prominent nose, a somewhat bulbous forehead, and a disconcerting habit of cocking his head like a quizzical beagle."[104] After graduating from Yale in 1773, Tallmadge worked as a schoolmaster in Wethersfield, Connecticut, where he met important Patriots such as Silas Deane, a member of the Continental Congress and later an envoy to France. But even after Lexington and Concord in April 1775, Tallmadge was reluctant to enlist. He told his friend Nathan Hale the following month that conflict with Britain might yield "a great, flourishing state," but he questioned whether "we ought to at present desire it."[105]

Benjamin Tallmadge by John Trumbull, circa 1783. *Sons of the Revolution in the State of New York, 1904.*

But Tallmadge's decision to visit the American lines around Boston in June seemed to resolve some of his doubts. While he wrote to Hale on July 4 and urged his friend to join the Continental Army, Tallmadge deferred signing up himself until the spring of 1776. When he was offered a lieutenancy in a Connecticut regiment led by his friend John Chester, Tallmadge accepted. After he fought at the Battle of Long Island in August, he was promoted to major in October when the officer holding that rank in General Jeremiah Wadsworth's brigade, which had absorbed Chester's regiment, was killed in a skirmish. It was then that Tallmadge first came into contact with Washington because majors of brigades met at the general's headquarters at eleven o'clock each day to receive orders. Tallmadge then accepted the lower rank of captain in one of four new cavalry regiments authorized by Congress, the Second Dragoons. It was in that role that he served as the contact for Sackett and received his first exposure to espionage.[106]

THE FIRST SUCCESSFUL LONG ISLAND SPY

The first spy to gather information successfully on Long Island as part of the Sackett network was Major John Clark. He was a young, tall Pennsylvania lawyer who had volunteered as a lieutenant in 1775 and gained notice for gallantry at the battles around Manhattan in 1776. After Clark demonstrated a talent for reconnoitering, Washington's favorite general, Nathanael Greene, made him his aide-de-camp and set him to work scouting in enemy territory. Clark established a network of contacts and was active on Long Island during much of 1777. He sent his messages to Washington through Benjamin Tallmadge, who was responsible for transporting Clark to the island from Connecticut.

Not much is known about Clark's activity after he crossed the Sound because he was extraordinarily secretive—even after the war. When he wrote an autobiographical sketch forty-five years later, he said nothing of what he did between January and September 1777. One of the few things that is known from that period is that on February 25 he paid a whaleboat captain to carry a message to Tallmadge. It noted that "there were no troops at Satauket, but part of two companies at Huntington.… There are but few who are not friendly to the Cause—That they had beat up for volunteers in the western part of the county but that only three had inlisted." On June 1, Washington recorded in his private accounts book that he had paid $946 for "secret services," some of it going to Clark.[107]

Caleb Brewster

Clark's intelligence was probably sent to Tallmadge by Caleb Brewster, a friend and early classmate of Tallmadge, who on April 7, 1777, was again promoted to major in his new regiment. Even before formation of the Culper Ring, Brewster, a boat captain who also became a captain in the Continental Army, had volunteered to provide General Washington with intelligence of British naval movements on Long Island Sound. "What I found from reading the Culper spy letters is that the first recruited spy was actually Caleb Brewster," Raynham Hall Museum historian Claire Bellerjeau said. "He wrote letters independently; he was not just somebody who carried letters."[108] Under the direction of Tallmadge, Brewster began using his whaleboats to carry spy messages in November 1778. The British knew a unit of Patriot whaleboats was operating on the Sound, but it wasn't until late 1781 that British spies identified Brewster as their leader and reported the information to headquarters.

Brewster was bold, using his real name in correspondence during the war even though the British offered a reward for his capture. He could usually rely on his knowledge of the Sound and bays and his crew's sailing and fighting skills to avoid having the British interfere with his duties. But he reportedly kept any secret messages in a weighted glass bottle tied to the boat in a way that it could be cut loose and sunk if the British appeared likely to capture them.[109]

Loyalist Lieutenant Colonel Richard Hewlett of DeLancey's Brigade stationed in Setauket informed General William Tryon in New York City in a letter received on September 3, 1777, that Clark was operating on Long Island and that Setauket Patriot leader Selah Strong was also spying there. Hewlett complained that rebels conducting a raid on Setauket had fired on soldiers trying to escape from a hospital and stolen British officers' horses. "There is a constant Correspondence between Connecticut & this County carried on to a most daring Degree I am well convinc'd," Hewlett wrote. "Mr. Strong has pretended to be our Friend....What Security can Government receive—while there are such Villains ready to stab her in secret."[110] The letter may have led to Strong's arrest on January 3, 1778.[111]

When Clark, who operated in the Philadelphia area for most of the war, left the island, Tallmadge needed another spy there or preferably a network of spies. He was fortunate in that he already had in place much of the infrastructure for what would become the Culper Spy Ring, particularly the cross-Sound connection through Brewster.[112]

Sackett had tried out several potential spies by sending them on information-gathering forays into Manhattan with mixed success. One never returned, while the others provided information of marginal importance. But Sackett learned some valuable strategies. He realized it was better to embed a spy behind British lines and leave him there with a cover story to explain his presence or have him masquerade as a Tory. But despite improving his spy craft, Sackett never developed a good relationship with Washington. Deciding his spymaster was better at developing successful espionage techniques than actually acquiring useful information, Washington terminated the arrangement with Sackett after two months following an unexplained fiasco. The general paid off Sackett with $500 from his Secret Service account.[113]

Despite the failure of the intelligence network, Washington had learned from its operation. He wrote to Sackett before firing him that "the good effect of intelligence may be lost if it is not speedily transmitted—this should be strongly impressed upon the persons employed as it also should be to avoid false intelligence."[114] Washington also realized that it was important to have multiple sources of information to ensure that what he was receiving was valid intelligence, particularly when it came to estimating troop strength, something often exaggerated. "A comparison of circumstances should be had, and much pains taken to avoid erroneous accounts," he wrote.[115]

FORMATION OF THE CULPER RING

After severing his connection with Sackett, Washington was forced to rely primarily on reconnaissance rather than espionage. But then the general got an unexpected gift in the form of an unsolicited letter written on August 7, 1778—a day that could be considered the start of the Culper Spy Ring. The letter was written by Lieutenant Caleb Brewster in Norwalk and sent directly to Washington—bypassing Tallmadge. Brewster offered to gather intelligence on Long Island.

While the letter has been lost, Washington's reply to the imposing and fearless mariner dated the next day fills in the blanks. The general instructed Brewster to "not spare any reasonable expense to come at early and true information; always recollecting, and bearing in mind, that vague and uncertain accounts of things…[are] more disturbing and dangerous than receiving none at all." He emphasized that he was particularly interested in sightings of enemy transport vessels, "whether they are preparing for the reception of troops and know what number of men are upon Long Island. Whether they are moving or stationary. What has become of their draft horses. Whether they appear to be collecting them for a move. How they are supplied with provisions. What arrivals. Whether with men, or provisions. And whether any troops have been embarked."[116]

Brewster's timing was perfect because Washington was preparing for an attack on British-held Newport, Rhode Island, by a combined Continental Army and French force now that the European power had entered the war against Great Britain. The attack fizzled when a storm damaged the opposing fleets and then scattered the vessels, which engaged in a disorganized battle. After that, the cautious French commander, Admiral Charles-Hector, the Comte (Count) d'Estaing, refused to attack Newport before his ships could be repaired in Boston. The arrival of British reinforcements doomed any immediate assault in Rhode Island.[117]

Brewster wrote his first intelligence report on August 27, 1778, several days before Sir Henry Clinton arrived in Newport with the British reinforcements. He detailed damage to British vessels limping into New York

Harbor after the storm and battle. He reported about one thousand British troops in Brookhaven and more than twenty-five warships at Huntington preparing to sail for Rhode Island. "While some of Brewster's intelligence was somewhat old…it was news to Washington," Alexander Rose wrote. "Thanks to his new agent inside them, New York's blank, forbidding walls had been breached, and intelligence was slowly leaking out."[118]

Washington was greatly pleased by Brewster's information. The general also realized he needed someone in the Continental Army to manage ongoing correspondence with Brewster after the departure of Sackett. The general asked Brigadier General Charles Scott, commander of a Virginia brigade stationed north of the city, to assemble a spy network. Washington detailed Tallmadge to assist Scott. With a field command that kept him busy, Scott put little effort or enthusiasm into the spy operation, so much of the work fell to the highly intelligent and energetic Tallmadge.[119]

Abraham Woodhull

It's not clear how long after Brewster reached out to Washington that the intelligence network that would become known as the Culper Spy Ring began to operate. In his memoirs, Tallmadge wrote that in 1778, "I opened a private correspondence with some persons in New York which lasted through the war…I kept one or more boats constantly employed in crossing the Sound on this business. My station was in the county of Westchester, and occasionally along the shores of the Sound." Letters from Tallmadge and his childhood friend Abraham Woodhull, who would become the chief spy coordinating with Tallmadge using the codename Samuel Culper, demonstrate that by October 1778 the espionage operation was in full operation.

"Brewster wrote the very first letter and was the first recruited," Bellerjeau said. "Then pretty quickly after that Tallmadge started talking about Woodhull. There's actually a letter where they don't call him Culper yet and just call him W."[120]

Woodhull initially showed little hostility toward the British. But that changed when his older cousin General Nathaniel Woodhull was killed by the British in August 1776 after surrendering while trying to move livestock east on Long Island to keep it out of British hands.

Washington wrote to Tallmadge on August 25 that "you should be perfectly convinced of the integrity of W—— previous to his embarking in the business proposed. This being done I shall be happy in employing him." Washington added that Tallmadge should not bring Woodhull to headquarters because "knowledge of the circumstances in the enemy might blast the whole design."[121]

Throughout the war, Woodhull was particularly zealous about protecting his identity and probably would have been horrified to learn that Washington had used the first letter of his real surname in a letter that might have fallen into British hands.[122]

Tallmadge appreciated the need for tightened security. With Scott's approval, he developed a list of codenames for the key players. Washington is believed to have invented the name for the network: Culper. It is thought to have been derived from the army commander's surveying work in Culpeper County, Virginia, when he was seventeen. Tallmadge became John Bolton while Woodhull became Samuel Culper.[123]

Sometime in the fall of 1778, Woodhull began traveling to Manhattan and reporting verbally to Brewster what he observed. Because many of his Loyalist neighbors were suspicious about the farmer's early release from custody in Connecticut, Tallmadge suggested that Woodhull sign a British loyalty oath to alleviate questions about his allegiance. Alexander Rose states that Woodhull followed Tallmadge's advice before writing his first Samuel Culper letter on October 29, 1778, but local historians say there is no record of that. "Just a conversation that went nowhere as far as I'm concerned," said Beverly Tyler, historian for the Setauket-based Three Village Historical Society, who has been researching the spy ring since 1974.[124]

When Woodhull switched from verbal reports to writing letters, his anxiety about security escalated exponentially. He repeatedly beseeched Tallmadge and Washington to destroy his letters upon receipt. Tallmadge dutifully destroyed the first letter from Samuel Culper written on October 29, 1778, after copying it and passing on the copy to headquarters so there would be nothing to trace back to Woodhull. But subsequently he dropped that precaution and just forwarded the originals to the general. Woodhull would have been appalled to learn that Washington kept most of them.[125]

Woodhull was very self-conscious about his lack of education and the language he employed in his letters, and he apologized for that in some of them. He was clearly intimidated by Tallmadge and his Yale education and the refined language used by the general. Woodhull's irregular spelling and punctuation reflected his limited education. And while his letters include archaic words such as *hath* and *doth*, Tallmadge and Washington never commented on it in their letters. They were more interested in his intelligence. Woodhull's facts were generally useful, even if his analysis of them was sometimes faulty.[126]

Conflicting Visions of Espionage

Tallmadge and Scott did not mesh well. They differed in personality and their approach to gathering intelligence. Scott, who unlike Tallmadge never showed enthusiasm for espionage and paid little attention to detail, never got along well with his subordinates and undermined them frequently. And while Tallmadge wanted to employ the carefully assembled network approach he learned from Nathaniel Sackett, John Clark and others, Scott favored the quick in-and-out mission strategy employed so unsuccessfully by Nathan Hale. Tallmadge wanted to put agents in place for long periods to provide more detailed information, while Scott thought sending spies out for one-time missions provided more immediate results and presented less danger to the others involved if one of them was captured. Initially, Washington sided with Scott, who continued to send out single agents on reconnaissance missions. But some never returned after being questioned by British sentries.[127]

On September 25, 1778, having concluded that Scott's approach was unworkable, Washington suggested to Scott that he try Tallmadge's embedded network approach. He instructed Scott to "endeavor to get some intelligent person into the City and others of his own choice to be messengers between you and him, for the purpose of conveying such information as he shall be able to obtain." As for the chief agent, Washington suggested Woodhull, Tallmadge's "Mr. C——," whose "discernment, and means of information, would enable him to give important advices."[128] Tallmadge used the endorsement from Washington to try to consolidate control over the fledgling espionage network, bypassing Scott in relaying messages.

With his own recruited spies providing little useful information, Scott decided to give up not only supervision of the intelligence-gathering but also the army. He wrote Washington on October 29 to say he was having trouble managing the spy operation and had family issues at home that needed his attention. "My unhappy misfortunes make it indispensably necessary that I should leave the army in a few weeks," he told the commander in chief.[129] Washington accepted Scott's resignation, undoubtably relieved. Washington then elevated Tallmadge, only twenty-four, to manage the spy ring as his "director of military intelligence."[130]

TALLMADGE IN CHARGE

Benjamin Tallmadge, son of Setauket's Presbyterian minister, was assigned to the Second Continental Connecticut Dragoons patrolling along the northern shore of Long Island Sound. He was a natural choice to oversee the spy operation. "With his Setauket-Presbyterian roots and his tested dedication to the cause of independence, Tallmadge was the obvious candidate to organize and run an espionage network in Manhattan and Long Island," biographer Richard F. Welch wrote. "Tallmadge readily accepted the assignment and devoted a considerable amount of his military career to obtaining, evaluating and forwarding reports from the British-occupied islands." As for who to recruit, Welch added that "Long Island patriots, primarily Suffolk County Presbyterians and Congregationalists, especially those with good reasons to travel into the city, were prime candidates for the role of intelligence agents."[131]

Tallmadge grew up in Setauket with ardent Patriots, including Abraham Woodhull, Caleb Brewster and Austin Roe. Tallmadge's patriotism was fueled by his religion but also the death of his eldest brother, who was captured during the battles in New York and starved to death in prison.

From 1778 to the end of the war five years later, Tallmadge and his dragoons were in almost constant motion in the lower Hudson Valley and along the Connecticut coast. They scouted, worked to suppress Tory bandits and responded to British raids while still participating in major army offensives. When Washington gave Tallmadge the important assignment of overseeing intelligence in late 1778, it kept them in constant contact and communication and led to mutual affection and deep devotion on Tallmadge's part.[132]

ROBERT TOWNSEND

Afraid of traveling to New York after being stopped and questioned by British sentries and with Washington urging that he uproot himself from Setauket and live in the city, Woodhull realized he needed to recruit someone else to spy there. His choice was inspired and fortuitous for the Patriot cause. Robert Townsend of Oyster Bay, purchasing agent in Manhattan for his prosperous merchant father, Samuel—excellent cover for gathering intelligence—agreed to take over the espionage in Manhattan.[133]

Woodhull knew Townsend, then in his late twenties, because both lodged at the Manhattan boardinghouse owned by Woodhull's brother-in-law Amos Underhill. Woodhull wrote on October 31, 1778, to General Scott, who had not yet been replaced as head of the spy operation by Tallmadge, that he had been "particularly successful in ingaging a faithful friend and one the first characters in the City to make it his business and keep his eyes upon every movement and assist me in all respects and meet and consult weekly in or near the city. I have the most sanguine hopes of great advantage will acrue by his assistance."

Alexander Rose stated definitively that Woodhull was referring to Underhill, who was married to his older sister Mary. But local historians Beverly Tyler and Claire Bellerjeau believe Woodhull was writing about Robert Townsend. "He uses similar verbiage later" to refer to Townsend, Bellerjeau said.[134]

Ink drawing of Culper Spy Ring member Robert Townsend done in 1813 by his nephew Peter. *Courtesy of Raynham Hall Museum.*

Robert Townsend remains something of a mystery. The only image of him is a small charcoal sketch done by his nephew Peter in 1813. Like other family members Peter sketched, Robert has a prominent forehead, a slim figure and short curly hair.[135] Authors have tried to fill in some of the blanks about the family's fourth son, sometimes out of thin air. Author Brian Kilmeade described him as "dark and lean" and as someone who "preferred to work quietly behind the scenes, managing the ledgers and accounts—anything that kept him out of the limelight and ribaldry that the other Townsend men shared" and being a man of "somber dress, quiet habit, and humble bearing."[136]

The most common adjective employed to describe Townsend is "bookish." "But that is simplistic," Bellerjeau argued.

> *He was a complex person. He was very highly educated with a large library. He had a great eye for observation; Washington commented on the accuracy of his reports. He was kind of a social rebel, but he did have a high moral standard. He was an abolitionist after the war but the effort failed at the time. He tended to be depressed and suffered from insomnia in his later life, according to family letters. But it was more that he was quiet and there were reasons not to be joyful after the war. The family had huge debt.*[137]

While most authors state that Robert Townsend swore an oath of loyalty to the Crown along with about three thousand other Long Island residents, including his father, he never did, Bellerjeau insists. He did help form a volunteer company to support the British and even had a red uniform and stood guard outside British headquarters, perfect cover for gathering intelligence. Bellerjeau said the enrollment papers for that unit that Townsend drafted, but never signed himself, are often mistaken as a loyalty oath that he signed.[138]

His nephew Peter wrote decades later that Robert "inclined at first to the Royal cause."[139] But that clearly changed over the years, presumably because of the treatment of his father by the Tories and his resentment over the harsh British occupation of Long Island, including the frequent takeover of the family home in Oyster Bay as a headquarters.

In managing his father's mercantile business in the city, Townsend focused on serving the British officer class, providing rum and other spirits, sugar and various commodities. Being in proximity to the redcoat leadership was an excellent place to be for a fledgling spy.[140]

Although Woodhull and Townsend both relied on a network of about a score of respectable citizen sources who would not arouse suspicion, they often found it necessary to personally scout for information.

Pennypacker and other earlier historians pondered how Townsend and Woodhull could frequently meet without attracting suspicion. Townsend's account books showed he changed his boarding place in New York usually about once a year, probably as a precautionary measure, Pennypacker wrote. He added that comparing Townsend's ledgers to Woodhull's showed that both men had accounts for staying with the same landlords simultaneously. One of them was Woodhull's brother-in-law Amos Underhill. Underhill bought a house and became a merchant in New York after the Continental Army was forced out of Manhattan in November 1776. Two years later, with a baby on the way, Amos and his wife, Mary, began to take in occasional boarders for extra income. With the war creating shortages of housing, goods and food that pushed the cost of living extremely high, even Abraham Woodhull was required to pay three pounds a week to stay there. This was one of the expenses of spying that he complained about in his letters to Tallmadge and Washington. But staying under the same roof as Townsend would allow the spies to meet without attracting suspicion.[141] "Robert was living at Abraham Woodhull's sister's boardinghouse, and so Robert and Woodhull knew each other all along the way," Bellerjeau said.

Townsend agreed to Woodhull's request to replace him as the principal spy in Manhattan with one condition: no one besides Woodhull, Tallmadge and the couriers—not even Washington—could ever know his identity. Understandably, both Woodhull and Townsend were in constant fear of being discovered. On October 31, 1778, Woodhull wrote to Washington, "I have to request that you will destroy every letter instantly after reading for fear of some unforeseen accident that might befall you and the letters get into the enemies hands and probably find me out and take me before I have any warning. I desire you will be particularly cairfull."

Washington clearly understood the need for secrecy. He wrote to Tallmadge about Woodhull on November 20, 1778, that "you will be pleased to observe the strictest silence with respect to C—— as you are to be the only person entrusted with the knowledge or conveyance of his letters."[142] In another letter to his spy chief, Washington wrote on July 10, 1779, that "there can be scarcely any need of recommending the greatest... secrecy in the business so critical and dangerous."[143]

To protect himself, Robert Townsend adopted the alias of Culper Junior, since Woodhull was already Samuel Culper. Woodhull then became Culper Senior. Although the army commander stated he never wanted to meet Woodhull or Townsend to protect them from discovery, Bellerjeau concluded that Washington may have deduced Townsend's identity because the general knew his father, Samuel.[144]

Townsend was widely praised by Woodhull and the other recipients of his intelligence. "He is the person in whom I have the greatest confidence," Washington wrote in one letter to Congress. In another, the general wrote that "his accounts are intelligent, clear, and satisfactory....I rely upon his intelligence." Tallmadge described Townsend as "a Gentleman of business, of Education and honor." Woodhull wrote of Townsend on June 20, 1779, that "he is a person that hath the interest of our Country at heart and of good reputation, character and family, I have reason to think his advantages for serving you, and abilities, are far superior to mine." Another Woodhull appraisal: "[H]e is allowed to be a person of good sense and judgment, and his firmness and friendship towards our Country I do assure, you need not doubt. I have known him several years and confident he is a sincere friend, and hath undertaken it solely for to be some advantage to our distressed Country."[145]

Many books on the spy ring state that Townsend was a Quaker and that was part of his motivation for engaging in espionage. Alexander Rose described him as "half Quaker" and "partly devout." These authors say that since members of the sect were known pacifists, Townsend's trading with the British while gathering information would not attract suspicion. But Claire Bellerjeau is adamant that Townsend was not even half Quaker. "I've never heard him say in any of his writings anything about a religious belief," she said. "He does not ever say that he goes to church. There's no question that his father Samuel, his mother Sarah and his sister Sally were Baptists. That's one hundred percent provable because they're on the Baptist church roll in 1789." She said there were other Townsends in Oyster Bay who were Quakers. "If you read anything written by a Quaker, they always start the letters saying something like 'thy respected friend' and they always use the words thee and thou. Robert Townsend never used that kind of language, and he never speaks about God. I don't think he went to church as an adult."[146]

Whether or not their religious beliefs were a factor, Woodhull and Townsend were clearly motivated primarily by their strong belief in the Patriot cause. They and the other members of the Culper network never asked to be paid, although Woodhull and Townsend did expect to be reimbursed for their expenses. One reason not to seek payment for espionage services was that spies providing information for pay were considered the lowest class of individuals, and Woodhull and Townsend clearly considered themselves better than that.

Townsend, however, did inquire about whether his service might be rewarded after the war. Woodhull told Tallmadge that his new recruit's "chief aim is to have such a recommendation at the close of this war as may entitle him to some imployment as compensation for the disadvantage and risque he plans."[147] A year later, Townsend inquired of Washington via Tallmadge about whether he would receive preferential treatment for a job from the new government should the war be concluded successfully. Washington replied in a letter of September 16, 1780, to Tallmadge that

> *it is impossible for me, circumstanced as matters are to give a positive answer to C—— Junior's request, as I cannot, without knowing his views, tell what his expectations are. Of this, both you and he may rest assured, that should he continue Serviceable and faithful, and should the issue of our affairs prove as favorable as we hope, I shall be ready to recommend him to the public, if public employ should be his aim, and if not, that I shall think myself bound to represent his conduct in the light it deserves, and procure him compensation of another kind.*

Neither man followed up after the Revolution.

Former Central Intelligence Agency senior case officer Kenneth Daigler wrote that compared to Woodhull, "Townsend was somewhat more pragmatic in his view of the business aspect of his activities. He fully expected to be reimbursed on a timely basis for his expenses and was often disappointed. Woodhull, however, was more idealistic in understanding about delays in repayment."[148] Bellerjeau disagreed with that assessment. "I think Woodhull writes much more about wanting money sent to him than Robert," she said. "Woodhull writes constantly about wanting to be paid and Robert doesn't do that at all."[149]

Pennypacker wrote that when the Culper spy operation was established, it

> *differed from that of Hale's time in that it became a business with the men who conducted it, and enabled them usually to have someone who could get the information when they feared they were suspected or for any*

other reason they believed it too hazardous to undertake themselves. It is remarkable that although their lives were every moment in danger so carefully were their secrets guarded that not only to the end of the war but for a hundred and fifty years thereafter, in spite of frequent efforts to discover their identity, the real men were never suspected. Primarily this was due to the caution of the men themselves…but it was also due to the care of General Washington in exacting from all who knew them the most solemn pledge that not to any one at any time or under any circumstances would they reveal their identity.

While there were some close calls, none of the Culper spies was ever caught by the British.

OPERATION OF THE ESPIONAGE NETWORK

The Culper Spy Ring operated via a circuitous but ultimately secure communications route. To avoid areas where interception and capture were more likely, the agents and couriers carried intelligence reports from New York City across the East River, eastward on Long Island to Setauket, across Long Island Sound and then west along the Connecticut shore to spymaster Benjamin Tallmadge and ultimately George Washington north of the city or in New Jersey. Requests for information from Washington to the initial principal spy, Abraham Woodhull, and later the primary spy in the city, Robert Townsend, followed the path in reverse.

The turnaround time could be a week or more. Washington complained repeatedly about untimely reports, and he and the members of the ring tried throughout the war to shorten the route without success. Setauket was the hub because it was the childhood home of Tallmadge, Woodhull and others they could trust and it was far enough east of the concentrations of Loyalists closer to Manhattan.

There are 194 known letters totaling 385 pages written by the Culper spies, Tallmadge, Washington and others, according to Bellerjeau, who keeps a spreadsheet. The latest addition came in mid-2020 when one later confirmed by experts was discovered in the collection of the Long Island Museum in Stony Brook. The letter was donated in 1951 and then overlooked until a curator came across it. It was written on November 8, 1779, by Benjamin Tallmadge to Robert Townsend and intended to be delivered personally by Abraham Woodhull. It is the only known surviving letter from Tallmadge to Townsend, according to Bellerjeau.

NAME	ALIAS	CODE #	POSITION	BORN	DIED
George Washington	None	711	Spymaster	1732 Virginia	1799 Mt. Vernon, VA
Benjamin Tallmadge	*John Bolton*	721	Chief of Intelligence	1754 Setauket	1835 Litchfield, CT
Abraham Woodhull	*Samuel Culper Senior*	722	Head Spy	1750 Setauket	1826 Setauket, NY
Robert Townsend	*Samuel Culper Junior*	723	NYC Spy	1753 Oyster Bay	1838 Oyster Bay, NY
Austin Roe	None	724	Courier, LI - NYC	1748 Setauket	1830 Patchogue, NY
Caleb Brewster	None	725	Whaleboat Captain	1747 Setauket	1827 Black Rock, CT
Anna (Nancy) Smith Strong	None	None	Spy Support	1740 Setauket	1812 Setauket, NY
Jonas Hawkins	None	None	Courier, Jan. -- June 1779	1752 Stony Brook	1817 Stony Brook, NY

General Washington's Long Island Spy Ring

Key players in the Culper Spy Ring. *Courtesy of Three Village Historical Society.*

There were certainly other letters that were destroyed after being received, as Woodhull and Townsend intended, and some were destroyed by couriers fearful of being apprehended. Others might have been lost after the war.[152]

Over the course of the conflict, the reports demonstrate an increasing level of spy craft sophistication. For the earliest letters, Tallmadge and Woodhull established a fairly simple process to hide the identity of the members of the network: giving them codenames. Tallmadge was John Bolton, Woodhull was Samuel Culper and Townsend was Samuel Culper Junior.

As the war wore on, security was increased by substituting numbers for people, places and things. The system devised by Woodhull and employed in his letter of April 10, 1779, used the figures 10 for New York, for example; 30 and 44 for post riders Jonas Hawkins and Austin Roe, who carried the dispatches; and 20 for Setauket.[153]

After inserting a few numerical ciphers in ten letters bound for New York and twenty going the other way, Tallmadge decided that a more secure arrangement was necessary. In July 1779, he upgraded the system by preparing a "dictionary" with a new, expanded code. It was loosely based on the Ave Maria cipher created by priest Johannes Trithemius, author

A page from the "dictionary" or codebook devised by Major Benjamin Tallmadge in early July 1779 after he determined that previous methods of transmitting information were inadequate. *Library of Congress.*

of the first book on the subject printed in 1518. The dictionary contained closely written columns of figures and words arranged on a double sheet of paper. The 710 words chosen by Tallmadge were the ones most likely to be used, such as Congress, gun, navy and Tory. He extracted them from a 1777 London edition of *Entick's Dictionary* and wrote them in alphabetical order in columns. Opposite each word was a number that would replace the word in the reports, such as "many" being replaced by 384 and "murder" being listed as 387. Fifty-three prominent proper nouns were also given numbers ranging from 711 to 763. Thus Tallmadge, who had gone by John Bolton, became 721. Woodhull, addressed previously as Samuel Culper and then Culper Senior, became 722. Robert Townsend, Culper Junior, was 723. Setauket tavern owner and courier Austin Roe was 724. Whaleboat captain Caleb Brewster was 725, George Washington 711, New York 727, Long Island 728, Setauket 729 and so on.[154]

There was also a coded alphabet for words not listed as well as a system to use letters to replace numerals. The letter A became E, B became F, and the numeral 1 became E and 2 became F and so forth. To make the system easier to understand, the writer would add a double line underneath transposed digits to set them apart from enciphered words and put a small flourish or squiggle above the code number for past and future tenses and plurals. Tallmadge's version was used for the duration of the war. Washington made reference to it in a letter dated July 27, 1779, and a copy of the code is included with his letters in the Library of Congress.[155]

Members of the spy ring and Washington's staff quickly adapted to using the improved code. An example of how it appeared is this sentence from an August 6 report to the general: "Sorry 626.280 cannot give 707 an exact account 431.625.635." Translation: "Sorry that I cannot give you an exact account of the situation of the troops."[156]

Alexander Rose states that Tallmadge's code was rudimentary compared to those being used in Europe at the time and could have been easily deciphered by experts there. But luckily for the Continental Army, British experts were not to be found on this side of the ocean. "The words and numbers were not randomized…and it contained 22 of the 27 most frequently used words…in the English language. Even a novice cryptologist knew better than to hand out such free clues," Rose wrote. "This bad habit soon ceased when it was realized that keeping common words as plaintext while enciphering the rarer, less easily guessable ones made messages far more secure.…Despite the Culper Cipher's weaknesses, it did the job it was meant for: turning plaintext into code strong enough to baffle an ordinary

BENJAMIN TALLMADGE'S
CODEBOOK DICTIONARY

ALPHABET		MONTHS		PROPER NAMES		NUMBERS		IMPORTANT WORDS	
Use of	Means	Use of	Means	Use of	Means	Use of	Means	Use of	
A	G	341	JANUARY	711	General Washington	1	E	15	Advice
B	H	215	FEBRUARY	712	Clinton	2	F	28	Appointment
C	I	374	MARCH	713	Tryon	3	G	60	Better
D	J	22	APRIL	721	Major Tallmadge, alias John Bolton	4	I	73	Camp
E	A	373	MAY	722	Abraham Woodhull, alias Samuel Culper	5	K	121	Day
F	B	336	JUNE	723	Robert Townsend, alias Samuel Culper Jr.	6	M	151	Disorder
G	C	337	JULY	724	Austin Roe	7	N	156	Deliver
H	D	29	AUGUST	725	Caleb Brewster	8	O	174	Express
I	E	616	SEPTEMBER	726	Rivington	9	Q	230	Guineas
J	F	462	OCTOBER	727	New York	0	U	286	Ink
K	Q	427	NOVEMBER	728	Long Island			309	Infantry
L	R	154	DECEMBER	729	Setauket			317	Importance
M	L			745	England			322	Inquiry
N	M							345	Knowledge
O	K							347	Land
P	N							349	Low
Q	O							355	Lady
R	P							356	Letter
S	Y							371	Man
T	Z							476	Parts
U	S							585	Refugees
V	T							592	Ships
W	U							660	Vigilant
X	V							691	Written
Y	W							708	Your
Z	X								

A sampling of the codes for people, places and other things listed in Benjamin Tallmadge's 1779 "dictionary" or codebook. *Courtesy of Three Village Historical Society.*

reader.…It was never intended to do more than provide backup security" for invisible ink. "Armed with their code and ink, the Culper Ring was already the most 'professional' of all of Washington's spies."[155]

"While this was a much more secure code," former CIA case officer Kenneth Daigler wrote, "it also involved more time to compose and to decode." So the full coding system was rarely used.[156]

The last—and best—added layer of security was using a special ink or "stain" that was invisible until treated with another solution. Unlike a code, it could never be broken. The ink used by the Culper Ring was invented by James Jay, brother of John Jay, who collaborated with Alexander Hamilton and James Madison to write the Federalist Papers and became the first chief justice of the Supreme Court. James Jay, a doctor who lived in London before the war, was an amateur chemist and had been knighted by King George III for his efforts in 1763. John Jay wrote to Washington about "a mode of correspondence, which may be of use, provided proper agents [chemicals] can be obtained. I have experienced its efficacy by a three years' trial."[157]

Jay's secret ink did not become visible by heating, as was the case with older methods such as using lemon juice, vinegar or milk. James Jay wrote to Thomas Jefferson after the war that his mixture "would elude the generally known means of detection, and yet could be rendered visible by a suitable counterpart"—the second chemical.[160]

Washington was excited at the prospect of improving the security of the spy ring, but it took him nearly six months, until December 1778, to receive a small initial supply of the solutions from Jay. The general did not have enough to provide any to the Culper spies until the following spring. In mid-April 1779, Woodhull finally received some stain and wrote that it "gives me great satisfaction."[161]

Jay had brought some of the chemicals back with him from London, but the supply soon ran out. When he could find more of the ingredients, Jay sent the commander in chief small batches of what they codenamed "medicine" in small doctor's boxes. Washington wrote from his headquarters in Morristown, New Jersey, to Jay in Fishkill on the Hudson River on April 9, 1780, to tell him that "the liquid with which you were so obliging as to furnish me for the purpose of private corrispondence is exhausted; and as I have found it very useful, I take the liberty to request you will favour me with a further supply....Should you not have by you the necessary ingredients, if they are to be procured at any of the Hospitals within your reach, I would wish you to apply for them in my name."[162]

Jay explained to Washington that part of the problem was that even if he had the chemicals to make what the general called the "sympathetic stain," it was difficult to create the solutions because it "require[d] some assistance from chemistry" and "I have no place where a little apparatus may be erected for preparing it" or the materials for making the apparatus. Washington quickly solved that problem by ordering a subordinate to have artillerymen build a lab for Jay.[163]

British intelligence officers and spies used a similar invisible ink. That is probably why Washington stated in a July 25, 1779 letter to Woodhull that accompanied a supply of ink that "I beg that no mention may ever be made of your having received such liquids from me or any one else...as I am informed that Govr. Tryon has a preparation of the same acid or something similar to it, which may lead to a detection if it is ever known that a matter of this sort has passed from me."[164]

The stain was first used about the time that Tallmadge developed his dictionary. Washington struggled to provide the funds to pay for the chemicals, so sometimes the Culper spies had to do without.[165]

Upon receiving one of the stain letters, Washington was alarmed. He wrote that

> *C———r, Jr. should avoid making use of the Stain upon a Blank sheet of paper (which is the usual way of its coming to me). This circumstance alone is sufficient to raise suspicions. A much better way is to write a letter in the Tory stile with some mixture of family matters and between the lines on the remaining part of the sheet communicate with the stain the intended intelligence. Such a letter would pass through the hands of the enemy unsuspected and even if the agents should be unfaithful or negligent, no discovery would be made to his prejudice, as these people are not to know that there is concealed writing in the letter.*[166]

It's likely that Tallmadge had not explained to his commander that Townsend sent his letters concealed in a predetermined position within an entire package of blank letter paper.

"We know with confidence that the ink was first sent to Woodhull in April of 1779," Claire Bellerjeau said. "But there is no way of truly counting how many letters were written with it."[167] Many of the surviving letters are copies made by Washington's aides, or if they were written using the stain, the invisible ink had already been developed.

The first postwar reference to the stain was in Morton Pennypacker's second breakthrough book on the spy ring published in 1939. The formula for Jay's stain remains a mystery. Alexander Rose believes it was made from gallic acid and powdered gum Arabic, while the reagent was composed of ferrous sulfate dissolved in distilled water.[168]

The spies feared their handwriting might betray them, so they practiced writing in different styles. The agents also urged that the letters they were sending be destroyed. But Washington preserved the majority of the letters. With one exception, the letters written by Washington to Tallmadge with information for the members of the Culper Ring were promptly destroyed by them. Eventually, it was Townsend's handwriting that enabled him to be positively identified as a member of the spy network by Pennypacker in 1939.

CARRYING THE MESSAGES

In the initial phase of the Culper network, chief spy Abraham Woodhull traveled from Setauket to Manhattan every few weeks to collect information and then returned home to turn it over to Caleb Brewster for the trip across Long Island Sound. Woodhull hated making the fifty-five-mile journey. Besides having to leave his aged parents unattended, it meant potential interception by robbers, Loyalist bands and British patrols. There was the need to show papers and answer questions at army checkpoints. There were expenses if he stayed at an inn along the way and his brother-in-law's house in Manhattan plus the ferry across the East River and often a permit from the British to leave the city. On October 31, 1778, two days after writing his first Samuel Culper letter, Woodhull wrote about the aggressive questioning he routinely had to endure at one British checkpoint, where he "received their threats for coming there that make me almost tremble" with fear of being unmasked.[169]

Even after Woodhull became so fearful of detection that he recruited Robert Townsend to gather intelligence in the city, he would still make trips occasionally to New York to compile information or serve as a courier connecting with Townsend.

But when a courier was available, Woodhull was able to remain relatively safe in Setauket and rely on Townsend and the rider. The most frequent and dependable courier was Setauket tavern owner Austin Roe, Culper code number 724. He began making his dangerous trips about April 1779. Roe continued at least once a week, ostensibly to purchase supplies for his business, until early July 1782, when the Culper correspondence ceased. Roe traveled to and from Setauket via North Country Road, Middle Country Road or South Country Road, depending on the latest information about British and Loyalist checkpoints and patrols. He crossed the East River by ferry to and from Brooklyn.

Roe overlapped for several months with Woodhull and Jonas Hawkins, another Setauket tavern owner recruited at the end of 1778. Having three couriers carry messages reduced the risk for all of them because they would be traveling less frequently through British lines. "Rather than having one person at a time do spy work and bring out messages himself, the Culper Spy Ring was much more sophisticated by having a person integrated into the area so he wouldn't stand out and having the messages come out by courier," Setauket historian Beverly Tyler said.

Early on, Caleb Brewster delivered the reports personally to Tallmadge, who was waiting at Fairfield. Later, when the officer was considered too valuable to retrieve the messages, he would deploy three of his dragoons as dispatch riders every fifteen miles along the route to relay the information to him.

The original site of Roe Tavern on Main Street in East Setauket. It was relocated in 1936. *Photo by Audrey C. Tiernan, copyright 2020.*

According to Alexander Rose, Kenneth Daigler and several other authors, Roe would usually or at least sometimes leave the information from Townsend in a secret location in one of Woodhull's livestock fields in Setauket, where a "dead drop" box was hidden in the underbrush or buried. Woodhull would retrieve it later while attending to his cattle.[170] But Raynham Hall historian Claire Bellerjeau countered, "I haven't seen any evidence of a dropbox" being used, and there was no need for the spies in Setauket to have one because they could just hand off the intelligence directly to each other.[171]

ANNA STRONG AND HER FAMOUS CLOTHESLINE

One of the best-known aspects of the Culper Spy Ring story is the purported role of Anna Strong's clothesline. According to family tradition, Anna Smith Strong, a neighbor and close friend of Abraham Woodhull, would hang out laundry to dry in a pattern that indicated where he should rendezvous with Caleb Brewster. Morton Pennypacker and some more current historians treat the story as fact while others say there is no historical documentation for it.

Strong was married to Patriot leader Selah Strong, who was imprisoned by the British in New York for "surreptitious correspondence with the enemy." Supposedly, she would hang a black petticoat on her clothesline to alert Woodhull, who lived across the bay, when Brewster had arrived from Connecticut to retrieve or drop off messages. She would add one to six white handkerchiefs to inform Woodhull in which of six coves Brewster would be waiting.

Pennypacker noted that he and other historians had spent years trying to track down information about how Woodhull knew where to find Brewster. "Finally a clue was found among the papers of the Floyd family and when this was compared with the Woodhull account book it was discovered that the signals were arranged by no less a personage than the wife of Judge Selah Strong," Pennypacker wrote. Strong family historian Kate Strong repeated the clothesline story in a chapter titled "In Defense of Nancy's Clothesline" in a 1969 book. She said it was corroborated by scraps of paper, deeds, journals and letters in her possession, as well as documents she saw or was told about by Morton Pennypacker.[170]

Many historians subsequently have repeated the clothesline story without skepticism. The most preposterous version is presented by former Central Intelligence Agency case officer Kenneth Daigler, who clearly never visited Setauket. He has Brewster looking at Strong's clothesline through a telescope "from his base in Fairfield," Connecticut. That account ignores the long distance and curvature of the Earth that would thwart even modern telescopes. And it ignores the significant amount of land between the Sound and the Strong property. Brian Kilmeade wrote in his 2013 bestseller *George Washington's Secret Six* that "the Strong estate, situated on a high bluff, would be visible to anyone passing by boat" on Long Island Sound.[171] But the Strongs' estate is not on a bluff by the Sound, and its servants' quarters, where the laundry would have been hung out to dry, are near the beach, not much higher than sea level. To his credit, Kilmeade does describe the clothesline story as "local legend."

Most Long Island historians who have spent decades researching the Culper network view the clothesline story the same way. "I have read all of the Culper letters and there is no reference to Anna Strong's clothesline," Bellerjeau said.[172] Tyler agreed: "The clothesline story is apocryphal; I treat it as folklore," although it is plausible. "Brewster couldn't meet directly with Woodhull because he's dressed in a Continental Army uniform and Woodhull is portraying himself as a Loyalist so they can't meet except at night after Anna Strong lets him know where."

Tyler continued, "She had to communicate with him in some way, whether it was the clothesline or some other regular method. She easily could have given the messages as to where Caleb Brewster was hiding his whaleboats by rowing across Little Bay to his house or taking her horse around and meeting with Abraham Woodhull." The two families were close because they were the only residents in the area, and Selah Strong was Woodhull's second cousin. "No matter where Brewster pulled in with his whaleboats—almost always more than one whaleboat and usually three—he went to the Strongs' home to check in, even though we have just one letter where he says he is at the Strongs," Tyler said.[175]

Whether guided by the clothesline or not, a related question is how did Caleb Brewster know when to come to Long Island to pick up a report for Washington? "These meetings were either on direct orders from Tallmadge or determined in advance by the Culpers," Bellerjeau said.

> *For example, in a July 1779 letter to George Washington, Benjamin Tallmadge wrote "I yesterday sent C. Brewster, intrusted over to Long Island for dispatches & to convey some instructions as well as guineas to Culper & Culper Jr." In an August 1779 letter, Tallmadge writes to Washington, "Culper Jur appointed the next time for 725* [Caleb Brewster] *to come on the 19th Instant." Following that meeting in August 1779 there is a letter from Woodhull to Tallmadge: "The next appointment for C. Brewster to be here is the 1st of September. It is very long but it cannot be altered now."*[176]

Tyler added that "he came across often as he had many contacts on Long Island and actually wrote to Washington asking for more boats and crews so he could be more effective on the Sound. It seems to be where he wanted to be, both intercepting British and Loyalist shipping and whaleboat raiders and picking up information from his various sources."[177]

SPEED VERSUS DISCRETION

As the war dragged on, Washington increasingly fretted that it was taking too long for the intelligence to reach him, while the British became more suspicious about the activity in Setauket. The commander wrote in a June 27, 1779 letter to Tallmadge that Culper Junior "should endeavor to hit upon some certain mode of conveying his information quickly, for it is of little avail to be told of things after they had become…known to every body."[178]

After repeated complaints from Washington, a shorter route was planned to cross the Sound near Cow Neck, present-day Port Washington. But it proved impractical, so the intelligence continued to move through Setauket.[179]

While Washington knew it was vital to his strategic planning to know expeditiously the number of British troops and navy vessels in the city and details of the forts protecting it, he also knew that the key to successful spying was extreme discretion. The necessity of that was demonstrated in the spring of 1779, when the spy operation was nearly uncovered after a Long Island Patriot privateer captain operating out of Connecticut, John Wolsey, was caught by the British. To gain his release, he provided information about suspicions of wrongdoing by Abraham Woodhull. Lieutenant Colonel John Graves Simcoe of the Queen's Rangers traveled to Setauket in April to investigate. Woodhull described his narrow escape in two letters dated June 5. He related in the documents—now full of code numbers for people and places—that "happily I [had] set out for N. York the day before his arrival, and to make some compensation for his voyage he fell upon my father and plundered him in the most shocking manner."[180] (This is in stark contrast to the AMC series *Turn*, in which Woodhull's Patriot father, Judge Richard Woodhull, is inaccurately portrayed as a Loyalist cozy with the British.)

THE RIVINGTON CONNECTION

Historians disagree over the role, if any, of publisher James Rivington in the Culper Spy Ring. Rivington, an emigrant from England, operated a print shop in Manhattan, where he published newspapers whose names changed over time but always demonstrated an extreme Loyalist point of view. He so angered the Patriots that in May 1775 a mob attacked his office, smashed his printing press and carried away his lead type to melt down for bullets.

Rivington retreated to England but returned in 1777 to resume his printing business and began publishing the *Royal Gazette*. The masthead of the biweekly publication with 3,600 subscribers and sixteen employees proclaimed the owner was "Printer to the King's Most Excellent Majesty." In outlandish coverage that would compare favorably with the "yellow journalism" around the turn of the twentieth century and tabloids like the *National Inquirer* in later generations, Rivington proclaimed his Tory bias with stories stating that George Washington had fathered illegitimate children—one of his favorite topics—that France's King Louis XVI was maneuvering to be crowned king of America or Patriot leaders like Washington and Benjamin Franklin had died. The newspaper office was located on the northeastern corner of Wall Street and Broadway. Rivington also operated two adjacent businesses, a coffeehouse and general store that sold stationery, which were frequented by British officers during the occupation.[181]

Beyond those facts, things get iffy. Some authors have Robert Townsend working for Rivington as either a paid or volunteer reporter. These include Kilmeade, who offers that Townsend, who "had always had a knack for writing," arranged to be hired by Rivington as a reporter in "a stroke of brilliance" because now he "had the perfect excuse for asking questions."[182] Others go

James Rivington, the printer of a Tory newspaper in New York City, in an engraving by A.H. Ritchie. His involvement, if any, in the Culper Spy Ring is widely debated. *Library of Congress.*

even further, elevating Townsend to being a co-owner of the newspaper and/or coffeehouse. Pennypacker and Alexander Rose have the two men jointly owning the coffeehouse, with Townsend spending time there chatting with British officers, who cultivated friendships with him in hope of getting a favorable mention in the *Royal Gazette*—perfect cover for a spy.[183] But Pennypacker carries the story only so far. He believed Rivington knew nothing about Townsend's spy activity. "That James Rivington ever imagined Robert Townsend to be in the service of George Washington there is no evidence to show," the historian wrote. "In fact it is very unlikely. Rivington was not the type of man that Townsend would trust with that secret."[184]

Kilmeade is the biggest outlier when it comes to Rivington's espionage role: he portrays the publisher as a full-fledged Culper spy. "At some point following his return to America from England at the end of 1777, it seems that his loyalty shifted," the television host wrote.

It remains unclear whether he was driven by a change of heart towards the American cause, a desire for monetary gain, or simply frustration at the Crown's objections and prohibitions to his printing criticisms of the leadership of General William Howe in the autumn of 1778. But what is certain is that Rivington secretly threw in his lot with the Americans and began to work alongside Robert Townsend gathering information and conveying it outside the city to General Washington's waiting hands.[185]

Kilmeade backs his contention by quoting a postwar letter from William Hooper, a North Carolina lawyer and signer of the Declaration of Independence, in which he stated that "there is now no longer any reason to conceal it that Rivington has been very useful to Gen. Washington by furnishing him with intelligence. The unusual confidence which the British placed in him owing in a great measure to his liberal abuse of the Americans gave him ample opportunities to obtain information which he has bountifully communicated to our friends."[186]

Claire Bellerjeau has spent a lot of time picking apart the Townsend-Rivington connection theories. She noted that during the first half of the war, prior to Benedict Arnold coming to New York after he defected to the British in the fall of 1780, Townsend operated a store on Hanover Square. In 1779, he formed a partnership with Henry Oakman. "In their ad for Townsend & Oakman from 1779, you can see that the location of their store is across the square from Rivington," Bellerjeau said.

Rivington's Gazette *and his coffeehouse were right there on Hanover Square. And Rivington was a very high-profile person. You see in Robert's ledgers that he regularly bought Rivington's* Gazette, *not because he liked Rivington better than other newspaper people, but because it was the standard for people. People might say that Rivington was the spy, and I think that is entirely possible because it would be a great way to be a spy to write a newspaper. But Robert clearly doesn't think that Rivington is on his team because early on in 1779 in one of his spy letters he writes specifically to look in Rivington's paper and you will see that somebody knows what we're doing or has guessed very nearly. In Rivington's* Gazette *he is writing that there are spies in New York and everybody should be on the lookout to turn them in. So Robert complains about Rivington. How is it that they are spies together? That just makes no sense.*[187]

Bellerjeau also noted there is no proof that Townsend and Rivington were partners in the coffeehouse. "I don't know where that comes from," she said. "There is zero evidence in his ledger books of any business connection with Rivington. The only thing we see is that he is buying his paper from Rivington. That's it." She added that it's possible that if they were silent partners it would not have been written down anywhere. "But I think you can say that they were not business partners because we have so many ledgers of the Townsends. Years and years, and every penny coming in or out is notated. And there is no money coming in from James Rivington or any kind of coffee purchasing going on. There's nothing like that."[188]

The authors who believe Townsend and Rivington had a business and/ or espionage link point to the fact that Rivington is one of the names listed for substitution in the spy ring codebook. Kilmeade noted that "Rivington's name was the last to appear among the Culper code monikers, 726, indicating that Townsend had recruited him soon after his own engagement, probably by the late summer of 1779, when the code was developed."[189]

Bellerjeau countered that "we know that Rivington is one of the proper names in the Culper code. That makes you think he's a spy, right? But you've got place names, people's names on both sides of the conflict. Is Rivington's name in there as a person or for the *Gazette*? As far as the Culpers are concerned, I think the word Rivington in the code meant the paper." Because Tallmadge may have placed a guard to protect Rivington after the British left New York in 1783, Bellerjeau said, "Maybe Rivington had an outside deal with Washington and Tallmadge. Maybe he wasn't part of the Culper Spy Ring but was doing other spy work for them." It would make sense for security to keep intelligence operatives separated, she added.[190]

When Benedict Arnold came to New York City after switching sides, Townsend left for several months for fear of being unmasked and arrested. "Arnold rounded up about forty suspected spies, and Robert definitely knew some of them," Bellerjeau said. "It really freaked him out when that happened. When he came back after this time away from the city, he moved to a new location. He ended his partnership with Henry Oakman, moved his entire business out of Hanover Square, probably because it was so public, and went way over to Peck's Slip by South Street Seaport." Townsend called the new location Bachelor's Hall. He lived above the store with his unmarried brother William and cousin John. He resumed his espionage activities, but initially would not write anything down for fear of discovery and gave only verbal reports.[191]

THE LADY OR AGENT 355

Some recent books on the spy ring, including Brian Kilmeade's 2013 bestseller, include the story of an Agent 355. She supposedly was a mysterious female Culper operative, even though a generic lady is mentioned only once in the letters. A coded letter from Abraham Woodhull to Washington dated August 15, 1779—a little over a month after Robert Townsend takes over as chief spy in Manhattan from Woodhull—includes this sentence: "I intend to visit 727 [New York] before long and think by the assistance of a 355 [lady] of my acquaintance, shall be able to out wit them all."[192]

That ambiguous reference has spawned a whole subgenre of the spy ring story. Morton Pennypacker suggested that not only was there a female Culper spy with the code number 355 but she also was the mistress of Townsend. And to make the story even more juicy, she was arrested, imprisoned on the infamous British prison hulk *Jersey*, gave birth to his illegitimate child onboard and then died.

Other writers have taken up the story, with some putting her in the social circle of British spy John André. Still others, including Alexander Rose, declare that the 355 referred to was Anna Strong. But he does not turn her into a secret agent. Rose does have Strong—without documentation—accompanying Woodhull into Manhattan and masquerading as his wife to make his trip less suspicious to the British sentries.[193]

Agent 355 is a recurring character in Kilmeade's book. "One agent remains unidentified," he wrote. "Though her name cannot be verified, and many details about her life are unclear, her presence and her courage undoubtedly made a difference."[194] With so little verified and so much unclear, it's questionable how the Fox News cohost was able to conclude that she made such a difference. In Kilmeade's telling, "she was somehow uniquely positioned to collect important secrets in a cunning and charming manner that would leave those she had duped completely unaware that they had just been 'outwitted' by a secret agent."[195]

Kilmeade dismissed the possibility that Anna Strong is the 355 referred to in the letter:

> *While Anna Smith Strong might have played a satellite role in the ring…a much more likely contender would be a young woman living a fashionable life in New York. Though of pro-American sentiments herself, she almost certainly would have been attached to a prominent Loyalist family….It is therefore possible that 355 was part of the glittering, giggling cluster*

of coquettes who flocked around the British spy John André as he moved around the city.[196]

Kilmeade even has his Agent 355 helping to uncover Benedict Arnold's treasonous plot to turn over West Point to the British.[197] One also has to wonder why Kilmeade attaches his Agent 355 to Townsend in the city when the only mention of a lady in the letters is in connection with Woodhull. In Kilmeade's version, as in Pennypacker's, Agent 355 is imprisoned on the prison hulk *Jersey*. While Pennypacker has her dying there, Kilmeade gives her a chance of surviving the ordeal.[198]

Many current historians who have researched the spy ring scoff at the Agent 355 theories as wild speculation unsupported by facts. Daigler called it "a romantic myth" that was discredited in the mid-1990s.[199]

Tyler emphasized that there is only the one reference to a lady, in the August 15, 1779 letter. "That is it," he said. "Everything else is made up—the whole business of Agent 355 and Robert Townsend." Tyler is one of those who believes the lady referred to is Woodhull's Setauket neighbor. "I'm fully convinced it was Anna Strong," he said. "She had relatives who were Loyalists in New York City and she portrayed herself as a Loyalist. During the war, as far as we can tell—since we don't know the details about the spies we have to make some assumptions—she accompanied Woodhull into New York City on occasion. Anna Strong was 355. She wasn't *Agent* 355." He said members of the spy ring "didn't refer to each other as agents." And the spies who did have code numbers were all numbered in the 700s. "Making up the word agent and tying it to the number 355 has no validity whatsoever."[200]

Bellerjeau also doubts there was anyone involved with the spy ring code-named Agent 355. But she conceded that "it's quite possible that there was a woman who was an agent and a significant role player. I wouldn't say that there is no agent, but she's never mentioned again. I think people want to have good stories about women so I can understand that people want to weave a larger story out of this one reference. It's the same thing with Anna Strong and her clothesline, even though there's no real evidence behind that." Bellerjeau noted that Woodhull tended to be indiscreet in his letters. "Mentioning a lady at all, any other person, should never be put in a letter, even in code," because it endangered that person and the entire espionage network, she said.[201]

Bellerjeau disagrees with Tyler's contention that the lady helping Woodhull would have been Anna Strong. She doesn't believe it would be anyone in Setauket "because it's so far out on the island and not that important a place. What special advantage could a person out in Setauket give you? The intelligence is about what's going on in Manhattan." As for Kilmeade's speculation that the lady was a socialite in Major John André's circle in the city, Bellerjeau said, "It's certainly possible because you're looking for somebody who's in a particular position to outwit. But would a lady of high society be an acquaintance with Woodhull, a vegetable farmer from Setauket? It doesn't seem likely." If there was a female Culper spy, Bellerjeau said, "I'm not surprised that Robert never said anything about it because he was being smart in his communications."[202]

HERCULES MULLIGAN

Historians agree that New York City tailor Hercules Mulligan was a spy for George Washington. But they don't agree on whether Mulligan was a member of the Culper Ring, gathered intelligence independently or operated both ways.

Born in Ireland in 1740, Mulligan immigrated with his family in 1746 to New York City, where the family owned an accounting business and prospered. After graduating from King's College (now Columbia University), Hercules initially worked for his father as an accounting clerk. Then the ambitious young man opened a tailoring and haberdashery business that catered to wealthy clients, including British officers stationed in the city after the occupation.

Although he married Elizabeth Sanders, niece of a British admiral, Mulligan was active in the Sons of Liberty, the Committee of Correspondence and other revolutionary organizations. He befriended Alexander Hamilton after he arrived from the West Indies in 1772. Hamilton lodged with Mulligan's family while attending King's College. Mulligan helped convince Hamilton to support the Patriot cause. In July 1776, Mulligan was one of the Patriots who toppled the lead statue of King George III that stood on Bowling Green and then broke it into pieces and melted them to cast bullets for the Continental Army. After the Battle of Long Island and the army's evacuation of New York in 1776, Mulligan decided he should join other Patriots in fleeing the city. Several days later, he was captured by a party of Tory militiamen and returned to Manhattan with a blanket over his head. Somehow Mulligan escaped imprisonment or other forms of retribution. He remained in the city, hiding his Patriot sympathies.[203]

In March 1777, after Hamilton was appointed Washington's aide-de-camp, he recommended to the general that Mulligan become a confidential correspondent in the city. Mulligan took full advantage of his access to British officers who were customers of his tailoring business and others billeted in his house.[204]

Mulligan proved valuable by informing Washington of General Howe's planned expedition to Pennsylvania in April 1777 as well as British and Loyalist plots to capture or assassinate Washington. Mulligan's network included his brother, Hugh, a banker and importer who did business with the British in New York and provided information on their supplies and shipping schedules. Another member was the Polish Jewish immigrant Haym Solomon, who served as an interpreter for the British and Hessians because he spoke a number of languages, including German. That allowed him access to vital British military intelligence. Another important member of the network was Cato, Mulligan's African American servant, who rowed across the Hudson to deliver intelligence reports.[205]

Mulligan learned of the plot to kidnap Washington when an officer came to his house at night in desperate need of a coat. He then carelessly revealed to Mulligan that he needed the coat for his mission to capture Washington later that day. The tailor dispatched Cato with a warning, and Washington changed his plans. Another example of Mulligan's usefulness was when the British learned of the American commander's plan to travel to Rhode Island along the Connecticut shoreline. Luckily for the Patriot cause, Hugh Mulligan was the person delegated by the British to load their boats with supplies for the interception mission. After Hugh informed his brother, Cato carried the message to Washington, who altered his route.[206]

Whether Mulligan was considered a member of the ring or not, he apparently began to cooperate at times with the Culper operatives in the summer of 1779. Woodhull mentioned in an August 12 letter that "an acquaintance of Hamiltons" had relayed information about British regiments embarking on transports.[207] That was about six weeks after Townsend, who had known Mulligan since childhood through his father, Samuel, began writing reports. According to Rose, Mulligan never wrote any known reports but provided information verbally to the Culper spies and via other routes to Washington.[208]

Daigler said there is documentation proving Mulligan did work with the ring on occasion. As evidence that he also ran his own separate network, he cited a letter from Tallmadge to Washington. On May 8, 1780, the spy chief stated that he did not know what Mulligan was doing and asked Washington for any information on that subject that might affect his own intelligence activities. Bellerjeau concluded that Mulligan was not part of the Culper Ring. "However, he and Robert knew each other, evidenced through two receipts," she said. "Did they know that they were both gathering intelligence? It's possible."[209]

The British never learned that Mulligan had been recruited by Hamilton, but the spy did have a number of close calls. He was arrested by the British in September 1776 during General Howe's roundup of New York Patriots. Mulligan was released after a month. When Benedict Arnold came to New York in 1780 after switching sides, he had Mulligan arrested as a spy but was unable to prove it.

After the British evacuation at the end of the war, Loyalists were attacked and their homes and businesses burned. Mulligan's connections with the British made him a target, but Hamilton protected him by inviting Washington to have breakfast with the Mulligan family at 23 Queen Street, now 218 Pearl Street, after Washington reviewed the victorious American troops at Bowling Green in 1783.

Hercules Mulligan died in March 1825 and is buried in the southwest quadrant of the cemetery at Trinity Church.[210]

6

THE CULPER LETTERS, 1778–1779

The 194 known Culper Spy Ring letters that survive are rare originals or copies made at the time. They were written to or by George Washington, his spymaster Benjamin Tallmadge, spies Abraham Woodhull, Robert Townsend and Caleb Brewster as well as other individuals. Most are owned by the Library of Congress and can be viewed on the library's website. (Go to https://www.loc.gov/collections/george-washington-papers and then put "Culper" or "John Bolton" into the search field.) The Litchfield Historical Society in Litchfield, Connecticut, where Tallmadge lived after the war, also owns some, as does Princeton University. Two are in the collection at the library at Stony Brook University. Many are copies made by Washington's aides, who destroyed the originals written in invisible ink. Unfortunately, images of all the letters with transcriptions have never been compiled into one volume or website.[209] Transcriptions of many of the letters can be found on a National Archives website. (Go to https://founders.archives.gov).

It should be noted that transcriptions are sometimes inaccurate because the handwriting is hard to decipher. Additionally, some of the transcriptions published by historians over the years reflect the authors' attempts to make them easier to read by correcting spelling or punctuation.

The Culper letters generally start out by confirming the author has received correspondence from the person to whom they are replying because in that era there was no guarantee that correspondence would be delivered, even if it wasn't a secret spy report.

And in an age before people could dash off emails and texts, writing was taken much more seriously. "When you read the Culper spy letters you notice how much care they took in their writing," said Claire Bellerjeau, historian at the Raynham Hall Museum in Oyster Bay.[212]

The contents of the most important letters are described in this and the following two chapters.

1778

As the spy ring came together, Washington clearly valued it. But initially he was frustrated by the vagueness of the information received from chief spy Abraham Woodhull. The fledgling operative wrote his first Samuel Culper letter on October 29, 1778. Washington instructed spymaster Benjamin Tallmadge on November 18 to inform Woodhull to "ascertain the following facts with as much precision, and expedition, as possible."[213] The commander in chief was interested in which British army corps were in Manhattan and on Long Island, whether forts were being built in Brooklyn on the East River, names of the commanders on Long Island and location of their headquarters, and whether troops were getting ready to move. He wasn't interested in Woodhull's initially inaccurate troop estimates, saying, "I can form a pretty accurate opinion of the numbers" just from knowing which units were present.[214]

Tallmadge replied that a bigger problem than getting reports from Woodhull was getting them across Long Island Sound. Whaleboat captain Caleb Brewster, who was on detached duty from the Continental Army to handle missions on the waterway, was dependent on getting volunteers from other units to man his boats when their commanders would give them the time.[215]

Nonetheless, Tallmadge said it was critical to make Brewster the only conduit between Woodhull and himself because of the agent's anxiety about discovery. Woodhull's "extreme cautiousness, and even timidity, in his present undertaking would not admit of having his business known to any persons who are not at present his confidants." If anyone else were to learn of his espionage work, Tallmadge, wrote, "he would most probably leave his present employment immediately" and "should leave the Island immediately" for refuge in Connecticut.[216] Washington agreed, writing that "you will be pleased to observe the strictest silence with the respondents respect to C——, as you are to be the only person intrusted with the knowledge or conveyance of his letters."[217]

As Woodhull quickly gained experience, his reports became more highly detailed, as Washington desired. A letter from Woodhull conveyed across Long Island Sound on November 23, 1778, less than a month after he began spying, for example, noted that

> *all of the best of their troops are on Long Island. There is about 300, most of them Hessians, at Brooklyn Ferry. 350 New Town, British; 1500 British Jamaica; 800 Yeagers, Flushing; 200 Jerico, most of them Dragoons; 400 foot, 70 Dragoons Oyster Bay; 150 Lloyd's Neck, N. Leveys* [new recruits or conscripts]; *400 Hempstead, Dragoons; Stripping Barns and out houses for boards to build huts for Winter. 40 wagons 100 troops this day at Smith Town collecting cattle, sheep, Boards, &c....Much provision is brought to town from the Jerseys privately; flour, beef, &c.*[218]

Washington, accustomed to and annoyed by inflated troop estimates from other spies and Woodhull initially, was impressed by the detail in the Culper reports. "His account has the appearance of a very distinct and good one and makes me desirous of a continuance of his correspondence," he told Tallmadge. But the general also raised an issue that persisted throughout the war: how to get the information quickly enough to be useful without compromising the security of those involved in getting it. "I am at a loss how it can be conveniently carried on as he is so scrupulous respecting the channel of conveyance." Washington delegated to Tallmadge the task of developing a method for "procuring his intelligence with expedition."[219]

Washington seemed annoyed at Samuel Culper's insistence on providing his personal views on the progress of the war and suggestions for specific military action. Washington clearly would not be eager to read something like this in a November 1778 letter: "I am firmly of the opinion that a sudden attack of ten thousand men would take the City and put an end to the War."[220] In almost every case, Washington ignored the tendered advice.

Caleb Brewster, the first of the Culper participants to provide reports to Washington, also provided detailed intelligence. He conveyed letters from the other spies across the Sound while continuing as a correspondent. On February 26, 1779, Brewster wrote from his base in Fairfield, Connecticut, that he had returned from Long Island that day and learned that

> *Genl. Erskine remains yet at Southampton. He has been reinforced to the number of 2500. They have three redoubts at South and East Hampton and are heaving up works at Canoe Place at a narrow pass before you get into South Hampton. They are building a number of flat bottom boats. There went a number of carpenters down last week to South Hampton. It is thought by the inhabitants that they will cross over to New London after the Continental Frigates. Colonel Hewlet remains yet on Lloyd's Neck with 350, wood cutters included. Colonel Simcoe remains at Oyster bay with 300 Foot and Light Horse. There is no troops from oyster Bay till you come to Jamaica.*

He goes on to say that there was a forty-gun British ship in Huntington, the brig HMS *Halifax* in Oyster Bay, with other vessels at shipyards to the west as far as Manhattan.[221]

Operating the espionage network required a significant outlay of cash by the spies and Washington. Woodhull's November 23, 1778 report to the general included this refrain: "My business is expensive; so dangerous traveling that I am obliged to give my assistants high wages, but am as sparing as possible."[222]

Not surprisingly, security concerns are frequently raised in the letters. Washington wrote to Tallmadge in December 1778 that "I should be glad to have an interview with Culper myself, in which I would put the mode of corresponding upon such a footing that even if his letters were to fall into the enemy's hands, he would have nothing to fear, on that account."[223] But when he learned that Woodhull feared that his prolonged absences from Setauket might attract the interest of the British, in his following letter, the general wrote that "when I desired an interview with him I did not know his peculiar situation. I now see that the danger that so long an absence would incur and I must leave it entirely to you to manage the correspondence in such a manner as will most probably insure safety to him and answer the desired end."[224]

Tallmadge answered the general on December 23, 1778, saying that any instructions for Culper could "be very safely conveyed to him, as from the regularity of his dispatches and the characters of the persons who I know are entrusted with their conveyance from N.Y. to Brook Haven, I dare venture to say there is not the least probability, and I had almost said hardly a possibility of a discovery."[225]

Woodhull could be conflicted over his not always compatible obsessions with security and reimbursement. He was not a wealthy man and laid out large sums to gather intelligence. And despite his best efforts, Washington often struggled to provide funding for Woodhull and later the lesser amounts requested by Robert Townsend. The result, historian Alexander Rose noted, was that "amazingly, for someone so strident about every other aspect of his security, Woodhull kept a cash book notated with the cost incurred by his espionage: travel, lodging, and food, mostly."[226] While Samuel Culper surely kept the book well hidden, having it at all was a serious breach of secure spy craft procedure.

Initially, Tallmadge met with Caleb Brewster in Fairfield and then personally carried the Culper reports westward to headquarters. But as his responsibilities grew, it became increasingly difficult for the spymaster to undertake the task himself. Washington suggested a solution: post an officer as a dispatch rider in Fairfield who would bring the reports back to headquarters "without his knowing the person from whom they came."[227] By the beginning of 1779, this arrangement was expanded by having dispatch riders stationed every fifteen miles between Fairfield and headquarters. The system was not flawless, however. One Culper letter arrived at headquarters several days late in mid-January because the dragoon's horse had gone lame and the rider needed to get some repairs made to his equipment.[228]

The Hawkins-Mount House in Stony Brook, home of Jonas Hawkins, a courier for the Culper Spy Ring. *Photo by Audrey C. Tiernan, copyright 2020.*

Tallmadge smoothed the operation on the Long Island side in December 1778 when he recruited Jonas Hawkins, owner of a Setauket tavern and store, as an occasional courier. Hawkins began to split the chore with another Setauket tavern owner, Austin Roe, a member of an old family in the community who was related to Hawkins and had bought his business from the Woodhull family. The Culper principals were always careful in their recruiting, adding only people to whom they were related or knew for years.[229]

1779

By the end of January 1779, the Culper Ring had perfected its roundabout transportation system to the point that it could get a letter from Manhattan to Washington at headquarters in a week—less than half the time it had taken in the beginning. Washington was also pleased to be getting more frequent reports.[230]

On March 17, 1779, Woodhull followed up on an earlier warning that British commander Henry Clinton was building transports with news that the general was on eastern Long Island looking to hire crews of Loyalists to raid the Connecticut coast. A week later, Washington told General Joseph Reed that "one of my most intelligent correspondants" had reported that "the enemy have some enterprize in view" in that region. Washington advised General Israel Putnam in Connecticut to reinforce the militia and man fortifications along the coast. But on April 1, he backed off from full alert status, writing, "Sir Henry Clinton is returned to New York…and accounts from New York mention that troops have been relanded upon Long Island.[231]

The letters show an irregular flow of cash traveled from Washington's headquarters to the Culper agents to facilitate operation of the ring as the general could find the money. For example, the commander wrote to Tallmadge on March 21 that "with this letter you will receive fifty guineas for S.C. [Samuel Culper] which you will cause to be delivered as soon as possible, with an earnest exhortation to use them with all possible economy, as I find it very difficult to obtain hard money."[232]

Washington's March 21 letter also included a long list of instructions to improve operation of the ring:

> *As all great movements and the fountain of all intelligence must originate at, and proceed from the Head Quarters of the enemy's army, C. had better reside at New York—mix with and put on the airs of a tory, to cover his real character and avoid suspicion....The temper and expectation of the tories and refugees, is worthy of consideration; as much may be gathered from their expectations and prospects. For this end an intimacy with some well-informed refugee may be politically advantageous—Highly so will it be to contract an acquaintance with a person in the Naval Department, who may either be engaged in the business of procuring transports for the embarkation of the troops, or in victualling* [feeding] *them.*[233]

Although Washington never indicated any displeasure with Woodhull's meandering letter-writing style, the country farmer was self-conscious about his use of the English language and cowed by the reputation of the commander receiving his letters. On April 10, 1779, he addressed these feelings when he wrote in one of his disjointed missives to Tallmadge that

> *whenever I sit down I always feel and know my Inability to write a good Letter. As my calling in life never required it....And much less did I think it would ever fall to my lot to serve in such publick and important business as this, and my letters perused by one of the worthiest men on earth. But I trust he will overlook any imperfections he may discover in the dress of my words, and rest assured that I indeavor to collect and convey the most accurate and explicit intelligence that I possibly can; and hope it may be of some service towards alleviating the misery of our distressed Country, nothing but that could have induced me to undertake it, for you must readily think it is a life of anxiety to be within the lines of a cruel and mistrustful Enemy.*[234]

Then it was back to business:

> *On the 25 Last Month 7 Sail Transports with about one hundred and seventy Scotch Troops of the Duke of Athol's Regiment arrived from Halifax under convoy of the Rainbow of 44 Guns, Sir George Collier, who is come to succeed Admiral Gambier. On the 26th, 23 Sail arrived from England (which place they left the 2th Jany.) under convoy of the Romulus of 44 guns. They were chiefly loaded with stores and provisions for the Army....On the 4th April arrived 7 Sail of transports from Cork with provisions. The enemy now have a very large supply of Provisions and Stores indeed I think enough for three months without any addition...*

All transports laying in the East or North River are completely victualed and waterd for sixty five days for their compliment of troops that they were accustomed to transport. The number of Ships, Brigs and Snows [square-rigged vessels with two regular masts and a short third mast for one sail called a snow or trysail] *in the Harbour differeth not much from two hundred, out of which thers two sloops of war, four Frigets* [frigates] *and two forty four guns ships and an old Indiaman with their usual number of guns for their defense, and an old 74*[-gun] *Store Ship, with only her upper teer of guns in.*

Woodhall also noted that "the Enemy seem to be in high spirits, and say now Great Britain is Roused and will support them and carry on the war at all events and appear to be more sanguine than ever."[235]

Woodhull's April 12, 1779, letter is notable because it's the first one to use a code that Woodhull introduced in a postscript of his April 10 letter. So now the number 10 represents New York, 20 represents Setauket and 30 and 40 represent two post riders.[236]

The April 12 letter also demonstrates that Woodhull lived in constant fear of detection. The document contained the same information as a report from two days earlier, which made Tallmadge so concerned about Woodhull's state of mind that he made a special trip across the Sound with Brewster on April 16 to check on him. Because a couple of British officers had decided to quarter in Woodhull's house temporarily, Tallmadge had to hide out in the woods nearby for five days. Woodhull brought food to Tallmadge when he could, and the spymaster gave money to Woodhull toward his expenses and told him how valuable his services were to try to relieve the spy's anxiety. They again discussed trying to find a quicker route for the intelligence. Tallmadge suggested placing a person vouched for by him and acceptable to Woodhull on Staten Island to forward messages without going through Setauket. Woodhull was open to the idea but said the courier would have to meet him in Manhattan because for a Setauket farmer to go regularly to Staten Island would generate dangerous suspicion. Nothing came of the idea, to Washington's annoyance.[237]

Tallmadge reported afterward to Washington that he had given a vial of invisible ink to Woodhull, who was practicing with it

when very suddenly two persons broke into the room. The consideration of having several officers quartered in the next Chamber, added to his constant fear of detection and its certain consequences made him rationally

*conclude that he was suspected and that those steps were taken by said
officers for discovery. Startled by so sudden and violent an obtrusion he
sprang from his seat, snatched up his papers, overset his table and broke
his Vial. This step so totally discomposed him that he knew not who they
were or even to which sex they belonged—for in fact they were two ladies
[his nieces] who, living in the house with him, entered his chamber in
this way on purpose to surprise him. Such an excessive fright and so great
a turbulence of passions so wrought on poor Culper that he has hardly
been in tolerable health since.*

Tallmadge continued on a more positive note that "he is much pleased with the Ink and wishes if any more can be spared to have a little sent him."[238]

If Woodhull didn't have enough problems worrying about being caught by the British, Tallmadge matter-of-factly stated that "Culper was the other day robbed of all his money near Huntington, and was glad to escape with his life."[239] Tallmadge believed the culprits were privateers he might know of who had been landing on Long Island "and plunder[ing] the inhabitants promiscuously," probably regardless of whether Loyalist or Patriot.[240]

After Woodhull just missed being apprehended in Setauket by Lieutenant Colonel John Graves Simcoe of the Queen's Rangers in April when privateer John Wolsey informed on him, Culper Senior kept a low profile in May, writing no reports. When he resumed writing on June 5, Woodhull said his life was saved only by pleading for help from "a friend of mine" who contacted a British officer and guaranteed Woodhull's Loyalist sentiments. The anonymous friend is believed to be Colonel Benjamin Floyd, a Loyalist militia officer who lived in southern Brookhaven Town. Floyd, a cousin of William Floyd, a signer of the Declaration of Independence, was distantly related to Woodhull. Once released, Woodhull wrote that "I daresay you will be filled with wonder and surprise, that I have had the good fortune to escape confinement. And am sorry to inform you that it hath rendered me almost unserviceable to you. [Because] I am now a suspected person I cannot frequent their camp as heretofore."[241] Once again voicing concern over his safety, Woodhull added that "I am very obnoxious to them and I think I am in continual danger."[242]

Woodhull proposed to remain entirely in Setauket but added, "I shall endeavor to establish a confidential friend to step into my place if agreeable." He told Tallmadge that once he found a substitute to gather information in New York, "most probable I shall come to you [in Connecticut]. And shall wish to join in the common defense."[243] That meant leaving his farm and his elderly parents, but if the British knew his true role it would be better to be a refugee than a corpse.

These incidents prompted Washington to reiterate his ongoing concern for Woodhull's safety. In a June 13, 1779, letter to Tallmadge, the general wrote, "Should suspicions of him rise so high as to render it unsafe to continue in New York I should wish him by all means to employ some person of whose attachment and abilities he entertains the best opinion, to act in his place, with a request to be critical in his observations rather than a mere retailer of vulgar reports."[244] The general tried to look on the bright side of Woodhull stepping back. If they had to find someone new, Washington mused, maybe that person might be more receptive to "a mode of conveying quickly" the intelligence via a less circuitous route than through Setauket. The general considered that still a matter "of the utmost importance."[245]

Washington wasn't content to wait for Woodhull to try to find a spy who would remain embedded in the city. Since the spring of 1779, the general had been searching for an agent himself. He reached out to Lewis Pintard, a merchant appointed, with the agreement of British General William Howe, in early 1777 to look after the care of American prisoners in New York. But Pintard, knowing he was under intense scrutiny by the enemy, refused to supply information.[246]

Washington's next choice, detailed in a June 27, 1779, letter to Tallmadge in Connecticut, was Manhattan resident George Higday. The general suggested the spy chief reach out to Higday, who the previous month had helped three stranded Continental Army officers cross the Hudson to safety in New Jersey.[247]

Tallmadge never got to pursue recruiting Higday because a week later on July 2, British Colonel Banastre Tarleton led a raid on Tallmadge's camp at Pound Ridge, Connecticut, with the presumed mission of capturing the spymaster. Before being driven away by the dragoons aided by the arrival of the local militia, the raiders inflicted ten casualties, captured eight dragoons and escaped with twelve horses and the flag of Tallmadge's unit. The most significant loss was one of the horses. It belonged to Tallmadge, and the saddlebags contained money from Washington for Woodhull and, worst of all, the general's June 27 letter mentioning Higday by name and where he could be located. The attack was likely precipitated by the British intercepting a June 13 letter from Washington to Tallmadge that was not written with the stain and mentioned "C———" and use of a "liquid" the general had been using for letters. The incident highlighted a grievous lapse in security by both men. When Tallmadge told his commander what had happened, the general responded in a mild tone, probably because of his own culpability, that "the loss of your papers was certainly a most unlucky accident and shows how dangerous it is to keep papers of any consequence in an advanced post. I beg you will take care to guard against the like in the future."[248]

Washington said he could replace the money for Woodhull and urged Tallmadge to warn Higday. The general's concern was justified. Higday was arrested on July 13 and wrote a confession letter from prison to General Henry Clinton to try to save himself. The fiasco prompted Tallmadge to rethink the operation and upgrade security measures by inventing a code, as discussed in chapter 4.[249]

While Washington searched unsuccessfully for an agent who could remain in New York, he did not know that Woodhull already had someone in mind: Robert Townsend. Woodhull wrote to Washington on June 20, 1779, three days after telling Tallmadge he might have to escape to Connecticut, that

I have communicated my business to an intimate friend, and disclosed every secret, and laid before him every instruction that has been handed to me. It was with great difficulty I gained his complyance, checked by fear. He is a person that hath the interest of our Country at heart and of good reputation, character and family as any of my acquaintance. I am under the most solemn obligations never to disclose his name to any but the Post [courier], *who unavoidably must know it. I have reason to think his advantages for serving you and abilities are far superior to mine....You will receive a letter from him in short time....He will expect an ample support at the same time he will be frugal; as long as I am here shall be an assistant and do all that I can.*

The post rider or courier Woodhull referred to was probably Setauket tavern owner Jonas Hawkins, who served as a Culper courier between January and the fall of 1779, but it might also have been Austin Roe. A pleased Washington replaced the more than ten pounds the spy had lost when he was robbed in April.[250]

Townsend and Woodhull were acquainted because both stayed at Amos Underhill's boardinghouse in Manhattan. Woodhull or both men came up with a simple code name for Townsend: Samuel Culper Junior, who became 723 in the list of proper names in the code. Henceforth, Woodhull would be Samuel Culper Senior.

On June 29, 1779, only nine days after Woodhull informed Washington that his "intimate friend" in New York had agreed to take up the spying

View of the kitchen in the Hawkins-Mount House in Stony Brook. *Long Island Museum photo.*

there, Townsend wrote his first intelligence report. It was a month before Tallmadge would supply his code dictionary, and the stain was not yet in use. So Townsend wrote the letter with regular ink in a way that made it appear it was penned by a Tory. The wording also was fairly innocuous to avoid incriminating anyone if it was intercepted. "We are much alarmed with the prospect of a Spanish war—Should that be the case, I fear poor old England will not be able to oppose the whole but will be obliged to sue for a peace," it said.[251] That was the kind of speculation typically seen in a Woodhull letter that would annoy the general. The one piece of potential useful information was that Townsend had heard from a Rhode Island resident that two divisions of British troops "are to make excursions into Connecticut."[252]

Woodhull passed on the same information from a different source in a July 1 letter. But Washington did not see it until late on July 7 because of the attack on Tallmadge's camp and the general being away from headquarters for a day. In the meantime, on July 5, the British attacked New Haven and burned some vessels and storehouses in an unsuccessful attempt to lure Washington out from his strong position along the Hudson River. The British then attacked Fairfield on July 8 and destroyed most of the town.[253]

Although Woodhull seemed oblivious to the occasional failings in the content of his own letters, he realized that Townsend's initial effort fell short of expectations. "He hath wrote in the style of Loyalty, I think through fear like me at first unaccustomed to the business," he told Tallmadge with his typical tangled syntax in a July 1 letter. "The longer one continues in the business if unsuspected of more real service can he be." Culper Senior pledged to "repeat again to him those instructions that I have received from time to time from you and use my utmost endeavor to acquaint him with the steps I used to take…that a person unaccustomed would not readily conceive of."[254]

Woodhull's seventeenth letter, dated July 9, 1779, stated that "I yesterday had the opportunity of seeing Mister Culper, Junr. and repeated again all my instructions ever received from you. He's determined to pursue every step that he may judge for advantage and is determined as soon as I can communicate to him your authority for my engaging him he will disengage himself from every other business which at present affords him a handsome living." He would be doing this "solely for to be some advantage to our distressed country." Woodhull noted that "I look upon myself all the time in danger" and after traveling to Manhattan—for what he hoped would be the last time—related information provided by Townsend. This included the arrival of a convoy from Halifax and another from the West Indies.[255]

After Townsend on July 15, 1779, asked Washington for a supply of the secret ink, the general forwarded a supply to Woodhull with a letter dated July 25 from West Point. "*Sir*: All the white Ink I now have (indeed all that there is any prospect of getting soon) is sent in phial No. 1….The liquid in No. 2 is the counterpart which renders the other visible by wetting the paper with a fine brush after the first has been used and is dry." Washington asked Woodhull to relay the ink as quickly as possible to Townsend.[256]

Washington frequently expressed satisfaction with the intelligence coming from Culper Junior once he had become comfortable in his role. It's not surprising, considering how specific it was. Townsend detailed the arrival of ships, the number of troops they carried and the provisions they brought, and he also related gossip he picked up from British officers and Tories about expected movements of enemy ships and troops.

In an early counterintelligence coup, Townsend in a July 15 letter to Tallmadge wrote that Manhattan sailmaker Christopher Duychenik, "formally chairman of the Committee of Mechanics, is amongst you and is positively an agent for David Mathews," a former mayor. Townsend was exposing a British spy posing as a Patriot but reporting to a former Loyalist mayor under the direction of former royal governor and now British Major

General William Tryon. Culper Junior added that "the particulars must be kept a profound secret, as few persons but myself know them, and it is known that I do."[257] He did not elaborate on how he knew about Duychenik, but it was the kind of information that could only be coming from someone important in the British command. It's not known what use Washington made of the information.

Woodhull, meanwhile, continued to implore Townsend to give up his partnership with Henry Oakman because he feared it would interfere with his spy work. Woodhull wrote to headquarters on August 12 that he had "begged him to disengage himself from all concerns that may interfere with the Public business he hath undertaken." Woodhull said Townsend would not give up his business because it would leave him "destitute of a support thereafter [in] employment when his services may not be required. I do not conceive his views as altogether mercenary yet [he] thinks he should have some compensation but his chief aim is to have such a recommendation at the close of this war as will entitle him to some employment" by the postwar American government."[258]

Woodhull and Townsend weren't the only members of the ring worried about security. Sometimes the couriers bringing the letters from the city to Setauket destroyed them along the way when they feared capture. Jonas Hawkins, the Setauket tavern owner, did this with Townsend's fifth and sixth letters to Washington. Townsend even brought the sixth letter across the East River to the nervous Hawkins, who nonetheless destroyed it before he could get it to Setauket. After that, Woodhull carried the seventh letter, dated September 11, 1779, out from the city himself.

In it, Townsend wrote that he was sorry the fifth letter had been destroyed, "tho' I can't say that it contained any intelligence that wou'd have been of material consequence—The bearer thought himself in danger. I believe it was merely imaginary." He noted that Hawkins, who dropped out of the spy network that month out of concern for his safety, suffered from such "timidity" that he would not come into New York so "I therefore met him at a place quite out of danger on Long-Island. I have now the pleasure of seeing our mutual friend Saml. Culper, Sen. who will run every hazard to forward this."[259]

Townsend then reiterated what was in his sixth letter, including details of the arrival of a fleet of seventy ships in the city with up to 3,000 soldiers. "They are all new troops, and in bad health," Culper Junior commented. "The general opinion is that there will be no Campaign opened from N. York. The most knowing and judicious of the Tories think that some troops

Transcription of Woodhull's Letter
to Benjamin Tallmadge 15 August 1779

Sir: Dqpeu Beyocpu agreeable to 28 met 723 not far from 727 &
received a 356, but on his return was under the necessity to destroy
the same, or be detected, but have the satisfaction to inform you that
there's nothing of 317 to 15 you of. There's been no augmentation
by 592 of 680 or 347 forces, and everything is very quiet. Every 356
is opened at the entrance of 727 and every 371 is searched, that for
the future every 356must be 691 with the 286 received. They have
some 345 of the route our 356 takes. I judge it was mentioned in the
356 taken or they would not be so 660. I do not think it will continue
long so. I intend to visit 727 before long and think by the assistance
of a 355 of my acquaintance, shall be able to outwit them all. The
next 28 for 725 to be here is the 1 of 616 very long but it cannot be
altered now. It is on account of their 660 that it is so prolonged. It
may be better times before then. I hope there will be means found
out for our deliverance. Nothing could induce me to be here but the
earnest desire of 723. Friends are all well,

and am your very
humble servant,
722.

Transcription of coded letter from Abraham Woodhull to Benjamin Tallmadge on August 15, 1779. *Courtesy of Three Village Historical Society.*

must be sent to the West Indies." In discussing troop disposition on Long Island, Townsend advised against an attack on the brigade manning Fort Franklin at Lloyd Neck because there were 450 members of the Queen's Rangers in Oyster Bay "who can be there by means of an alarm gun in two hours."[260]

Townsend also addressed Woodhull's suggestion that he disengage himself from the dry goods business. "I intended to have disengaged myself from business agreeable to the solicitations of my friend Samuel Culper, Sen.; but find it will be attended with more difficulty than I expected, owing to my having a partner, as I can make no excuse to do it. Until I can, will continue to write as usual."[261]

Woodhull thought Townsend was being too hard on the jittery Hawkins. His August 15 letter to Tallmadge stated that "every man is searched" leaving Manhattan because the British "have some knowledge of the rout our letters take. I judge it was mentioned in the letter taken [in Tarleton's raid on Tallmadge's camp] or they would not be so vigilant."[262]

Washington disagreed with Woodhull's suggestion that Townsend disengage from his business. On September 24, 1779, the general wrote from headquarters at West Point that

> it is not my opinion that Culper Junior should be advised to give up his present employment. I would imagine that with a little industry he will be able to carry on his intelligence with greater security to himself and greater advantages to us, on the cover of his usual business, than if he were to dedicate himself wholly to the giving of information. It may afford him opportunities of collecting intelligence that he could not obtain so well in any other manner. It prevents also those suspicions which would become natural should he throw himself out of the line of his present employment.[263]

Again addressing the issue of security in the same letter, Washington wrote that it would leave the reports

> less exposed to detection, but relieve the fears of such persons as may be entrusted with its conveyance to the second link in the chain…[if] he should occasionally write his information on the blank leaves of a pamphlet, on the first, second, and other pages of a common pocket book, or on the blank leaves of each end of registers, almanacks, or any new publications or book of small value…on paper of a good quality.…He may forward them without risk of search or the scrutiny of the enemy, as this is chiefly directed against paper made up in the form of letters.

Washington also provided "a further hint" that "he may write a familiar letter on domestic affairs, or on some little matters of business, to his friend at Setauket or elsewhere, interlining with the stain his secret intelligence, or writing it on the opposite blank side of the letter.…This last appears to be the best mark of the two, and may be the signal of their being designated for me. The first mention mode, however, with that of the books, appears to me the least liable to detection." On the issue of rewarding Townsend's work, Washington wrote that he "may rest assured of every proper attention being paid to his services" after the war.[264]

Rather than writing his stain reports in books and pamphlets as suggested by Washington, Townsend came up with his own variation. He would write his message on a sheet from a ream of high-quality paper and reinsert it in a predetermined place in the package. But Tallmadge complained to Washington that on occasion he wasn't told of where in the package the letter would be and had to waste a lot of his reagent chemical swabbing different sheets to find the dispatch. Writing paper was also expensive, while there were plenty of old books and pamphlets available. Townsend told Tallmadge on October 21 that he would switch to one of the methods recommended by the general.[265]

The growing concern for the safety of the Culper operatives, especially when writing coded letters without the stain, was validated by Woodhull's twenty-fifth letter to Washington on October 10, 1779. "It is too great a risque to write with [regular] ink in this country of robbers," he wrote.

> *I this day just saved my life. Soon after I left Hempstead Plains and got into the woods I was attacked by four armed men, one of them I had frequently seen in N. York. They searched every pocket and lining of my clothes, shoes, and also my saddle, which the enclosed was in, but thank kind Providence they did not find it. I had but one dollar in money about me. It was so little they did not take it, and so came off clear. Don't mention this for I keep it a secret for fear it should intimidate all concerned.*[266]

Woodhull, however, did not believe the added threat posed by robbers or Loyalists would persist. "I do not think it will continue long so I intend to visit New York…and think by the assistance of a 355 [lady] of my acquaintance, shall be able to outwit them all."[267] (The possible identity and role of this mysterious woman, referred to only once in all of the Culper letters, is discussed in the previous chapter.)

In September, a minor player was added to the spy ring: Woodhull's uncle Nathan Woodhull, who served as an informant and scout. Culper Senior wrote Tallmadge on the nineteenth about his relative, who was a captain in a local Loyalist militia unit, a good vantage point for spying on British troop movements. "Pevbep Yqqhbwmm"—his uncle's name spelled in Culper code—had returned from New York to report that "there's a council of war holding of all the general officers." He added that "a large number of troops were embarking" on transports. Two months later, Abraham Woodhull said he had sent a person to check troop positions between Setauket and Huntington who subsequently provided a lengthy report. Rose concluded that person was Nathan Woodhull.[268]

In October, Washington stated it was vital to "establish a very regular communication with Long Island" and wrote four letters requesting information on British movements from the Culper spies. Washington made the inquiries because he had learned of the expected approach of a French fleet under the command of the Comte [Count] d'Estaing from the Caribbean and hoped to coordinate a surprise attack with the allies on Clinton's forces in New York. But that hope evaporated when he received a letter from Townsend on October 9. Culper Junior reported that the British garrison had also learned about the approach of the French fleet and "was much alarmed." Clinton ordered warships to Sandy Hook off the entrance to New York Harbor to counter any attempts by the French fleet to sail through the Narrows. But the French admiral decided that rather than sail directly to New York he would join in an attack with General Benjamin Lincoln on Savannah, Georgia. The October 9 assault turned into a debacle.[269]

Washington decided in the fall of 1779 that the spy operation needed to be more professional. In early October, he summoned Tallmadge to West Point, where they developed a memo to be sent to Culper Senior and Culper Junior. On October 14, Tallmadge forwarded these instructions to the pair:

> C—— Junr, to remain in the City to collect all useful information he can—to do this he should mix as much as possible among the officers and Refugees, visit the Coffee Houses, and all public places. He is to pay particular attention to the movements by land and water in and about the city especially. How their transports are secured against attempt to destroy them—whether by armed vessels upon the flanks, or by chains, Booms, or other contrivances to keep off fire Rafts.

Washington goes on to ask about "the number of men destined for the defense of the City and Environs," the location of redoubts and how many cannons they contained, whether pits have been dug in front of the lines, the state of British provisions and other details that take several hundred words to list. "C—— Senior's station to be upon Long Island to receive and transmit the intelligence of C—— Junior."

Washington also wanted "proper persons to be procured at convenient distances along the Sound from Brooklyn to Newtown [today's Elmhurst in Queens] whose business it shall be to observe and report what is passing upon the water." He concludes with another admonition for discretion: "there can be scarcely any need of recommending the greatest Caution and secrecy in a Business so critical and dangerous." He then reiterated how the messages should be transmitted and stressed that they should be given "to no one but the Commander-in-Chief."[270]

As Townsend's interactions with Jonas Hawkins show, relationships among the spy ring members were not always smooth. The often prickly Woodhull on October 29, 1779, urged Tallmadge to "forget not to urge 725 [Caleb Brewster] to his duty, which I must say he hath lately neglected."[271]

Brewster is mentioned in another complaint from Woodhull in the same letter, but not as an offender. Culper Senior, who did not like to see deprivations of noncombatants, even if they were Loyalists, wrote Tallmadge:

> *Night before last a most horrid robbery was committed on the houses of Coll. [Colonel] Benj. Floyd and Mr. Seaton, by three whale boats from your shore, commanded by Joseph Hulce and Fade Danolson, and one other master of a boat, name unknown to me. 725 can well inform you of their names. From the best judgment I can form they took to the value in money, household goods, Bonds and Notes, of Three Thousand Pounds. They left nothing in the houses that was portable. They even took their clock and all their looking glasses....I cannot put up with such a wanton waste of property, I know they are enemy's to our cause, but yet their property should not go amongst such villains. I beg you would exert yourself and bring them to justice.*[272]

Tallmadge commented on the incident in his own letter to Washington on November 1, 1779. "I have additional accounts of the same from others," he wrote.

> *In addition to the crime of plundering the distressed inhabitants of Long Island the perpetrators of such villainy never bring their goods before any court for tryal and condemnation, but proceed to vend them....This species of Privateering (for it goes by this name) is attended with such numberless bad consequences, that to a gentleman of your Excellency's feelings, I am confident I need not state them. If being so plundered by the enemy that the inhabitants have hardly a subsistence left, be not sufficient (for the marauders from our shore make no distinction between Whig and Tory further than what interest may point out) it truly cannot be reputable to leave it in the power of individuals to punish at pleasure, and enrich themselves by the plunder they take....I would further observe that the boat that crosses for dispatches from C—— has been chased quite across the Sound by those plunderers, perhaps for the sake of being the more secret in their Villany.... Indeed if some stop cannot be put to such nefarious practices C—— will not risque, nor 725 go over for dispatches.*

Tallmadge continued, "I should be happy to have permission to take the men who have been concerned in this Robbery, and have them delivered over to the authority." He added that Colonel Floyd had recently been brought over to Connecticut as a Tory prisoner and had been released on parole. "From a long and intimate acquaintance with this gentleman I believe him to be of more service to the Whig interest in Setauket than every other man in it, though from his family connection I believe he has been in favor of Royal Government....I hope some steps may be taken to prevent such contact in the future."[273] Tallmadge wanted to do more than protect Floyd; he suggested to Washington that they try to recruit him for the spy ring.

Two days later, Washington instructed New York governor George Clinton to take "proper measures...to bring [the perpetrators who had robbed Floyd] to justice, and prevent such acts of violence in future."[274] Tallmadge then instructed Woodhull to "take all the pains possible to secure Col. Floyd" as a spy. But Culper Senior refused, arguing that the Loyalist had not really changed sides and approaching him could be dangerous for the members of the ring. He told Tallmadge that he had "no love for Col. Floyd, not for no Tory under heaven."[275]

Townsend's November 3 letter contained a brief mention of interesting geographical confluence: "General Clinton and the [unnamed] Admiral were at Oyster Bay on Monday observing the Harbour. It is positively said a number of Transports are to be sent there to winter." The British commanders were in Townsend's hometown, likely on his family's property and not far from his family home, but the spy made no mention of that.[276]

Woodhull's twenty-seventh letter, dated November 5, 1779, is short but reflects his unease at British troop movements in the Huntington area, not far away enough from Setauket for his liking. "Much talk about their coming to this place soon, and we are greatly alarmed about it," he wrote. "Should they come here I shall most certainly retreat to your side [Connecticut] as I think it will be impossible for me to be safe." He added that he would be meeting with Culper Junior on the tenth to "order affairs so that the damage I hope will not be great if it should become necessary to quit the Island. Depend I shall not do it without absolute necessity."[277]

Woodhull wrote again—six pages—on November 13 about his planned meeting with Townsend, which failed to occur:

> *On the 10th I was to see Culper Junior, at a house he appointed twelve miles west from here, and set out with all my letters to meet him, and just before I arrived at the appointed place I suddenly met a foraging party of 40 horse* [calvary] *and 200 foot* [infantry soldiers] *and about 100*

wagons. Was much surprised but after answering a few questions passed them unmolested. But to my great mortification Culper Junior did not come that day. I waited all the next, sent a person westward to several houses where I thought likely to find him, but could hear nothing of him. I am much concerned. Fear some accident hath befallen him, but yet wish to entertain a favorable thought that he may be sick.

Culper Senior goes on to talk about the condition of the local people:

The inhabitants of this Island at present live a miserable life.... Plundering...increases at no small rate. I am tired of this business, it gives me a deal of trouble, especially when disappointment happens....I am perfectly acquainted with a full year's anxiety, which no one can scarcely have an idea of, but those that experience. Not long since, there was not a breath of your finger betwixt me and death. But so long as I reside here my faithful endeavors shall never be wanting.[278]

Woodhull's November 29, 1779 letter recounts that a British foraging party did come to Setauket, as he had feared. "This place is very distressed," he wrote. "Their coming was like death to me at first but have no fears about me at present and soon intend to visit N.Y. There is about 400 [soldiers] in the town and following the wagons. They take all the forage and oats."[279]

That same day that Woodhull wrote with minor news, Townsend also wrote and delivered a bombshell. The British "think America will not be able to keep an Army together another campaign...[because the] currency will be entirely depreciated, and that there will not be provision in the country to supply an Army [for] another campaign. That of the currency I am afraid will prove true, as they are indefatigable increasing the quantity of it. Several reams of paper made for the last emission struck by Congress have been procured from Philadelphia."[280]

Townsend had uncovered the latest British plan for counterfeiting Continental currency, a strategy directed by Lord Germain in London. There were counterfeiting efforts throughout the war, including advertising the availability of free fake Continental bills in Loyalist newspapers. The earlier counterfeits were printed on thicker paper and never quite matched the authentic currency. But what Townsend found this time was different: the British had acquired the same paper used by Congress to print legitimate money. After receiving Townsend's letter, Washington warned Congress about the report from "a confidential correspondent in New York."[281]

Eventually—not until March 18, 1780—Congress recalled all of the currency in circulation to thwart the British scheme.[282]

Woodhull had calmed down considerably from his November jitters by the time he wrote to Tallmadge on December 12. "Hope if the weather is favorable you will incline to come over, as we greatly desire to see you," he said. "I have the pleasure to inform you my fears are much abated since the troops have been with us. Their approach was like death to me." Lieutenant Colonel Simcoe of the Queen's Rangers, who had come to Setauket to arrest him and assaulted his father when the spy could not be found, had been captured and was a prisoner in New Jersey. Woodhull remarked that if he was there "without fear of Law or Gospel would kill Col. Simcoe for his usage to me."[283]

7

THE CULPER LETTERS, 1780

As the war dragged on into 1780, George Washington continued to pursue his goal of finding a faster route to get reports from the Culper Ring to his headquarters.

The general wrote from Morristown, New Jersey, on February 5, 1780, that with his headquarters farther west, it was taking even longer to get intelligence from the spies. Washington pushed for a route across the Hudson River or Staten Island to New Jersey—a change that would make Woodhull superfluous.

He told Woodhull that

> it is my further most earnest wish, that you would press him [Townsend] to open, if possible, a communication with me by a more direct route than the present. His accounts are intelligent, clear, and satisfactory, consequently would be valuable, but owing to the circuitous route through which they are transmitted I can derive no immediate or important advantage from them, and (as I rely upon his intelligence) the only satisfaction I derive from it, is, that other accts. [accounts] are either confirmed or corrected by his, after they have been some time received. I am sensible of the delicacy of situation, and the necessity of caution.

Washington added that if Townsend could not come up with trustworthy people to shorten the loop, "I think I can name one or two men to him who will receive and convey to me through others such intelligence as he may think important."[284]

Phillips Roe House in Port Jefferson, home of a member of the Culper Spy Ring. *Photo by Audrey C. Tiernan, copyright 2020.*

While relaying the usual information about enemy activity and telling Washington about a meeting with Townsend in New York City, Woodhull wrote at the end of February about the condition of prisoners on the *Jersey* and other British prison hulks anchored along the Brooklyn shore. "Our prisoners on board of ships hath suffered much this winter, and to complete the total destruction of the sick, the hospital ship on Thursday last about 4 o'clock took fire in the stern, said by means of a stove, and was immediately consumed. How many perished I cannot say. Reports are from 3 to 50."[285]

Woodhull was never reticent about offering military advice to the commander in chief. In a postscript to a letter from March 13, 1780, Culper Senior wrote,

> *I have just heard that the enemy hath made a demand from Smith Town of a thousand cords of wood and that all the wood lying near our harbor is to be cut for them—and two regts.* [regiments] *is to be stationed in this Town* [Brookhaven]. *If it should take place it will I fear entirely ruin our correspondence. To prevent which I shall give you early intelligence of their motions from time to time, that you may be prepared to give them a fatal blow at the beginning, or we shall be totally ruined.*[286]

With Woodhull providing little information of importance and sensing Washington's increasing frustration with the circuitous route through Setauket, Townsend pursued the idea of a more direct conduit for intelligence out of Manhattan. But then in April 1780 Townsend somehow communicated directly with Washington without going through Woodhull that he was withdrawing his services.

His decision is not explained in the Culper letters that have survived. Historian Morton Pennypacker, however, came up with an explanation by looking at other correspondence. It turned out that Culper Junior, in looking for a way to get messages to the general more quickly, enlisted the help of his teenage cousin James Townsend. When messages were ready on March 22, 1780, the younger Townsend managed to get safely across the Hudson River but did not meet his contact at the appointed time. For several days, Townsend fretted that his cousin had been captured and the British had learned their secrets. In fact, James Townsend had become bewildered and was cowered by the importance of the messages he carried. Possibly inebriated, he also had become confused about which house was the intended destination for his letters. He entered the wrong structure and got into a conversation with two young men there who questioned him. Being that he was in a Loyalist area, Townsend, thinking the men were Tories, related his cover story that he was a Loyalist looking to recruit men for the British army.

The two men, who were in fact Patriots, took him prisoner. His pockets were searched, and their contents, including two folded sheets of paper on which Robert Townsend had written a poem, were forwarded to Continental Army headquarters. The papers he carried seemed unremarkable, but Washington realized that they were stain letters written in the manner laid out in his instructions to the Culper spies. The general applied the second solution to reveal the real contents of the letter, but the stain had been applied sloppily so the reagent blurred the writing and made it illegible. It took some effort by Robert Townsend to persuade Washington to arrange the release of his relative because the general feared that British spies in the Continental Army camp might learn of the spy ring. Washington was angry with Culper Junior over the dangerous and embarrassing episode. And Robert Townsend found the whole incident so troubling that he abandoned not only his efforts to shorten the route to Washington but also his espionage efforts entirely.[287]

After Tallmadge filled him in, Woodhull went to the city to visit Townsend in early April. It didn't go well. Woodhull complained afterward in a letter to Tallmadge on April 5 that Culper Junior was uncooperative, and he received nothing but "a short memorandum from C. Junr. on a scrap of paper which he said contained all worthy of notice." Angry at being cut out of the action and Townsend's lack of judgment in sending his inexperienced young relative on such an important mission, Woodhull complained that he thought Townsend "exceedingly to blame and guilty of neglect. And have given him my opinion in full upon the matter [and] hope that the like may never happen again." Townsend's response was that he would "continue no longer" in the espionage business.[288]

Woodhull tried again on April 19, traveling into the city to see Townsend. But he reported to Tallmadge that he had "returned this day after making every effort with his utter denial."[289] Tallmadge then tried to arrange a meeting with Townsend and Woodhull on May 1 but Culper Junior would not cooperate. Ever trying to please everyone, Woodhull headed back to the city a few days later to try again. He reported to Tallmadge on May 4 that "I have had an interview with C. Junr. and am sorry to find he declines serving any longer" as a report-writing participant. "If any other person can be pointed out…who can be safely relied on to supply C. Junr's place, I will make myself known to him, and settle a plan for the purpose."[290] The only positive outcome of the visit was that Townsend did agree to "give verbal information as he can collect."[291]

Townsend's decision to abandon almost all intelligence work prompted Washington to essentially disband the Culper network. He wrote to Tallmadge from Morristown on May 19, 1780, to say that

> as C. junior has totally declined and C. Senior seems [not] to wish to do it, I think the intercourse may be dropped, more especially as from our present position the intelligence is so long getting to hand that it is of no use by the time it reaches me. I would however have you take an opportunity of informing the elder C. that we may have occasion for his services again in the course of the Summer, and that I shall be glad to employ him if it should become necessary and he is willing. I am endeavoring to open a communication with New York across Staten Island.[292]

Not surprisingly, Woodhull was displeased when he received word of Washington's decision from Tallmadge, although he phrased his displeasure in polite terms:

> I am happy to find that 711 [Washington] is about to establish a more advantageous channel of intelligence than heretofore. I perceive that the former he intimates hath been but of little service. Sorry we have been

at so much cost and trouble for little or no purpose. He also mentions my backwardness to serve. He certainly hath been misinformed. You are sensible I have been indefaticable, and have done it from a principle of duty rather than from any mercenary end—and as hinted heretofore, if at any time theres need you may rely on my faithful endeavors.

Woodhull then goes on to report military news.[293]

After Washington operated without intelligence from the Culper spies for several weeks, his anger at the spy ring cooled and he rushed messages to Tallmadge to reengage them. From headquarters in Bergen County, New Jersey, on July 11, 1780, Washington wrote that "as we may every moment expect the arrival of the French Fleet a revival of the correspondence with the Culpers will be of very great importance. If the younger cannot be engaged again, you will endeavor to prevail upon the older to give you information of the movements and position of the enemy upon Long Island."[294]

It took three days for Washington's letter from New Jersey to reach Tallmadge in Cortlandt Manor in northern Westchester. The spy chief told his commander that he would set out the next morning for Fairfield, Connecticut, "where I will endeavour to put matters on such a footing… as may answer your Excellency's expectations." He added that "we are something in arrears" to Woodhull "and in order to enable him to prosecute the business, it may be necessary to afford him a small supply of money."[295]

When he arrived in Fairfield early on July 15, Tallmadge found Caleb Brewster, who immediately started across the Sound carrying messages for Woodhull and Townsend. Reaching Setauket, Brewster found Woodhull was ill, but Austin Roe rode to New York City to deliver the message to Townsend. At the same time, a British spy was carrying a message from East Hampton to New York with news that a French fleet had arrived off Rhode Island.[296]

When Roe met with Townsend in New York, Culper Junior agreed to resume his spy work. He obtained updates from his sources and wrote a message that many historians cite as his most important. When it reached Woodhull, Culper Senior enclosed his own message for Washington. It was most likely the shortest he ever dispatched to the commander in chief and his most excited: "Sir. The enclosed requires your immediate departure this day by all means let not an hour pass: for this day must not be lost. You have news of the greatest consequence perhaps that ever happened to your country."

Townsend's news was that eight thousand British troops were then embarking at Whitestone in Queens for Newport, Rhode Island, while

Abraham Woodhull's message–probably his shortest ever–to General George Washington forwarding a July 20, 1780, report from Robert Townsend about a planned British attack on Rhode Island: "Sir. The enclosed requires your immediate departure this day by all means let not an hour pass: for this day must not be lost. You have news of the greatest consequence perhaps that ever happened to your country…" *Library of Congress.*

Admiral Graves with eleven ships was already sailing there to take on the French fleet that the English believed consisted of only seven vessels. On July 10, seven French ships of the line and four frigates under Admiral Chevalier de Ternay, along with thirty-six transport vessels carrying about six thousand French soldiers commanded by Lieutenant General Comte de Rochambeau and their supplies, arrived off Newport. Surprisingly, the British commander, Sir Henry Clinton, would not learn for another week that the French had arrived that day. But Clinton had known since June 12 that the French fleet was on its way. The information had come from General Benedict Arnold, who had learned it from Washington several days before he switched sides.[297]

Townsend did not follow his usual procedure when transmitting this crucial information. Rather than writing in stain on a blank piece of paper and hiding that page in the middle of a ream of blank paper or writing in the blank areas of a book or pamphlet, Townsend wrote a letter addressed to Loyalist Colonel Benjamin Floyd about replenishing supplies that Floyd needed. Between the lines he wrote his real message with the stain. The legible part of the letter read "New York, July 20th, 1780. Sir, I received your favor by [Mister Roe, crossed out but still legible] and note the contents. The articles you want cannot be procured, as soon as they can I will send them. I am, Your humble Servant, Samuel Culper."[298]

As a prominent property owner, Floyd was a target for plundering by both sides. At least three times, Patriot raiders came from Connecticut or elsewhere in New England to steal his cattle, sheep, cash and some of his slaves. In September 1778, former governor and now Major General William Tryon and General Gerald DeLancey led two thousand soldiers backed up by several battalions of militia to eastern Long Island to seize cattle belonging to Patriot sympathizers. They stopped along the way in Brookhaven to dine with Floyd, and while they ate, soldiers cleaned out all of Floyd's apples, corn, potatoes, turnips, cabbages and much of his poultry and burned all of his fences, presumably for cooking fires.[299]

Despite Woodhull's distrust of Floyd, some historians say that Floyd, over the course of the war, shifted from being a Loyalist to a Patriot and aided the Culper Spy Ring. However, that doesn't mean he actively gathered or carried intelligence information. There is no documentation of his role. Setauket historian Beverly Tyler noted that there is no evidence that Floyd had any involvement in the spy ring and doesn't "believe there is any real evidence that Benjamin Floyd was a Patriot during the war."[300] But Oyster Bay historian Claire Bellerjeau noted that when Floyd was taken prisoner by Patriots and held in Connecticut in February 1779, Woodhull wrote a letter to Washington urging his release because "I am very likely to stand in need of his services."[301] And she pointed out that in the fall of 1779, Woodhull wrote to Tallmadge asking him to protect Floyd's property from whaleboat raiders because he was helpful to the cause of independence. "Tallmadge, Townsend and Woodhull all said they saw him as a person who was helpful to them," Bellerjeau said, although none of the Culper letters elaborates.

Whatever Floyd's role, it's not clear how Townsend's July 20 letter addressed to Floyd and another dated August 6 also addressed to him were delivered to Washington. It's unlikely they were delivered to Floyd in southern Brookhaven Town and then turned over to Woodhull in the northern part of the town to be sent across the Sound to Washington because of the extra time it would have involved. It's more likely they were conveyed directly to Woodhull, bypassing Floyd, who was never the intended final recipient anyway. A third possibility suggested by Bellerjeau is that Floyd received them in New York directly from Townsend and then as a Loyalist who would not attract suspicion arranged to get them to Washington more directly than going through Setauket. Otherwise, she argued, why would Townsend take the time to write a bogus letter when it would be so much easier just to write the letter in stain and hide it in a ream of paper as usual.[302]

In the most generally accepted version of what happened with Townsend's July 20 letter, Roe carried the letter directly to Woodhull and reached him in time to get the message across the Sound the same evening.

However the Culper warnings about the British plans for attacking Newport were transported, the news reached Continental Army headquarters and the Patriot commander in Newport, General William Heath, earlier from other sources. When Brewster reached Connecticut with the reports, the whaleboat captain couldn't find Tallmadge and arranged for a dragoon to carry it to Washington's headquarters in Preakness, New Jersey. It was received there on July 11 by the general's aide Alexander Hamilton. With Washington absent, Hamilton dispatched a courier to convey a warning about the British plans derived from "different channels" to General Lafayette, who was on his way to Rhode Island. But the dispatch rider did not catch up to Lafayette before he arrived in Newport. So Heath's first warning came with the July 24 arrival of the sloop *Gates*, whose captain sailed from Stonington, Connecticut, and evaded the British blockade of Narragansett Bay after learning of the British plans from a Continental Army colonel who had been captured and then released on parole. The express rider conveying Hamilton's report delivered it to Lafayette in Newport late on the day after the arrival of the *Gates*.[303]

Learning of the British intentions at Newport, Washington arranged some clever subterfuge. A Patriot who would not be suspected posed as a Tory farmer and dropped off a package at a British outpost, claiming he had found it along the road. Inside the official dispatch pouch was a fictitious plan for an imminent attack by twelve thousand Patriot troops on New York City. According to some of the earlier histories of the spy ring, when the documents reached headquarters, Clinton took the bait. He ordered the lighting of signal fires along the northern shore of Long Island to recall the fleet, then anchored in Huntington Bay. By allowing the French to land and establish themselves in Rhode Island unmolested, the Culper Ring had provided its most important contribution in the war effort, according to Morton Pennypacker, Brian Kilmeade and some other current historians.[304]

But Revolutionary War historian Christian M. McBurney wrote that the British decision to call off the attack was more the result of a lack of coordination between Clinton and the senior Royal Navy commander in

North America, Admiral Marriott Arbuthnot. Regardless of why Clinton abandoned the assault, he accepted the spurious report that Washington planned to attack New York City as legitimate. And the intelligence received in Newport prompted General Heath to mobilize thousands of militiamen and spurred Rochambeau to more rapidly upgrade Newport's fortifications.[305]

Clinton tried to explain his aborted attack in a letter to Lord George Germain, secretary of state for America, adding he remained hopeful of mounting another effort. "Many causes conspired to retard the arrival of transports" in Whitestone, the British commander wrote. "During this time all hopes of success from a coup de main [sudden surprise attack] were of course wasted away."[306]

Clinton said the British fleet had gotten as far east as Huntington Bay when he received the intelligence about the arrival of the French and called off the attack. And then "on the 31st therefore I returned to White-stone, where I disembarked the troops, keeping the transports in readiness to receive them again, if necessary; and the army encamped near the shore. During this time, Washington, by a rapid movement, had, with an army increased to 12,000 men, passed the North-river, and was moving towards King's-bridge [at the northern tip of Manhattan], when he must have learned that my armament had not proceeded to Rhode-Island. He (I apprehend in consequence of this) re-crossed the river."[307]

Likely prompted by the urgency of the maneuvering around Newport, Tallmadge continued to address Washington's desire for a shorter route for reports. The Culper spies were now taking even more care about putting pen to paper, with Townsend willing to write letters only with the stain. The spy chief told Washington on August 1 that "I have been endeavoring to open communications with New York by crossing over to Cow Neck [current day Sands Point]....If this can be effected, Dispatches may be bro't [brought] from New York to the White Plains in 12 hours...as the whole land course on both sides would not exceed 34 miles, & the Sound not more than 10 miles over." (Actually, the distance across the Sound there is only about three miles.) He added that Townsend had "near relations living [near] Cow Neck whom if I can also engage, I am sure of Cr. Jr.'s services." Another benefit would be "a change of men through whom letters may pass," apparently a reference to Townsend's annoyance with Austin Roe for arriving late for several meetings, making Culper Junior even more skittish about writing reports. Tallmadge pointed out that Townsend "has consented to give intelligence but does not say how long."[308] Had Townsend seen that correspondence with its reference to him having relatives in Cow Neck, it would likely have made him more anxious about being discovered had it fallen into the enemy's hands.[309]

Ultimately, nothing came of Tallmadge's idea for the Cow Neck route, so intelligence reports continued to follow the existing route through Setauket. The system of having three dragoons posted every fifteen miles along the Connecticut shore to serve as relay couriers had its problems in addition to the time it took. A letter from Washington on August 27 noted that one of the express riders had been captured by the British and taken to New York. Fortunately, he was not carrying any secret correspondence.[310]

On August 11, Washington wrote to Woodhull: "I am very much pleased that the Correspondence with C____ [Junior] is again opened. I have the greatest dependence in his good intentions and I am persuaded when he pleases to exert himself he can give the most useful intelligence. The shorter the line of communication so much the better."[311]

Woodhull responded on August 16, 1780, after a visit to New York: "Sir, I have this day returned from New York and am happy to inform you that Culper Junior hath engaged to serve as heretofore....I have the satisfaction to assure you that the judicious Torys in New York are more dejected now than ever I knew before, on account of the neutrality entered into by the Powers of Europe." He mentioned that Clinton and about seven thousand men were still camped in the area of Whitestone "to hold themselves in readiness together with the fleet that still lays at Whitestone." He added as an afterthought that Washington should be getting "papers regular as heretofore. Should have sent them now but lost them out of my pocket on the road."[312] It was clearly good for all concerned that the correspondents were writing with the stain.

How dangerous the spy work could be was illustrated in a letter Caleb Brewster wrote to Tallmadge from Fairfield on August 18, 1780. While waiting for messages from Culper Senior, his whaleboat crew was attacked by two men. "I left one man taken and one wounded," he said of his losses. "We killed one on the spot." He asked for at least two replacements and ideally seven, preferably Continental soldiers, because "I have got two boats in fine order." Washington replied through Tallmadge that as far as he knew the only Continental boat crews operating in the area were those already under Brewster's command. But if the lieutenant found any others he could "take what hands he wants from them" in Washington's name.[313]

Always a man of action, Brewster did not wait for reinforcements. He wrote on August 21 from Fairfield that he had just returned from Long

Island after taking three boats across the Sound to Setauket. He reported that the hamlet was "full of troops." Brewster was looking for the two men named Glover and "Hoyght" who had attacked his crew "but could hear nothing of them. They never stayed to bury their dead man. They carried another away with them mortally wounded."[314]

Woodhull continued to give troop dispositions and also make suggestions for attacking them. Noting that there were about 470 troops around Setauket, Culper Senior thought them an attractive target. "There's every appearance of their continuing here sometime as they appear quite easy and off their guard," he wrote. "Am fully of an opinion that 500 good men would make prisoners of them all." He said Brewster could cross the night before an attack to get updated intelligence on the enemy disposition from him. Woodhull pressed the issue again in a September 5, 1780, letter in which he said the number of troops in Setauket had dropped by 34 because of the departure of the contingent of Queen's Rangers. "For God's sake attack them, you'll certainly be successful, if you are secret about it. Trust not to small boats at this season, you have three strong vessels on your shore that will be sufficient to bring five hundred men. Setauket is exceedingly distressed. Pray offer some relief."[315]

Tallmadge was eager to undertake such a mission. He wrote to Washington on September 9 that "I need not repeat to your Excellency how exceedingly happy I should be to assist in such an Expedition, should it be thot. advisable." But Washington never acted on Woodhull's recommendations, deciding the risks were too great for the potential reward.[316]

In the aftermath of the discovery of Benedict Arnold's treason and the hanging of British spy John André, there was much consternation within the Culper network. None of the participants was sure how much information on the spies Arnold had gathered before jumping to the British side. He had questioned Lafayette on the subject, but the French general responded he had been sworn to secrecy and he did not know any names anyway. Once he was wearing the red coat of a British general, Arnold began an aggressive campaign to locate Washington's spies in New York. He had a score of men, including Hercules Mulligan, in Manhattan and Long Island arrested (see chapter 5).[317]

With paranoia sweeping through his spy organization, Tallmadge wrote to Washington from Bedford on October 11, 1780, that even though Arnold

knows not a single link in the chain of my correspondence, still those who have assisted us in this way, are at present too apprehensive of Danger to give their immediate usual intelligence. I hope as the tumult subsides matters will go on in their old channels. Culper, Junr. has requested an interview with me on Long Island on the 13th. but in the present situation of affairs I believe it would be rather imprudent....I have wrote Culper, Junr. assuring him that his name or character are not even known by any officer but myself in the army.

Washington agreed with Tallmadge's decision not to meet with Townsend. "The enemy would act with more than common rigor just now should an officer be taken under circumstances the least suspicious—I should be exceedingly glad to hear from C. Junior, because all my accounts from other quarters are very defective as to the number of troops to be embarked or, indeed, whether an embarkation is seriously in contemplation."[318]

Washington also wrote to Congress that "unluckily, the person in whom I have the greatest confidence is afraid to take any measure for communicating with me just at this time, as he is apprehensive that Arnold may possibly have some knowledge of the connection and may have him watched."[319]

Because he had mentioned in a September 21 letter to Arnold that he was receiving "private accounts from New York," Tallmadge was worried that he had given away too much information despite not naming anyone. He remained concerned about the fate of his agents until he received a letter in early October from Woodhull relating that he and Townsend were both safe. "The present commotion that has arisen on account of the infamous Arnold together with little or no intelligence at this time was the reason he did not write," Woodhull said of Townsend. He added that he had arranged to meet Culper Junior to discuss their future plans.[320]

Townsend replied to Tallmadge's letter about Arnold not knowing the identity of anyone in the Culper network on October 20. He wrote somewhat testily that the spy chief's "assurances are as much as I could expect. When I conclude to open another route you shall be informed of it....I am happy to think that Arnold does not know my name....I was not much surprised at his conduct, for it was no more than I expected of him....His name will stink to eternity." As for the hanging of André, Townsend continued, "I never felt more sensibly for the death of a person whom I knew only by sight, and had heard converse, than I did for Major André. He was a most amiable character. General Clinton was inconsolable for some days; and the army in general and inhabitants were much exasperated....I believe General Washington felt sincerely for him, and would have saved him if it could have been done with propriety." Townsend included another reminder of his desire for increased security: "I hope and expect that all my letters are destroyed after they are perused."[321]

Woodhull commented on Townsend's fears and intention to take another interlude from spying in an October 26, 1780 letter to Tallmadge.

> *I have this day returned from New York, and am sorry to inform you that the present commotions and watchfulness of the Enemy at New York hath resolved C. Jur. for the present to quit writing and retire into the country for a time.—Most certainly the enemy are very severe, and the spirits of our friends very low. I did not think myself safe there a moment, and as nothing is like to be done about New York, perhaps it may be not be much disadvantage to drop it for a time, and if need requires C. Junr. will undertake again, and in the interim if anything in particular is wanted to be known, shall be ready to serve and faithfully transmit what I may know.*[322]

In a November 12 letter, Culper Senior wrote to Tallmadge that Townsend's caution was probably justified with Benedict Arnold now in New York hunting for Patriot spies. Reiterating that he had "informed you of the severity and watchfulness of the Enemy," Woodhull noted that "several of our dear friends were imprisoned, in particular one that hath been ever serviceable to this correspondence. This step so dejected the spirits of C. Junr. that he resolved to leave New York for a time. I earnestly endeavored to prevent it but could not, so that I have no person there now that I can send the Express to that [I] can rely upon."[323]

Although more than forty suspected spies were taken into custody, Rose concluded that the "particular one that hath been ever serviceable" was probably tailor/spy Hercules Mulligan. He wrote that since Mulligan knew Townsend and also knew he was spying for Washington and had supplied information to the Culper Ring, Townsend was justifiably nervous about the arrest and the possibility of being unmasked.[324]

With Townsend incommunicado, Woodhull focused on enemy activity on Long Island, making recommendations for targets to attack. He and Brewster recommended to Tallmadge that he attack Fort St. George. The colonial manor of William "Tangier" Smith in Mastic had been fortified into a triangular stockade manned by Tory refugees from Rhode Island. They also recommended destroying a three-hundred-ton supply of hay stored in Coram, about seven miles south of Setauket. Brewster wrote from Fairfield on November 13 to Tallmadge that he had just returned from Long Island where Woodhull had made a reconnoitering trip and confirmed that "forrage is at Corum yet in stack where tavern is kept. Their remains about 40 Ruffigeus [refugees from Patriot-controlled Rhode Island] yet at Mastick on Mr. Smith's place. They have no connon, nothing but muskets."[325] With Washington's approval, Tallmadge acted on the intelligence. He captured the fort—despite it having cannon—and burned the hay, as discussed in chapter 15.

THE CULPER LETTERS, 1781–1783

Abraham Woodhull shared good news at the beginning of a new year. He wrote on January 14, 1781, that Robert Townsend "intends to undertake the business again in the spring." He tempered his upbeat message by pointing out that "it is now a full year that I have supported this correspondence and afforded frequent dispatches—and the expenses incurred amount to one hundred and seven pounds eighteen shillings, and all I have received is 29 guineas. The balance is due me and in want thereof, wish it could be forwarded soon."[326] Woodhull had been paid only slightly more than a quarter of what he said he was owed. With a guinea equal to twenty-one shillings or one pound and one shilling, his expenses in 2020 dollars totaled more than $24,000.

On March 18, Woodhull followed up with more good news: "C. Jur. is again in 727 [New York] and entering into business again as heretofore, and you may soon I hope receive his dispatches."[327] But then Culper Senior wrote on April 23 that Townsend had visited him in Setauket to tell him "that he will not 691 [work] anymore on any account whatsoever."[328] Woodhull's summary of the situation was overstated: Townsend was willing to provide reports, but only verbally.

Townsend's caution was reasonable considering he had learned that the British had information that might have uncovered the spy ring. One of Clinton's agents, William Heron, actually a double agent known as "Hiram, the Spy" who worked both sides, had reported to headquarters on February 4, 1781, that "private dispatches are frequently sent from New York to the

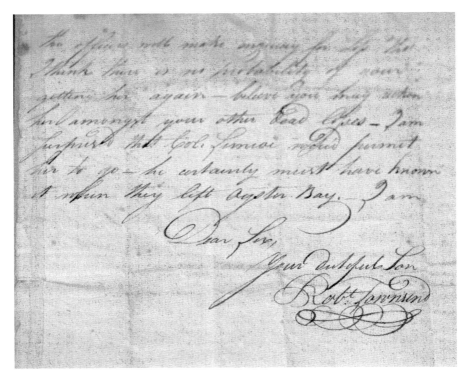

Culper spy Robert Townsend's signature on a letter to his father on display at the Raynham Hall Museum in Oyster Bay. *Photo by Audrey C. Tiernan, copyright 2020.*

Chieftain here [George Washington] by some traitors. They come by way of Setalket, where a certain Brewster receives them at, or near, a certain womans."[329] The unidentified woman clearly was Anna Strong, the only woman living near Woodhull and who was in regular contact with Caleb Brewster. As accurate as the information from Heron was, nothing came of it, to the relief of the Culper operatives. But Heron had increased the risks for the ring because his intelligence led to new British checkpoints, increased patrols and recruiting of dozens of new informers. From the information Heron supplied and what Benedict Arnold knew, it was clear that Tallmadge was in charge of getting information out of the city and to Washington via Setauket.[330]

The spy ring correspondence continued to include discussion of reimbursement—or lack thereof—for money laid out for paying sources, buying supplies, transportation and other costs. Tallmadge wrote to Washington on April 25, 1781, that at a meeting with Woodhull the chief spy had proposed that he remain mostly on Long Island and Townsend, who he thought might be lured back fully into the operation, would stay exclusively in New York. "That some confidential person must of course be employed to carry dispatches as it would cause suspicions which might lead to detection if either of the Culpers should be frequently passing from New York to Setauket, &c. [etc.] they being men of some considerable note," Tallmadge wrote.

> *What he* [Woodhull] *will of course want will be a sufficient sum of money to defray the contingent expenses which as living at New York and traveling on Long Island is very dear, the expenses accruing must be considerable. C. Senior observes that he is already considerably in advance for the business....He further observes that if in the present state of our public affairs it should be found difficult to furnish money for the purpose, he will advance 100 guineas or more if needed, receiving your excellency's assurance that it shall be refunded by the Public, with reasonable interest, after the War.*[331]

Washington replied on April 30 that he wanted to resume operations with the Culper network: "Fully impressed with the idea of the utility of easy, regular and accurate communications of the kind in contemplation, I shall make no difficulty in acceding to the proposal." Washington authorized a "liberal reward for the services of the Culpers, (of whose fidelity and ability I entertain a high opinion)," as long as "their exertion should be proportionally great."[332]

The results were not immediately what Washington had been seeking. Woodhull wrote Tallmadge on May 8 after a trip to New York that "I can only obtain verbal accounts for you and that but seldom, as the enemy have lately been made to believe that a line of intelligence is supported here. They are jealous of every person that they may see from this part."[333]

On May 12, Tallmadge reported to Washington that he was looking for another person to help the operation on Long Island who was located closer to the city than Woodhull. Woodhull contacted someone suggested by Tallmadge, but the person could be in the city only occasionally, so he did not work out. But a new spy ring member was recruited who signed his reports S.G. That was George Smith of Nissequogue, who had been a lieutenant in the Suffolk County Loyalist militia before becoming disenchanted with the British. Smith had been suggested by Brewster to Tallmadge. He apparently acted as a replacement for Brewster when the captain was not available to carry messages. Smith was active at least through August 1782.[334]

Another fringe recruit was Nathaniel Ruggles, a Yale-educated schoolmaster and physician who helped refugees from Long Island resettle in Connecticut at the beginning of the war. Brewster and Tallmadge apparently persuaded him to relocate temporarily to Old Man's, now Mount Sinai, a few miles east of Setauket on Long Island in the spring of 1781. He made several trips to New York before his cover was blown within a few months by Ebenezer Hathaway, captain of the Loyalist privateer *Adventure*. Ruggles was never arrested, so he must have escaped back to Connecticut before being caught.[335]

Washington would continue to be frustrated in his desire for a shorter route for relaying the intelligence and someone to write reports in place of Townsend. Culper Senior wrote Tallmadge after returning from the city on May 19 that

> it is a matter of grief to me that I cannot completely execute your request. When at New York myself, together with Culper Junior racked our invention to point out a proper person and made several attempts but failed—no person will write. The enemy have got some hint of me for when passing at Brooklyn Ferry was strictly examined and told some villain supported a correspondence from this place. I do assure you am greatly alarmed—and wished to be relieved from my present anxiety. I shall not think it safe for me to go to New York very soon—and can only supply you with verbal accounts as hath been the case for some time.[336]

With the organization stymied, Tallmadge began mulling the idea of relying primarily on temporary agents like Nathaniel Ruggles who would be willing to spend short periods on Long Island before returning to Connecticut. Their reports would be much less precise than those of the Culper agents at their peak, and these men would probably want to be paid for their work rather than just for expenses. But Tallmadge calculated the short stays would minimize their chances of being caught. Several acquaintances of Caleb Brewster took on the role, but their effectiveness is unknown.[337]

By June 1781 the Culper operation had come to a standstill. Woodhull wrote on the fourth to Tallmadge that like Townsend he felt forced to stop for self-preservation: "We live in dayly fear of death and destruction. This added to my usual anxiety hath allmost unmanned me—I must now (as painfull as it is to me) disappoint your expectations....I dare not visit New York myself and those that have been employed will serve no longer, through fear." Woodhall said he was "fully persuaded by various circumstances and observation" that continuing to make reports "regular without any interval" would lead to his "ruin." He concluded that "you must acknowledge and readily conclude that have done all that I could, and Stood by you, when others have failed And have not left you in the darkest hour."[338]

Tallmadge was able to persuade Woodhull to continue on an irregular basis. But from July 7, 1781, to May 5, 1782, he wrote no letters. Besides still being fearful of detection, he became engaged in November 1781 to a cousin, Mary Smith of Setauket, which gave him more to lose. Townsend submitted only occasional verbal reports. So for the rest of the war, Washington looked elsewhere for most of his intelligence. The new spies he employed were not driven by the patriotic fervor of the Culper Ring members but by mercenary motives.[339]

1782

When Woodhull finally resumed writing on May 5, 1782, it was directly to Washington in Virginia. The Continental Army remained there with its French allies after the successful Siege of Yorktown, which lasted from September 28, 1781, to October 19, 1781, and proved to be the final gasp of the British effort to retain control of America. Woodhull's letter was brief but contained momentous news: "A cessation of arms is ordered, to take place within these lines both by Land and Sea—and terms of peace are given to Congress, but the conditions is here unknown, but generally supposed Independence is offered. The Enemy still continue to fortify, nevertheless, both on [New] York and on Long Island. I have nothing further to inform you of but hope soon to have peace in our land."[340] The "cessation of arms" was news to Washington. An official declaration from London would not reach New York until August.[341]

Washington reactivated the Culper Ring in the spring of 1782. He was concerned that the new British commander in chief, Sir Guy Carleton, was improving the defenses in New York when the Continental Army general expected him to be preparing to evacuate. The Culper agents were agreeable to the resumption of spying and even writing reports again because they were less fearful of being detected and hanged since the British had shifted

The tavern owned by Culper Spy Ring courier Austin Roe was built in East Setauket in 1703 and relocated nearby in 1936. President George Washington spent the night there on April 22, 1790, during his tour of Long Island. *Photo by Audrey C. Tiernan, copyright 2020.*

their emphasis and many of their troops to the South prior to the defeat of Cornwallis at Yorktown.[342]

Woodhull wrote to Tallmadge on July 5 after receiving a report from Townsend and arranging for Austin Roe to reconnoiter in the city. He said that the British actions seemed to be purely defensive. He reported that the enemy was

> *fortifying on the banks of the rivers near the City and it is expected they will contract their lines and only attempt to defend a part of* [New] *York Island near the town if they should be attacked. They have a number of ships ready to sink in the river if an enemy should appear. There's only two ships of any consequence in the harbor, the* Lion *and* Centurion. *Their design appears only to act on the defensive and be as little expense to the Crown as possible. God grants their time may be short for we have much reason to fear within these lines that Carleton's finger will be heavier than Clinton's....He is called a tyrant at N. York by the inhabitants in general and makes them do soldier's duty in the City.*[343]

Carleton informed Washington on August 2 that the new government in London had accepted the principle of American independence.

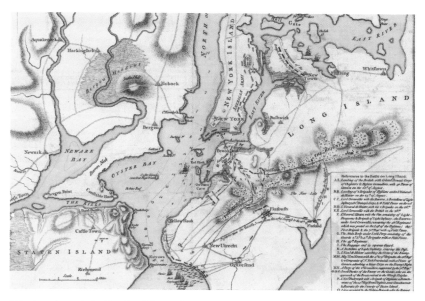

The location of the Battle of Long Island shown in a detail from "A plan of New York Island, with part of Long Island, Staten Island & east New Jersey, with a particular description of the engagement on the woody heights of Long Island, between Flatbush and Brooklyn, on the 27th of August 1776 between His Majesty's forces commanded by General Howe and the Americans under Major General Putnam, with the subsequent disposition of both armies" by William Faden, 1776. *Library of Congress.*

The Battle of Brooklyn by Mark Maritato depicts Colonel William Smallwood's Maryland Battalion in action. *Courtesy of the artist.*

Captain Caleb Brewster receives intelligence for General George Washington from chief Culper spy Abraham Woodhull in a mural at the Setauket School. *Courtesy Three Village Central School District. Photo by Beverly Tyler.*

"U.S. Army Artillery Retreat from Long Island." *Library of Congress.*

A Dutch door at the Mastic Beach home of Declaration of Independence signer William Floyd, which his family abandoned during the British occupation. The house was expanded after the war. *Photo by Audrey C. Tiernan, copyright 2020.*

Left: The desk owned by Declaration of Independence signer William Floyd at his Mastic Beach home. *Photo by Audrey C. Tiernan, copyright 2020.*

Below: The hallway at Rock Hall in Lawrence. The house, owned by the Loyalist Martin family, was occupied by Patriot troops early in the war. *Photo by Audrey C. Tiernan, copyright 2020.*

Left: The parlor at Rock Hall in Lawrence features period furnishings based on inventory records. *Photo by Audrey C. Tiernan, copyright 2020.*

Below: Parlor at Raynham Hall Museum in Oyster Bay, which was occupied by British officers many times during the Revolution. *Photo by Audrey C. Tiernan, copyright 2020.*

Detail of a parlor desk at Raynham Hall in Oyster Bay. *Photo by Audrey C. Tiernan, copyright 2020.*

Bedroom at Raynham Hall Museum occupied by British Lieutenant Colonel John Graves Simcoe during the Revolution. *Photo by Audrey C. Tiernan, copyright 2020.*

Top: A detail of the Raynham Hall bedroom where John Graves Simcoe stayed. *Photo by Audrey C. Tiernan, copyright 2020.*

Bottom: A replica map and other items in the Raynham Hall bedroom used by John Graves Simcoe. *Photo by Audrey C. Tiernan, copyright 2020.*

The rear doorway of Hewlett House in Hewlett, former home of Loyalist Lieutenant Colonel Richard Hewitt. *Photo by Audrey C. Tiernan, copyright 2019.*

Bedroom at Sagtikos Manor in West Bay Shore where British General Henry Clinton is believed to have slept. *Photo by Audrey C. Tiernan, copyright 2019.*

A groove carved into an attic staircase by a British soldier's musket ball fired at Sagtikos Manor owner Isaac Thompson. *Photo by Audrey C. Tiernan, copyright 2019.*

A fireplace at Sagtikos Manor. *Photo by Audrey C. Tiernan, copyright 2019.*

Left: A desk in Sagtikos Manor. *Photo by Audrey C. Tiernan, copyright 2019.*

Below: Interior of the Old House in Cutchogue, built in the late 1600s. *Photo by Audrey C. Tiernan, copyright 2020.*

Target Rock, a glacial erratic boulder left behind by the glaciers and used by British warships for target practice during the American Revolution. *Photo by Audrey C. Tiernan, copyright 2019.*

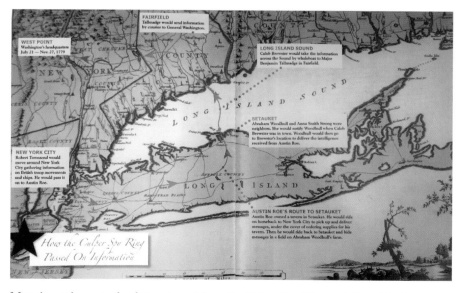

Map shows the route that letters to and from the Culper Spy Ring took from Manhattan to George Washington's headquarters. *Courtesy of the Three Village Historical Society.*

Miniature portrait of Benjamin Tallmadge, General George Washington's spymaster. *Collection of the Litchfield Historical Society, Litchfield, Connecticut.*

The tavern room, which was constructed in 1754, at the restored Terrell-Havens-Terry-Ketcham Inn in Center Moriches. Benjamin Havens, who ran the inn during the Revolutionary War, is believed to have been a member of the Culper Spy Ring. The house was expanded after the war. *Photo by Audrey C. Tiernan, copyright 2020.*

Diane Schwindt, who demonstrates colonial cooking at the Terrell-Havens-Terry-Ketcham Inn in Center Moriches, carves a chicken in the kitchen, which dates to 1693. *Photo by Audrey C. Tiernan, copyright 2020.*

The interior of the Thompson House in East Setauket. *Photo by Audrey C. Tiernan, copyright 2020.*

Above: The fireplace at the Sands-Willets House in Flower Hill. *Photo by Audrey C. Tiernan, copyright 2020.*

Left: The beehive oven at the Sands-Willets House. *Photo by Audrey C. Tiernan, copyright 2020.*

Above: Interior of the
Brewster House in
East Setauket. *Photo
by Audrey C. Tiernan,
copyright 2020.*

Right: "Evacuation of
New York by the British,
November 25, 1783."
Library of Congress.

EVACUATION OF NEW YORK BY THE BRITISH, NOVEMBER 25, 1783.

Roslyn mill owner Hendrick Onderdonk speaks with George Washington during the president's 1790 tour of Long Island in a mural painted in 1937 by Robert Herbert Gaston. *Courtesy Roslyn Public Schools and Howard Kroplick.*

"Evacuation day and Washington's triumphal entry in New York City, Nov. 25th, 1783," by lithographer Edmund P. Restein. *Library of Congress.*

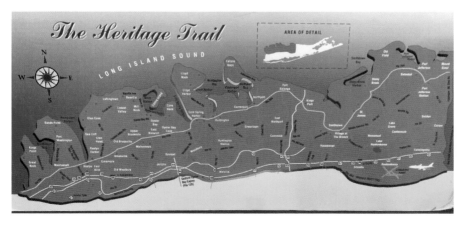

Map of the George Washington Spy Trail designated by the state in May 2017. It is marked by twenty-two brown signs along Route 25A between Great Neck and Port Jefferson. *Courtesy of the Ward Melville Heritage Organization.*

Washington remained skeptical despite Woodhull's assertions that Carleton was preparing only defensive fortifications. He wrote to Tallmadge on August 10: "I wish you without delay to open again, or at least to renew effectually, the channel of Intelligence through the C——s or any other Friends you can rely upon, in such a manner, as to keep me continually and precisely advised of every thing of consequence that passes within the Enemy's Lines....I know your correspondents, have heretofore, in general, been well-informed, that the only [great] difficulty has been in the circuitous route of communication." Tallmadge responded by having George Smith convey Washington's request to Woodhull and Townsend.[344]

By September, information was again coming from Woodhull to Tallmadge about the British plans for dealing with the coming peace. The reports detailed British officers selling their heavy baggage and furniture and Loyalists departing on ships for new lives in Canada and other parts of the empire.[345]

The last of Robert Townsend's letters known to have survived was written on September 19, 1782. Culper Junior carried it himself into Westchester County, where he delivered it to Tallmadge for forwarding to Washington. He wrote that the hopes of Loyalists that the war would not end and leave them abandoned had proven empty. He said the last regularly scheduled packet ship from England, rather than "bringing better news to the Loyalists, has indeed brought the clearest and unequivocal Proofs that the independence of America is unconditionally to be acknowledged, nor will they be any conditions insisted on for those who have joined the King's Standard." He said British troops were embarking for the West Indies and "a fleet is getting ready to sail for the Bay of Fundy about 1 October to transport a large number of Refugees to that Quarter....I never saw such general distress and dissatisfaction in my life as is painted in the countenance of every Tory at N.Y."[346]

Even though the war was essentially over, Tallmadge, based on the intelligence he was getting from his spies, urged his commander to approve a "stroke" against Colonel Benjamin Thompson's Loyalist troops based in Huntington. He said they were "very much off their Guard" and losing men through desertion.[347] Washington told Tallmadge to go ahead and sent him reinforcements. But the raid scheduled for December 5 was canceled when strong winds that blew for forty-eight hours prevented the crossing. Meanwhile, Caleb Brewster and other Patriots battled with three boatloads of Loyalists trying to get back to Long Island after trading and spying on the Connecticut shore. Brewster was severely wounded.[348]

1783

Once Washington was convinced that Carleton had no plans to hold onto New York, the Continental Army commander had little interest in hearing from Woodhull or Townsend. Woodhull continued to send reports that were usually only one page and appeared hastily written. The last report from Culper Senior was dated February 21, 1783.[349]

A month before the peace treaty was signed, Tallmadge in a letter dated March 31, 1783, asked the commanding general to be permitted to be one of the first to enter New York when the British evacuated the city so he could "insure the safety of certain Characters in New York" who appeared to their neighbors "to be of the Tory character" but who had "served us very essentially, & who may otherwise be treated amiss—It is a favor which they will by all means expect, & some of them will not wish to have the nature of their services divulged."[350] Washington agreed about the "propriety in your going early into Town."[351]

At Washington's request, Tallmadge asked Woodhull for an accounting of the spy ring's expenses. Culper Senior submitted it on July 5. He said the total spent was a little over £500—about $94,000 in 2020 adjusted for inflation[352]—over the course of the war with more than £125 still unreimbursed. Woodhull had spent a little more than £154 himself for travel, boarding in Manhattan and even keeping a horse there, as per Tallmadge's instructions, for nine months to facilitate rides by couriers. Couriers Jonas Hawkins, Austin Roe and George Smith accounted for £145, £116 and £4, respectively. Townsend's total was almost £52, mostly for buying reams of writing paper. There was also £18 for someone listed just as J.D., who could have been Setauket residents Joseph Davis or Jonas Davis or Joshua Davis, a whaleboat captain on Long Island Sound who filled in for Caleb Brewster when he was unavailable. Brewster spent a little over £6 on supplies "when here in distress by bad weather." The list included £4 for Selah Strong, which might have gone to expenses incurred by his wife, Anna. Woodhull told Tallmadge that he did not keep track of the dates the expenses were incurred because "I only kept the most simple accounts that I possibly could for fear it should betray me." But he added that his expense invoice was "a just one" and he wanted to "assure you I have been as frugal as I possibly could."[353]

Tallmadge verified the numbers and passed them on to Washington on August 16, 1783, in what would be his last significant letter to his commander. He stated that he was "convinced that he [Woodhull] has been as attentive to the public interest as his circumstances and peculiar situation would admit."[354]

After providing the final accounting of what was due to the Culper operatives for their "secret Services," he concluded by saying, "should I not have an opportunity to pay my personal respects to Your Excellency before You retire from the Army, give me leave at this Time, with the warmest Gratitude, to assure Your Excellency that I shall ever entertain a lively sense of the many marks of attention which I have rec'd from Your Excellency's hands."[355]

The commander in chief replied on September 11 that he needed more documentation from Tallmadge and then would try to provide funds for the outstanding amount. But he cautioned it would be "no very easy matter" because the states—there was no federal budget under the Articles of Confederation—showed little interest in paying for past services. He told Tallmadge that there was no other officer to whom he was more indebted.[356]

Washington was less generous in his remarks about the Culper spies:

> *I have no doubt, because I suppose S.C. [Samuel Culper] to be an honest Man, that the Monies charged in his Account have been expended, & therefore should be paid; but the Services which were rendered by him (however well meant) was by no means adequate to those Expenditures— My Complaints on this head, before I knew the amount of his charges, you may remember were frequent; and but for the request of Count de Rochambeau…I should have discontinued the Services of C.S. long before a cessation of hostilities took place, because his communications were never frequent, and always tedious in getting to hand.*[357]

Washington's comments read as an ungracious rebuke of the Culper agents in startling contrast to his earlier praise of the ring and his requests to resurrect it after periods of inactivity. Author Alexander Rose explained it by noting that "after 1781, the Culper Ring had declined precipitously in importance. Nearly all of the expenses still owing dated from that time onwards, so Washington was referring to that two-year period, not the Culpers' service as a whole." Tallmadge never shared Washington's comments with the Culper spies.[358]

Setauket historian Beverly Tyler said,

> *It is obvious to me in my readings of the letters that Washington was also looking for a way, in his own thinking, to justify changing his mind about compensating (money or jobs or something else) the members of the Culper Ring after the war. There is some human nature involved here, sort of*

Washington thinking, "It's over, let's all of us move on. Good work was done, most of the time, and we need to understand the needs of the country from here on in."[359]

After the war, Woodhull was eventually reimbursed for his expenses, while Townsend never asked for further reimbursement or pursued his earlier interest in a federal job. James Jay asked Congress to reimburse him for his expenses, but the request was rejected.[360]

Washington's total expenditure for intelligence gathering during the war was £1,982 (about $375,000 in today's money). More than a quarter went to the Culper Ring, which shows its prominence, even if the commander soured on it toward the end of the conflict.[361]

With the accounting completed, Tallmadge focused on protecting his agents in the city. Before the redcoats evacuated, Tallmadge, as proposed in his March 31 letter to Washington and with his commander's approval, entered Manhattan under flag of truce soon after the signing of the Treaty of Paris on September 3, 1783, which officially ended the war. His goal was to protect from mistreatment those aforementioned "certain Characters in New York [who had] served us very essentially." He rode down Broadway for the first time in seven years escorted by a few of his dragoons. He said he was surrounded by "British troops, tories, cowboys, and traitors" but was treated "with a great respect and attention" by military officers, especially when he had dinner with General Carleton and his staff one evening.[362]

Tallmadge wrote later that he "saw and secured all who had been friendly to us through the war, and especially our emissaries, so that not one instance occurred of any abuse, after we took possession of the city."[363] Among those who might have been secured was newspaper publisher James Rivington, who had given the appearance of being a "notorious Tory" but did not go into exile with other Loyalists.

The signing of the peace treaty did not immediately lead to the departure of the British. Their last troops did not depart New York until November 25, 1783. Continental soldiers marched into the city the same day, greeted by wildly cheering crowds.[364] November 25 would be celebrated as a holiday known as Evacuation Day in New York City into the early decades of the twentieth century.

THE END OF THE WAR

By 1780, the British had shifted their emphasis from the Middle Atlantic region to the South, where they believed there was a higher concentration of Loyalist residents who would support their efforts. To bolster their strength in that region, the British removed most of their troops from eastern Long Island. This allowed refugees to begin returning from Connecticut long before the final major battle of the war at Yorktown, Virginia, in the fall of 1781 and the signing of the Treaty of Paris on September 3, 1783, which officially ended the war. The returnees discovered that most of their homes and property had been ravaged by the occupation forces.[365]

One of the most notable early returnees was Patriot leader Selah Strong. He ventured back to his Setauket home by June 1780, having been elected president of the Town of Brookhaven trustees. That month he presided over a town board meeting.[366]

More evidence that the British presence had been reduced before the signing of the peace treaty was that five months earlier they had auctioned about two hundred "excellent dragoon horses in high condition" at the Hempstead Plains, Huntington and other places.[367] When it became clear the occupying troops would be leaving, Loyalists began to evacuate the city and Long Island in the spring of 1783, months before the official end of the war.

It wasn't until November 25—almost three months after the signing of the Treaty of Paris—that Washington's army reoccupied New York City. But the

"Entrance of the American Army into New York, Nov. 25th 1783." *Library of Congress.*

British retained control of areas of Queens County, which included present-day Nassau County and Suffolk, for nine more days until the final British evacuation on December 4. "This long delay was owing to the removal of so many loyalists, who dared not remain here after the passage of so many violent resolutions by whig [Patriot] meetings in various parts of the Union," wrote nineteenth-century historian Henry Onderdonk Jr. "Ships were sent for from the West Indies, and even Europe."[368]

The delay contributed to Long Island being occupied by the British longer than any other area of the thirteen colonies during the Revolution. The last soldiers to leave were those stationed in Queens. As the British regulars and Loyalist troops marched toward the evacuation transports, they maintained their order, some serenaded by their bands and others in silence.[369]

In Setauket, Patriots celebrated the departure of the occupying troops by roasting an ox for a daylong celebration on the green. The master of ceremonies was native son Benjamin Tallmadge, promoted to the rank of lieutenant colonel at the end of the war. He had recently attended the December 4, 1783, gathering at Fraunces Tavern in Manhattan, where Washington had bid farewell to his officers, and the intelligence chief wrote the only known account. After a blessing was offered by his father, Tallmadge undertook the carving and served the meat. "All was harmony and joy," Tallmadge wrote, "for all seemed to be of one mind. A Tory could not have lived in that atmosphere one minute. By sunset the whole concourse—a vast multitude—dispersed and returned to their own homes in quietness and peace."[370]

After the occupying troops left, Suffolk Patriots engaged in reprisals— official and otherwise—against their Tory neighbors. In Queens, the victors attempted to be less vindictive and tried to reintegrate most Loyalists into the communities of the new nation. But some inhabitants of both counties who still actively resisted independence or had been threatened with violence, lawsuits or potential prosecution for treason because of their cooperation with the British chose voluntary exile.

The more pessimistic Loyalists began leaving for Britain or other colonies as early as the summer of 1782. But the government in London did not want a flood of impoverished refugees arriving in the mother country, so it began planning for resettlement in Canada. The head of a family would be offered five hundred acres and bachelors three hundred acres. They would also be given three weeks' rations and a year's worth of supplies, clothing, medicine and firearms. Initially, only a modest number of Tories accepted the offer to resettle in Nova Scotia because they could not conceive of Britain giving up America. Only after the fighting stopped in mid-February 1783 did a rush of refugees prepare to leave. While many sold their possessions at bargain prices, others chose suicide. Carleton

The home of Declaration of Independence signer William Floyd in Mastic Beach. It was abandoned by the family during the American Revolution and expanded after the war. *Photo by Audrey C. Tiernan, copyright 2020.*

wisely refused to evacuate New York until anyone who wanted to leave could do so.[371]

As many as 100,000 Loyalists abandoned the former thirteen colonies in the year before or at the end of the war. Among them were about 35,000 residents of the new state of New York, including about 29,000 in New York City. Because of the more forgiving attitude in Queens, it is estimated that only about 5 to 6 percent of that county's residents left. Four years before the end of the war, New York legislators passed the Forfeiture Act of 1779, allowing the future state to legally prosecute, or in effect persecute, prominent Loyalists and confiscate their property. More than 50 Queens residents ultimately were indicted under the law as enemies of the new nation. Residents who did not appear in court to answer the indictment were subject to having their property confiscated, but that was the fate of only about a dozen Queens residents. Further pressure came from passage of the Voting Act of May 1784. It allowed those who lived in counties occupied by the British to be disenfranchised from voting if they were proved to have been disloyal to the Patriot cause unless they had been the victims of compulsion.[372]

A few of the Loyalist refugees who left Long Island at the end of the war sailed for Britain or the British West Indies. But most headed for Canada, particularly Nova Scotia and New Brunswick.[373]

The first fleet carrying Loyalists from the New York region sailed for Canada late in the spring of 1783. It took two days to load families and their possessions before the *Two Sisters* left Oyster Bay on May 27, 1783. A second ship that arrived in Oyster Bay to transport Loyalists was set afire by angry Patriots. *Two Sisters* arrived in New York Harbor, where it waited two weeks for a dozen other ships carrying Loyalists from other areas to congregate. Then on June 11, the fleet sailed for Canada.

A second large fleet sailed from New York to Nova Scotia in the fall. The dozen ships carrying 2,500 Americans loyal to King George III were commanded by Lieutenant Colonel Richard Hewlett, owner of a large tract in present-day Lawrence and East Rockaway who had commanded a battalion of Loyalist troops on Long Island. The officer protected his 664-acre Queens estate from confiscation by the state by deeding it to his son Oliver, who had remained neutral during the war. Hewlett settled along the Saint John River and called the community he founded Hampstead after the town he had been forced to leave: Hempstead. The new county incorporating the new town was named Queens. Hewlett lived as a farmer and received half-pay from the British army for his service. After he died in

1789 at the age of fifty-nine, one of his sons, Joseph, remained in Canada while his wife, Mary, and a daughter returned to Long Island.[374]

Long Islanders, whether Patriot, Loyalist or neutral, suffered greatly during the more than seven years of occupation. But the state legislature believed Long Island hadn't suffered enough. After the return of peace, the lawmakers levied a tax of £37,000 on the island for not supporting the war effort sufficiently—something difficult to do when enemy troops were occupying the land.[375]

10

IMPACT OF THE INTELLIGENCE

How important was the Culper Spy Ring to achieving American independence during the Revolution? It was crucial, at least in a few instances. But there were differences of opinion about its overall value at the time and among modern historians.

Benjamin Tallmadge, George Washington's spy chief who supervised the Culper operation, rated the operation as vital to the war effort. In the memoirs he wrote for his children, Tallmadge stated that "how beneficial it was to the Commander-in-Chief is evidenced by his continuing the same to the close of the war."[376] Of course, Washington could have kept it going for lack of an alternative. And there were times when Washington suspended the network when the agents balked at providing reports for fear of discovery by the British.

During the war, Tallmadge pointed out times when the Culper spies provided critical information. In April 1779, for example, he wrote, "Some pieces of useful intelligence respecting the movements of the Enemy in the late intended Expedition to New London, in which I have reason to believe in a great measure defeated their intentions, have been communicated by Culper."[377]

The commander of the Continental Army vacillated in his opinion of the spy ring's usefulness over the course of the war. Washington wrote in a July 11, 1780, letter that he found the intelligence "of very great importance." In another letter, he stated, "I rely upon this intelligence."[378] And on April 30, 1781, the general wrote that of their "ability I entertain a high opinion."[379]

The home of chief Culper spy Abraham Woodhull about 1900. It was destroyed by fire in 1931. *Courtesy of the Three Village Historical Society.*

Yet throughout the conflict, the general complained about how long it took for him to get the information from the spies through the circuitous route via Setauket, saying it often was moot by the time he received the reports because of rapidly changing circumstances.

By the end of the war, with the Culper Ring operating only sporadically, Washington's opinion had veered to highly negative. In a September 11, 1783 letter to Tallmadge, the general questioned whether the results he had obtained were worth the expense: "The Services which were rendered by him [chief Culper spy Abraham Woodhull] (however well meant) was by no means adequate to those Expenditures…because his communications were never frequent, and always tedious in getting to hand."[380]

Modern historians and authors have been kinder than Washington on the usefulness of the Culper Spy Ring. But there are still differences of opinion.

The most positive assessment by far comes from Fox News anchor Brian Kilmeade. The subtitle of his 2013 bestseller *George Washington's Secret Six* is *The Spy Ring That Saved the American Revolution*, which most historians agree is hyperbole. "With the ability to get the intelligence that they did and with their efficiency in relaying the information, they allowed Washington to anticipate the British moves," Kilmeade told the author in a 2014 interview for a *Newsday* article. "So they helped break the back of the British military."[379]

Researchers who have spent years studying the spy ring recoil from such assertions by the amateur historian. They point—as Washington did—to how long it took for the information to make the circuitous transit and how in most cases it only seconded reports Washington already had from other sources or proved worthless because the military situation had already changed significantly.

But Kilmeade is not alone in giving a lot of credit to the Culper Spy Ring and other intelligence efforts during the war. Former CIA case officer Kenneth Daigler wrote: "That American intelligence activities were a significant factor in defeating the British in the Revolutionary War is well documented by historical record."[380] Daigler credited the agents and Tallmadge for developing professional methods of transmitting information and keeping their activities secret. "That the ring was a valuable source of intelligence for Washington cannot be debated," he wrote.

> *His appreciation of its information during the war was well-documented, even though in a letter to Tallmadge on September 11, 1783, after the conflict ended, he did question whether the ring had been worth the funds expended on it. To put his comment in perspective, Washington was by nature a rather frugal individual and as a gentleman of the time probably did not view spies, even his own, as being of the highest character. Also, intelligence agents, like infantrymen, are seldom as appreciated as much after the conflict as in the heat of it.*[381]

Author Alexander Rose noted that "after 1781, the Culper Ring had declined precipitously in importance."[382] So Washington's assessment was skewed negatively by that rather than looking at the network's output over the entire war. Revolutionary War historian Christian M. McBurney concluded that "the Culper spy ring performed highly dangerous work brilliantly, but there were other sources who conveyed the same intelligence in a timely fashion."[383]

Even if other sources sometimes provided the same intelligence earlier, Raynham Hall Museum historian Claire Bellerjeau said that "it was valuable for Washington to get the same information from several sources. It was their corroboration that made it valuable."

"I think it's hard for us to imagine—in a world where we can instantly communicate through text, email and other means—how important it was for Washington to have information coming out of New York City and Long Island," Bellerjeau continued. "The 193 letters that survive include 383 pages of information! Troop movements, ship arrivals, and a stream of vital intelligence was being delivered and its worth to the Patriot cause, while hard to show through a single sentence on a particular page, in its totality was of incredible value."[386]

"Washington considered the Culper Spy Ring as the most important source of information about the British forces in New York City and on Long Island," Setauket historian Beverly Tyler said. "Washington was able to trust the information being passed to him, although he consistently wanted the information to be transmitted faster and tried a number of times in 1779 and 1780 to facilitate a different route for the intelligence, including going directly north from Manhattan and going through Cow Neck [modern-day Sands Point] and Oyster Bay rather than Setauket. Neither possible change worked." And while the general received some of the intelligence from other sources before getting confirmation from the Culper spies, Tyler said, "he knew from the many dealings with the Culpers that their intelligence was accurate and trustworthy and that this was the most important consideration."

Tyler continued,

> *Washington's correspondence with Tallmadge shows how important the Culpers were to him. It was not any of the individual pieces of intelligence such as the British planning to attack the French fleet in Newport, nor the fact that the British were about to flood New York with counterfeit Continental dollars, nor the information that Townsend sent to Tallmadge to watch out for a man named John Anderson [British spy Major John André], it was the trustworthiness of the total intelligence that Washington received from the Culpers that made their work invaluable. The Culpers were probably the only intelligence network that was operating in British territory for the entire Revolutionary War, and Washington appreciated their efforts, kept corresponding with them and consistently worked through Tallmadge to make their operation safer and more effective.* [387]

As for specific circumstances in which the Culper information proved vital, Abraham Woodhull's reports about troop disposition across Long Island had to be of value to Washington in his planning. And Woodhull and Caleb Brewster's recommendation of specific targets for whaleboat raids across Long Island Sound were clearly useful when Benjamin Tallmadge was planning them and executing some of them, particularly the raid on Fort St. George in Mastic, as discussed in chapters 5 and 15.[388]

Another instance where Culper intelligence was clearly valuable was a July 15, 1779 letter in which Townsend exposed a Tory spy. Christopher Duychenik was posing as a Patriot but providing intelligence via former Loyalist New York City mayor David Mathews to William Tryon, the former New York royal governor who was a major general in a Tory militia unit making raids along the Connecticut shoreline. According to Daigler, the letter shows that the spy ring had internal information from the Tory intelligence system being run by William Franklin, the illegitimate son of Benjamin Franklin and former royal governor of New Jersey.[389]

Another example involved thwarting British efforts to counterfeit Continental currency. The British tried to counterfeit the paper bills throughout the war. Previously, however, they had not acquired paper that exactly matched what the Patriots used for their printing, so careful examination always revealed the counterfeits. But in a November 29, 1779 report, Townsend relayed information that the British had acquired paper that exactly matched that of the Continental currency and could now produce counterfeits that could further devalue the already devalued paper money. Washington advised Congress of the problem in a December 7 letter, and lawmakers decided in March 1780 to recall all extant currency.[390]

Original July 20, 1780, invisible-ink letter written by Robert Townsend (Samuel Culper Junior) to Abraham Woodhull (Samuel Culper Senior) warning of a planned British attack on Rhode Island disguised as a letter to Tory Colonel Benjamin Floyd. *Library of Congress.*

In early March 1780, Manhattan spy Hercules Mulligan provided information to the Culper operatives or to Tallmadge directly that the British planned to capture Washington while he was traveling to meet with French General Rochambeau, allowing Washington to change his route.[391]

And then there was Robert Townsend's July 1780 message that eight thousand British troops were embarking from Queens with the destination of Newport. Admiral Graves and eleven ships were already under sail for Rhode Island to take on the French fleet that was expected to arrive there to establish its American base of operations. While Washington's headquarters was alerted to the British plans prior to getting the information from Townsend and Woodhull, their reports confirmed the intelligence and spurred the Continental Army to act. As detailed in chapter 7, Washington developed a plan to bluff the British that most historians agree prompted the enemy to call off the attack in Rhode Island.

It's not hard to make a compelling case that the Culper Spy Ring was important to the war effort. And that, along with the tension created by the fear of detection while snooping on the world's biggest military power, may explain why so much has been written about it, even if some of the facts have gotten twisted along the way.

II

AFTER THE REVOLUTION

Geroge Washington's intelligence chief and the two primary Culper spies—Benjamin Tallmadge, Abraham Woodhull and Robert Townsend—all lived for more than a half century after the beginning of the American Revolution. And after the war, they talked little or not at all about their roles in the espionage network.[392]

After the Continental Army disbanded, Tallmadge returned to his hometown of Setauket. In the spring of 1784, he married Mary Floyd, eldest daughter of wealthy Mastic landholder and signer of the Declaration of Independence William Floyd. The couple lived in Litchfield, Connecticut, where Tallmadge became wealthy as a merchant, banker and investor in midwestern land.

All Tallmadge ever said about the Culper Spy Ring was a few paragraphs in a memoir he wrote for his children that mentioned how in 1778 "I opened a private correspondence with some persons in New York which lasted through the war."[393]

Tallmadge was a founder of the Society of the Cincinnati with other Continental Army and navy officers. He cofounded the Litchfield Auxiliary Society for Ameliorating the Condition of the Jews and was a

Benjamin Tallmadge painted by E. Ames. *Library of Congress.*

benefactor of local churches. From 1801 to 1817, Tallmadge served as a Federalist in Congress, where he opposed slavery. After leaving the House of Representatives, he established a training school for Native American and Asian missionaries. After the death of his first wife, he married Maria Hallet of New York. Tallmadge died at age eighty-one in 1835 and is buried in Litchfield.[394]

Abraham Woodhull remained in Setauket, where he continued to farm with the assistance of enslaved African Americans he freed before his death in 1826, a year before slavery was outlawed in New York State. He and Mary Smith had three children.

Although he apparently never talked about it himself, Woodhull's involvement in the spy ring was known after the war. In his 1839 *History of Long Island*, published thirteen years after Woodhull's death, Benjamin F. Thompson, a grandson of Woodhull's aunt, noted that Tallmadge "opened this year [1777], a secret correspondence [for General Washington] with some persons in New York, and particularly with the late Abraham Woodhull,

The grave of chief Culper spy Abraham Woodhull, who died on January 23, 1826, at the Setauket Presbyterian Church. Bricks from the foundation of the Woodhull homestead on Little Bay, which was destroyed by fire in 1931, were used in his memorial. *Photo by Audrey C. Tiernan, copyright 2020.*

of Setauket, which lasted through the war."[395] Setauket historian Beverly Tyler believes "many other members of the Brookhaven and Suffolk County communities, not to mention New York City residents, knew about his Revolutionary War work. I'm even convinced that former Loyalist Benjamin Floyd knew, possibly as early as 1778, since he spoke up for Woodhull after Simcoe attacked his father while looking for Woodhull."[396]

After serving as a judge of the Court of Common Pleas for six years, Woodhull was a Suffolk County magistrate from 1799 to 1810. A surviving account book shows that the government finally repaid his outlay for expenses of the spy ring in 1790. Mary died in 1806, and in 1824 Woodhull married Lydia Terry. He was seventy-five when he died in 1826 and was buried in Setauket (see chapter 14.)[397]

Robert Townsend never discussed his role in the American Revolution. And he never pursued or received the federal position Washington had said he would seek for him after the war. His nephew Dr. Peter Townsend often asked him about the Revolutionary War. Robert would comment about others but never what he had done.

After the war, Robert went into business with his brother Solomon in New York, but their relationship disintegrated. Robert then moved back to Oyster Bay, probably in 1789, to live with his parents and sisters Sarah and Phebe and manage the family mercantile business. His father, Samuel, who served as a state senator for five terms, died in 1790.[398]

Robert Townsend never married. But some writers state that he had an illegitimate son named Robert Townsend Jr. with an immigrant from Nova Scotia named Mary Banvard, who was the housekeeper in his Manhattan apartment. There was a Robert Junior, born on February 1, 1784, when Robert Townsend was thirty and Mary Banvard was twenty-four. The baby was raised by his mother, who later married someone else. Robert Junior became a carpenter and after getting into politics was elected to a term in the New York State Assembly in 1836. Some historians doubt that Robert Townsend fathered this child. "There has been some crazy stuff written about Robert Junior over the years," said Claire Bellerjeau, historian at the Raynham Hall Museum, Townsend's Oyster Bay home. "I think he was a Townsend, but I don't think Robert was the father. He did pay for Robert Junior's education, carpenter's apprenticeship and his tools, and he left more to him in his will than anyone else." But Bellerjeau believes someone else fathered Banvard's child and Robert Townsend supported him.[399]

Robert Townsend maintained a low profile within his family for his entire lifetime and that continued after his death. A family history prepared in

Claire Bellerjeau, historian at the Raynham Hall Museum in Oyster Bay, by the grave of Culper spy Robert Townsend, at left, in the Fort Hill Cemetery in the woods at the end Simcoe Street in Oyster Bay. *Photo by Audrey C. Tiernan, copyright 2020.*

the nineteenth century described him with one sentence: "Robert, son of Samuel, died unmarried, March 7, 1838."[400] After his death at the age of eighty-four, he was buried in the Fort Hill Burying Ground in Oyster Bay, not far from the family home, at the end of Simcoe Street, named for Lieutenant Colonel John Graves Simcoe, the commander of the Queen's Rangers, who had occupied the Townsend home.[401]

It was not until 1930, with the publication of *The Two Spies, Nathan Hale and Robert Townsend* by the Suffolk County historian Morton Pennypacker, that the names of all the major players in the spy ring were revealed publicly for the first time. The Philadelphia native, who worked as a printer and then an ad salesman, moved to Long Island in 1920 and began studying the region's history. In his book, he stated that Culper Senior was Abraham Woodhull of Setauket and Culper Junior was Robert Townsend of Oyster Bay. But Townsend's involvement wasn't proven for another nine years until Pennypacker published *General Washington's Spies on Long Island and New York*. The proof came after Pennypacker acquired a trunk filled with Robert Townsend's account books. According to the East Hampton Library, the repository for Pennypacker's papers, he befriended the last two residents of Raynham Hall, the Townsend family home in Oyster Bay, and they gave him the account books. Pennypacker compared examples of Townsend's writing from the documents with Culper Junior letters preserved among the papers of George Washington.[402] The historian wrote:

> It was found that the paper upon which they were written was identical. The same watermark, the same shade, the same weight, same laid marks minutely varying one from the other on the same sheet....The handwriting, looking so similar, was not declared identical until the world's greatest expert, Albert S. Osborn, had examined it....The movements of Culper Junior corresponded with those of Robert Townsend as revealed in his documents, and the stain invented by James Jay had been twice tested on documents still carefully preserved among Townsend's effects....It was certain that the identity of Culper Junior, that most active spy of the Revolution, had been revealed.[403]

After the Revolution, Samuel Townsend's most famous involuntary wartime guest, Lieutenant Colonel John Graves Simcoe, became the governor of Upper Canada, now southern Ontario. He founded what became the city of Toronto, where the residents still celebrate Simcoe Day because he abolished slavery in Canada. A lake is named in his honor.[404]

Caleb Brewster never tried to keep his involvement in the Revolution or the Culper Spy Ring a secret, even during the war. "Everyone knew about Caleb Brewster because he basically wrote his name large on any of the messages that he did and basically dared the British to find him," Beverly Tyler remarked.[405]

After surviving his whaleboat adventures on Long Island Sound, Brewster married Anne Lewis, a woman from Fairfield, Connecticut, where her father owned a wharf Brewster had used during the war. The couple had eight children. Brewster, who received a pension from Congress for gallantry in a whaleboat raid, worked as a blacksmith in Fairfield until 1793. Then he became captain of the cutter *Active* with the new U.S. Revenue Marine established by Congress to enforce customs laws and combat smuggling. He held that position until 1816 except for three years during the administration of John Adams when he quit to protest the president's policies. He died in 1827 at age eighty and is buried in Fairfield.[406]

After serving as chief courier for the Culper operation, Austin Roe continued to operate his tavern in East Setauket. He apparently never told anyone of his intelligence activities. Roe served as a lieutenant in a Suffolk County militia regiment where his fellow Culper courier Jonas Hawkins, who continued to run a store and inn at his home, was a captain and his immediate superior. Eventually, Roe was promoted to captain. President

Austin Roe, the chief courier for the Culper Spy Ring, is buried in Cedar Grove Cemetery in Patchogue. *Photo by Audrey C. Tiernan, copyright 2020.*

George Washington stayed at Roe's Tavern during his tour of Long Island in 1790 (see the next chapter). In 1798, Roe moved to Patchogue, where he founded Roe's Hotel. The father of eight died in 1830 at age eighty-one from gangrene in his left leg when he was thrown from his horse. He was buried in his family's private cemetery located on Roe Boulevard in Patchogue; in 1890, his body was exhumed and reburied in Cedar Grove Cemetery in Patchogue.[407]

Anna Strong spent the rest of her life in Setauket with husband Selah, with whom she raised nine children. She died at age seventy-two in 1812, three years before her husband. They are buried nearby in the Smith-Strong family graveyard (see chapter 14). The story about the laundry on her clothesline alerting Abraham Woodhull about where Caleb Brewster had landed was handed down through her descendants.[408]

After the British left New York, James Rivington published a different version of his newspaper, dropping the *Royal* from the *Gazette*. But he only put out twelve issues before Patriot leaders he had angered during the war shut him down, despite George Washington greeting him publicly after the British evacuation. Rivington lived in poverty until he died at age seventy-eight in 1802.[409]

12

PRESIDENT WASHINGTON'S
1790 TOUR

As the first president of the fledgling United States, George Washington decided in April 1790 to revisit Long Island, the site of his great defeat in 1776.

Historians have spent a lot of time analyzing Washington's reasons for coming. Many believe that besides seeing the countryside and agricultural activity, a major reason for his trip in the second year of his presidency was to thank members of the Culper Spy Ring. Traveling as far east as Brookhaven, the president spent a night at the Setauket tavern owned by Austin Roe, a courier in the spy ring. "There were other such connections [with Culper members]…during the five-day tour," wrote Carl Starace, former Islip town historian, past president of the Sagtikos Manor Historical Society and editor of the *Long Island Forum* from 1964 to 1991.[410]

Even if a primary motivation was to thank some members of the Culper Spy Ring, the president, now fifty-eight, did like to meet the people and travel about the new nation now bound together by the Constitution rather than being thirteen confederated states.

Washington offered his own explanation in a diary entry dated October 5, 1789, just before he spent a month touring New England: "Had conversation with Colo. [Colonel Alexander] Hamilton on the propriety of my making a tour through the eastern states during the recess of Congress to acquire knowledge of the face of the country the growth and agriculture there and of the temper and disposition of the inhabitants towards the new government."[411]

Whatever his motivations, the president wanted to see Long Island. It was primarily farmland, which would have been of interest to Washington as a gentleman Virginia planter. As he traveled around the island, the president commented continually in his diary about the poor quality of the soil on southern Long Island east of Brooklyn. In contrast to large plantations like Washington's Mount Vernon, most of the agriculture on Long Island was done on small family farms that sometimes relied on slaves or indentured servants. But Washington did not mention anything about who was working the farms he passed. Crops and livestock were the main products along with firewood. Besides agricultural and soil details, Washington's diary is full of precise topographical detail in keeping with his early career as a surveyor. He was less concerned with the proper spelling of the names of people and places, which was typical for the time. For example, he uses three different spellings for Setauket and two for Huntington.[412]

During Washington's trip to New England the previous fall, his arrival was usually celebrated with feasts and pageantry. The tour of Long Island from April 20 to April 24, 1790, was much more subdued. It was in part a reflection of the fact that life was quiet on Long Island, which would not have its own newspaper, *Frothingham's Long-Island Herald* in Sag Harbor, for another year. So news traveled slowly. But Washington did not seem to go out of his way to meet a lot of the population. He traveled, not inconspicuously, with

President Washington's coach in *Historic Long Island in Pictures, Prose and Poetry* by Paul Bailey, 1956. *Courtesy of Babylon Town Historian Mary Cascone.*

his military aide, Major William Jackson, and several servants in an elegant cream-colored coach drawn by four large gray horses, but there were no large publicized public events. Residents did come out to greet him along the way, informally.[413]

The president made a loop of about 165 miles over five days. He traveled from Manhattan to southern Brooklyn to Jamaica and along the South Shore to Patchogue. From there he headed north to Setauket and came back along the North Shore with stops in Smithtown, Huntington, Oyster Bay, Roslyn and Flushing before crossing the East River at the Brooklyn ferry landing. Washington traveled about seven and a half hours each day. He had his main meal at 3:00 p.m. Because of a scarcity of taverns and inns, he ate some meals and stayed at some private homes, often paying for the services rendered and noting the fact in his diary.[414]

On April 20, Washington traveled from Manhattan as far as Jamaica, where he spent the night at William Warne's tavern. On April 21, Washington wrote,

> *the morning being clear & pleasant we left Jamaica about Eight O'clock & pursued the Road to South Hempstead passing along the South edge of the plain of that name—a plain said to be 14 miles in length by 3 or 4 in breadth witht.* [without] *a Tree or a Shrub growing on it except fruit trees (which do not thrive well) at the few settlements. The soil of this plain is said to be thin & cold, and of course not productive, even in Grass.—We baited* [fed the horses] *in South Hemstead (10 miles from Jamaica), at the House of one Simmonds, formerly a Tavern, now of private entertainment for Money.*

The president was probably referring to Simmonson's Inn, believed to have been at the southwest corner of today's Fulton and Main Streets.[415]

Washington ate dinner on the twenty-first at the home of Patriot militiaman Zebulon Ketcham, age fifty, and his wife, Hannah Conklin Ketcham. It was an unpainted Shingle-style structure in Huntington South, now Copiague. The president wrote: "We dined at one Ketcham's wch. [which] had also been a public House, but now a private one—received pay for what it furnished—this House was about 14 miles from South Hempstead & a very neat and decent one."[416] Washington's mention of a "public house" refers to its previous use as an inn or tavern that would serve travelers. What Washington ate at the Ketcham House was not recorded. But the table on which he ate is owned by the Huntington Historical Society

The Zebulon Ketcham House now in Amityville was visited by President George Washington during his 1790 tour of Long Island when it was in its original location in Copiague. *Photo by Audrey C. Tiernan, copyright 2020.*

and displayed at its David Conklin Farmhouse Museum, a structure built around 1750. "Some historians report that the president presented a gold ring to one of the Ketcham children, while others have said that he presented a coin to the child. The whereabouts of the mysterious ring or coin, precious mementos, are unknown," wrote Babylon town historian Mary Cascone.[417] The house was located near today's Deauville Boulevard and Montauk Highway. It was moved later to South Bayview Avenue in Amityville, where it is now a private home, despite a marker on the original site erected by the Babylon Town Board in 1927 declaring the house was razed in 1857.[418]

Washington slept that night at Sagtikos Manor, home of Judge Isaac Thompson in West Bay Shore, where British officers had been quartered during the war (see chapter 15). Some local historians speculate that Washington spent the night with Thompson because he had been involved in the Culper Ring.[419]

On the twenty-second, Washington "halted a while" at the home of Samuel Greene, which still stands at 93 West Main Street in West Sayville and is used as office space. A historical marker commemorates Washington's stop.[420]

On his 1790 tour of Long Island, President George Washington "halted a while" on April 21 at the home of Samuel Greene in West Sayville. *Photo by Audrey C. Tiernan, copyright 2020.*

The president then dined on oysters—according to local accounts but not mentioned by Washington—and other fare at Hart's Tavern at the north end of River Avenue in Patchogue. According to a story handed down through the Hart family, when Washington arrived, a group of boys was roasting sweet potatoes on a fire at the side of the road. A son of the Harts walked over to the coach and offered the president a sweet potato, which he ate with pleasure before giving the boy an English shilling that was kept by the family.[421] There is no record of what became of the coin.

Heading north after his meal, Washington passed "the East end of the Brushy Plains" on his way through "Koram" [Coram] to "Setakit" or alternatively "Setaket." The president noted that "the first five miles of the Road is too poor to admit Inhabitants or cultivation being a low scrubby Oak, not more than 2 feet high intermixed with small and ill thriven Pines.—Within two miles of Koram there are farms, but the land is of indifferent quality much mixed with sand.—Koram contains but a few houses—from thence to Setaket the soil improves, especially as you approach the Sound; but is far from being of the first quality—still a good deal mixed with Sand."[422]

On the night of April 22, the president slept at Austin Roe's Tavern in Setauket. According to historian Morton Pennypacker, Roe, principal courier traveling between Manhattan and Setauket for the spy ring, fell from his horse and broke his leg while rushing to meet Washington. The accident has generated debate among historians about whether Roe actually got to meet Washington at his establishment. Historian Kenn Stryker-Rodda wrote that "it is ironic that Roe, who had written at least 2,000 miles as a courier should, on the day of Washington's visit, have fallen from his horse and sustained a broken leg so that he was unable to play host in person."[423] (As noted in the previous chapter, a later fall from a horse proved fatal for Roe.) But Setauket historian Beverly Tyler countered, "I don't believe that Roe wasn't able to host Washington. I agree with the report by Pennypacker on Roe breaking his leg (good folklore/family history) but even with a broken leg, with Washington spending the night at the tavern, Roe would have returned to the tavern if humanly possible."[424] Whether he met the tavern owner or not, the president wrote in his diary that Roe's establishment was "tolerably dect. [decent] with obliging people in it." Washington made no reference to whether Roe was there or his involvement in the Culper network, even if he was aware of that fact.[425]

While there's no evidence that the president knew of Roe's role in the spy ring, Tyler thinks it's likely that he did. But Tallmadge biographer Richard F. Welch disagrees because "George Washington told Benjamin Tallmadge he did not want to know the identities of the Culpers. It seems most likely he didn't want to know the names of the couriers as well."[426] Tyler countered,

It is of course true that Washington didn't want to know the names of the Culper spies during the war. However, after the war is a different matter. The fact that Selah Strong, Patriot leader during the war and Brookhaven president of the town trustees and town supervisor, met Washington at Coram and led the entourage to the Roe Tavern gives added strength to the story that he knew. The Culper Spy Ring did not exist in a vacuum. Woodhull, Roe, Brewster and probably Anna Strong had a lot of friends and relatives who assisted their efforts.[427]

Welch responded:

Selah Strong's escort of George Washington to the Roe Tavern proves nothing by itself. Did Strong know the identities of the Culper network? Is there any solid, contemporary evidence this was the case? Did Washington

Above: Platt's Tavern in Huntington, where President George Washington dined during his 1790 tour. The structure was moved to Halesite in the 1850s and destroyed in a fire around 1914. *From the Collection of Karen Rae Levine.*

Left: The chair that President George Washington sat on when he dined at Platt's Tavern during his 1790 tour. It is displayed at the Soldiers and Sailors Monument in Huntington. *Photo by Audrey C. Tiernan, copyright 2020.*

Site of Platt's Tavern at the intersection of Main Street and Park Avenue in Huntington. *Photo by Audrey C. Tiernan, copyright 2020.*

have a meeting with Woodhull in Setauket? If not, why not? He was far more important than a courier. Without any evidence to the contrary, it is difficult to accept as a fact that George Washington knew who he was meeting when he went to Setauket.[428]

On the twenty-third, the last full day and night on Long Island, the president wrote,

About 8 o'clock we left Roe's, and baited the Horses at Smiths Town [Smithtown] at a Widow Blidenberg's [Blydenburgh] a decent House [tavern] 10 miles from Setalkat—thence 15 miles to Huntington where we dined—and afterwards proceeded seven miles to Oyster-Bay, to the House of a Mister Young [Youngs] (private and very neat and decent) where we lodged.—The house we dined at in Huntingdon [Huntington] was kept by a Widow Platt, and was tolerably good. The whole of this day's ride was over uneven ground and none of it of the first quality but intermixed in places with the pebble stone.

Vintage postcard of the Youngs Homestead in Cove Neck where President George
Washington stayed during his 1790 tour of Long Island. *Author's collection.*

Although Washington did not mention it in his diary, he apparently spoke
to residents on the Huntington village green, thanking them for their support
of the Patriot cause. The Platt Tavern was moved to Halesite in the 1850s
and burned down around 1914.[429]

Daniel Youngs's home still exists on Cove Neck Road east of Oyster Bay
in what is now the village of Cove Neck, although it only remained in the
family until 1929. Considering that Youngs had been an officer in a Tory
militia unit during the war, Washington's decision to spend his last night
on the island there seems unusual. Youngs was a captain in the local militia
before the Revolution and signed on to support the Patriot cause in 1776.
But after participating in the Battle of Long Island, he did not enlist into the
Continental Army or flee Long Island during the occupation. As a result,
he was compelled to take an oath of allegiance to King George III and
became a captain in the local Loyalist militia. The unit was responsible for
providing the British army with supplies, which were brought to Youngs's
dock on Oyster Bay to be loaded onto schooners for shipment to New York.
But Youngs apparently did a very inefficient job in gathering and shipping
supplies for the British, perhaps because of secret support for independence.

Some historians even suspect Youngs might have been a secret agent
for Washington. Beverly Tyler is not one of them. "We don't know if Mr.

Youngs had any connection to the spy ring or if it was just a convenient place that offered a night's lodging," he said.[430] Raynham Hall Museum historian Claire Bellerjeau added that "there is no evidence that Youngs was a spy. Washington stopped there because the Youngs were a prominent family and they had a nice house in a convenient location."[431]

Oyster Bay town historian John Hammond, one of those convinced that Youngs was supporting the Patriot cause in some fashion, said that even if Youngs was not a spy for Washington, the two men had another possible connection: both were probably Masons. Washington was a well-known member of the order, serving as the head of his Masonic Temple in Virginia. Hammond hasn't seen any proof that Youngs was a Mason, but he said there is evidence pointing in that direction. "The 1790 Long Island tour had Masonic connections," Hammond said.

> *Blydenburgh's Tavern out in Smithtown was the place where the Smithtown Masonic lodge used to meet. When he stopped at Daniel Youngs' homestead, he left a Masonic trinket of some kind, and you would never leave a Masonic object with a non-Masonic family. One hundred years later, Judge Billy Youngs donated it to the Matinecock Lodge in Oyster Bay. Unfortunately, the secretary of the lodge did not describe at the time what the object was, and it was ultimately lost.*[432]

The Youngs family kept objects used by Washington, including a bed, a drinking glass and tableware.[433]

Washington's choice of lodging with Daniel Youngs raises another question: why did he not stay at the home of Samuel Townsend a short distance down the road in Oyster Bay? The Townsends were the most prominent family in the area, and their house was large for the time and centrally located, which is why the British used it as a headquarters during the war. It was also the home of Samuel's son Robert, one of the primary Culper spies. And if Washington was trying to meet members of the spy ring to thank them, the Townsend home would seem to have been a natural place to secure lodging. But Bellerjeau explained that there was a good reason for why the Townsend home would not have been able to accommodate Washington: "1790 was the year Samuel died. He died in late November, seven months after Washington stopped in Oyster Bay, but it had been 'a long and painful illness,' according to his obituary."[434]

Also, some historians, including Richard F. Welch, as noted earlier in this chapter, point to Washington writing to Tallmadge that he did not want to know the names of the Culper operatives and might not have known that Robert Townsend was Culper Junior. But Bellerjeau argues that the president probably did know. "It's true that in the Culper letters, Washington says that he does not want to know the spies' identities," she noted. "That being said, he knew Samuel Townsend very well, and I find it hard to believe that Washington—and Samuel, for that matter—didn't know Robert's identity as Culper Junior."[435]

On April 24, Washington wrote in his diary that he "left Mister Young's before 6 o'clock and passing Musqueto Cove [now Glen Cove] breakfasted at a Mister Underdunck's [Onderdonk] at the head of a little bay; where we were kindly received and well entertained.—This Gentleman works a Grist & two Paper Mills, the last of which he seems to carry on with spirit, and to profit." Hendrick Onderdonk lived in Roslyn, where his house is now the core of Hendrick's Tavern, formerly the Washington Manor restaurant, near Onderdonk's mills. A plaque on the exterior wall of the restaurant at 1305 Old Northern Boulevard commemorates Washington's visit. Onderdonk's gristmill still exists at 1347 Old Northern Boulevard. Owned by Nassau County, it is being restored.[436]

After eating a midday dinner in Flushing, Washington wrote that "before sundown we had crossed the ferry and was at home" back in Manhattan.[437]

What Washington's motivations were for the Long Island tour in 1790 and whether he had contact with any of the former Culper Spy Ring members may never be known definitively. But Beverly Tyler noted, "Remember that his tour of Long Island took him to only four overnight stays, including Squire Thompson's in Bay Shore, whose mother was the aunt of Culper spy Abraham Woodhull and Roe Tavern in East Setauket. A coincidence? Not really!"[438]

Whatever reasons the president had for coming to Long Island in the spring of 1790, the sites that Washington visited and other Long Island locations that played a role in the Culper Spy Ring or the American Revolution in general are the subject of the second part of this book.

PART II

LONG ISLAND'S REVOLUTIONARY WAR SITES

13

NEW YORK STATE'S
GEORGE WASHINGTON SPY TRAIL

Thanks to the persistence of the president of a Stony Brook nonprofit organization, those interested in the Culper Spy Ring and other Revolutionary War history can now follow a fifty-mile state-designated trail that ties together the North Shore's heritage.

Officially designated by the state in 2017, the George Washington Spy Trail is marked by twenty-two brown signs along Route 25A between Great Neck and Port Jefferson. The logo is a depiction of Washington's carriage used during his 1790 tour of Long Island. The route leads to the homes of the Culper spies and other historic sites such as the location where Nathan Hale is believed to have landed after his trip across Long Island Sound to begin his ill-fated spy mission. The trail and its website are designed to promote history and boost the economy by increasing tourism.

The seed for the trail concept was philanthropist Ward Melville's 1948 purchase of the Brewster House in Setauket (see chapter 15). More than three decades later, the nonprofit organization Melville created to operate its historic properties and modern shops, the Stony Brook Community Fund, began restoration of the vacant structure.

As the restoration was being planned, Gloria P. Rocchio, president of the Community Fund since 1980, realized little was known about the history of the house and the Brewster family. She began researching at the East Hampton Library and other resource centers. When Rocchio learned that Setauket tavern owner Austin Roe traveled along the road by the Brewster House—now Route 25A—when he was carrying messages for the Culper Spy Ring, she had an inspiration.

Left: One of twenty-two signs marking the fifty-mile New York State George Washington Spy Trail from Great Neck to Port Jefferson. *Photo by Audrey C. Tiernan, copyright 2020.*

Below: Jeffrey Sanzel, the head of Theater Three in Port Jefferson, portrayed George Washington for a press conference at Coindre Hall in Lloyd Harbor on February 15, 1996, to publicize that state legislators had introduced bills to create a "Long Island's Heritage Trail." *Courtesy of the Ward Melville Heritage Organization.*

"I said 'Boy, that is a great thread to tie all of the communities on the North Shore together, and wouldn't it be wonderful to celebrate all of that history,'" she recalled.[439]

To make her dream of a tourist route pegged to the spy ring but including other historic sites along 25A from the Queens border to Port Jefferson a reality, she formed the North Shore Promotion Committee in 1995 with Michael Davidson, president of the Long Island Convention and Visitors Bureau. Rocchio became the committee president.

After obtaining more information on the history of the road from the Society for the Preservation of Long Island Antiquities (now Preservation Long Island), Rocchio gathered the leaders of a number of organizations and historical sites for a press conference on February 15, 1996, at the historic Coindre Hall mansion in Lloyd Harbor. At the event, which featured a Washington reenactor traveling by carriage, State Senator James Lack and Assemblyman Stephen Englebright announced they had submitted legislation to create what was originally to be called "Long Island's Heritage Trail."

When the legislation was approved, Rocchio's promotional group began designing signage they hoped to have erected along the route. Their plan evolved to label the corridor George Washington's Spy Trail after learning that Washington had followed the route to return to New York during his April 1790 visit to Long Island, which many historians believe he arranged to thank members of the spy ring.

Rocchio traveled to Washington's Mount Vernon plantation in Virginia to meet with the staff there to research the type of coach Washington would have used on his 1790 trip.

Then on April 23, 1998, the group held a press conference at the George Washington Manor restaurant in Roslyn, housed in a structure where Washington stayed during his trip, to unveil its proposed design for the sign with artwork of the coach. The state didn't accept the design because it was multicolored with a yellow background. Transportation officials went instead with a brown sign in keeping with those used for other historic sites and attractions but retained a carriage. The state officially designated the corridor as the George Washington Spy Trail in May 2017.[440]

"It took them more than seventeen years to approve everything," said Rocchio, whose Stony Brook organization is now named the Ward Melville Heritage Organization. "We were able to get twenty-two signs installed from Port Jefferson to the Queens line. It's a tribute to George Washington and this wonderful area. Route 25A between Stony Brook and Smithtown is still pretty much the way it was when Washington traveled it, and hopefully it will stay that way."[441]

What is now the North Shore Promotion Alliance, still headed by Rocchio, handles the marketing of the trail and maintains its website: https://washingtonspytrail.com. Travelers can also call 631-498-4730 and enter the number of a site and hear a recorded description. The website proclaims that "a visit to the North Shore takes one back to 1778 when Long Islanders lived under an uneasy military occupation by the British commanders and troops."

14

SPY RING SITES TODAY

Many sites associated with the Culper Spy Ring can still be visited on Long Island. They are listed alphabetically by town.

BROOKHAVEN TOWN

BENJAMIN TALLMADGE BIRTHPLACE
30 Runs Road, Setauket

George Washington's spy chief was born at this private home, once the manse, or minister's home, for the adjacent Presbyterian Church, on the southwestern shore of Setauket Harbor. It cannot be seen from Runs Road but is visible from the Brookhaven Town dock on the southern end of the harbor just off Shore Road. Tallmadge lived in the house until he left for Yale University. As detailed in chapter 11, after the Revolution he lived in Litchfield, Connecticut, where he is buried.[442]

ABRAHAM WOODHULL HOMESITE
Dyke Road, Strong's Neck, Setauket

The location of farmer and Culper spy Abraham Woodhull's home is commemorated by a historical marker that reads "Site of home of Abraham Woodhull, chief of Long Island spies under General Washington. Built by Richard Woodhull, 1690. Burnt in 1931."

The house of George Washington's spymaster Benjamin Tallmadge in East Setauket is now a private home. *Courtesy of Beverly Tyler.*

Site of the home of chief Culper spy Abraham Woodhull on Strong's Neck in Setauket. The house was destroyed by fire in 1931. *Photo by Audrey C. Tiernan, copyright 2020.*

Likely because of the death of his elder brother Richard at age thirty-two, Abraham inherited the family home and ran the farm. A modern two-story house now occupies the site.

Looking east across Little Bay you can see a flagpole on the shore that lines up with the smokestacks of the Port Jefferson power plant. That little promontory was the location of the servants' quarters of Selah and Anna Strong's manor and, according to the legend, where Anna hung her laundry in a pattern to tell Woodhull where Caleb Brewster had landed his whaleboat to pick up messages from the Culper Spy Ring. (The area is depicted in a William Sidney Mount painting of eel fishing in Setauket.) A modern house occupies the site of the servants' quarters.[443]

SMITH-STRONG HOUSE/ST. GEORGE'S MANOR
Strong's Neck in Setauket

A house built in the 1830s may have replaced the original circa 1690 home occupied before and after the Revolutionary War by Selah and Anna "Nancy" Smith Strong, a couple involved in the Culper Spy Ring, according to Setauket historian Beverly Tyler. "When they did an archaeological dig here for a year, they could not find another foundation for a house," Tyler said. "So either this house replaced the one that was here during Anna Smith Strong and Selah Strong's time or it's the original house with a different façade, new chimneys, etc."

The original house was initially the home of Anna Smith Strong's great-grandfather William "Tangier" Smith. Selah Strong was a town trustee between 1767 and 1777, when an election was held after the British took control of Long Island and Loyalist-leaning candidates were elected after most Patriots fled to New England.

During the war, British officers occupied the house, according to family history and documents. Tyler believes the family moved into the adjacent servants' quarters. Selah Strong initially remained on Long Island but was arrested by the British and confined in the "Sugar House" prison in Manhattan in late December 1777 or early January 1778 for "surreptitious correspondence with the enemy."

"According to the family stories," Tyler said, "his wife got him released, reportedly by appealing to her Tory relatives, and he fled to Connecticut until June of 1780 when he returned to Long Island. What he was doing, whether he was part of the Army or part of the spy ring working with Caleb Brewster and Benjamin Tallmadge, nobody knows."

The Smith-Strong House in Setauket. A structure built in the 1830s may have replaced the original circa 1690 home occupied before and after the Revolutionary War by Selah and Anna "Nancy" Smith Strong, a couple involved in the Culper Spy Ring. *Photo by Audrey C. Tiernan, copyright 2020.*

Tyler believes Anna lived in the servants' quarters with her children for the duration of the war, although some authors agree with the family history that the children were with Selah in Connecticut, which the local historian insists makes no sense.

In May 1780, three years before the official end of the Revolution, Strong was elected president of the Brookhaven town trustees and was reunited with his wife when he returned for a June meeting. He remained on Long Island because the British had lost much of their interest in Long Island at that point, being more concerned about the fate of General Cornwallis in the Southeast, Tyler said.

If the legend about Anna Strong using the laundry on a clothesline to signal Abraham Woodhull about where Caleb Brewster had landed his whaleboat was true, Tyler said it would have been done at the servants' quarters on Little Bay, which was visible from his home.

Family correspondence shows that she would order material for the British officers who were occupying her manor. So "they were actually funding Austin Roe to go into the city to get stuff for them as well as his tavern and then bring out the spy messages," Tyler said.

Selah Strong continued in his town government role until 1797. Anna died in 1812 and Selah in 1815. They are buried nearby in the Smith-Strong family graveyard. Jack Strong, a descendant of Anna and Selah Strong, is the current occupant of the house.[444]

SMITH-STRONG GRAVEYARD
Cemetery Lane off Dyke Road on Strong's Neck in Setauket

Also known as St. George's Manor Cemetery, the privately owned site on the east side of Little Bay is open to the public with prior approval (email Ray. Strong@Evercore.com). Culper Spy Ring participants Anna Smith Strong and Selah Strong are buried on land that belonged to her ancestors.

A sign at the entrance reads: "William Tangier Smith, the patentee, his wife, Madame Martha, patriots Captain Selah Strong & his wife Anna Strong known as Nancy, and many of their descendants are buried in this historic site."

Weathered rectangular marble markers topped with urns mark the two Strong graves. Hers contains a plaque from the Anna Smith Strong Chapter of the Daughters of the American Revolution that describes her as a "Revolutionary Patriot" born in 1740 and who died in 1812.

The graves of Culper Spy Ring participants Anna Smith Strong and Selah Strong in the Smith-Strong Graveyard in East Setauket. *Photo by Audrey C. Tiernan, copyright 2020.*

ROE TAVERN
On a private road off Old Post Road, East Setauket

The tavern owned by Austin Roe, the Culper Spy Ring's primary courier, was originally on Main Street (Route 25A) at the corner of Bayview Avenue in East Setauket. A historical marker denotes the location. It states that "Roe Tavern stood here 1703 to 1936. Washington spent the night here April 22, 1790. Austin Roe, innkeeper, was one of Washington's spies." A white ranch house now stands on the property.

The tavern was built circa 1705 by Selah Strong, grandfather of the namesake future town supervisor during the war. Thomas, son of the first Selah, sold it to the Woodhull family, which sold it to Austin Roe. A dormer was added after the Revolution before the house was moved. At some point after the war and Washington's visit, Roe moved to Patchogue and opened the Roe Hotel.

The original structure was moved by a writer, Wallace Irwin, who owned it in the 1930s and didn't like the traffic noise outside. It was relocated several hundred yards to a private road off of Old Post Road. In its new location, the house faces in the same direction that it did at its original site. But additions were built on the west side and in the rear, according to local historian Beverly Tyler. The bedroom where Washington stayed was on the second floor to the left of the entrance door.

The building with its wood-shingled roof has been owned for about a decade by Arthur Billadello, a reenactor with the Brigade of the American Revolution. New York State Assemblyman Stephen Englebright has been trying to have the tavern moved again to a site on Route 25A between Memorial Park and its original location.[445]

HAWKINS-MOUNT HOUSE
1556 Stony Brook Road, Stony Brook

The home of Jonas Hawkins, a courier for the Culper Spy Ring, was built in the mid-1720s by his father, Eleazer. Three major additions were added over the next two centuries.

Jonas, who constructed the most prominent addition to accommodate a tavern, store, post office and possibly an inn, was one of seventy-three men who signed the association document on June 8, 1775, pledging themselves to protect against British tyranny. Hawkins and his wife, Ruth, remained in Setauket throughout the war, and he worked with chief spy Abraham

Woodhull at least between January and June 1779, according to local historian Beverly Tyler. The house also served as a store and "ordinary" or inn. Jonas traveled into the city to buy items for his store, "which gave him an excuse to go into New York and bring out spy messages," Tyler said. Jonas was not given a spy ring code name, although he is mentioned by name, in code, in a Culper letter.

Jonas was the grandfather of William Sidney Mount. The famous artist was born in 1807, and his family lived in Setauket where the Emma Clark Library is now located. After Mount's father, Thomas, died when he was six, Mount's mother moved with her five children into the house of her uncle Jonas. After completing his education, Mount returned to the house and had a studio with a skylight built in the attic. After William's death, the house remained in the family for more than fifty years. It was eventually acquired by local philanthropist Ward Melville and placed on the National Register of Historic Places in 1965.

The house is now owned by the Ward Melville Heritage Organization and operated by the Long Island Museum (https://longislandmuseum.org), which conducts occasional tours.[446]

PHILLIPS ROE HOUSE/DROWNED MEADOW COTTAGE MUSEUM
West Broadway and Barnum Avenue, Port Jefferson.

The Phillips Roe House was built circa 1755–60 with post-and-beam construction. Roe was a member of the Culper Spy Ring, but his role in the network is unknown, Setauket historian Beverly Tyler said. A relative, Nathaniel Roe or Nathaniel Roe Jr., who lived nearby and was either Phillips's brother or cousin, was also a member of the spy network with an unknown role.[447]

Loyalist Nehemiah Marks wrote to British Major General Oliver DeLancey on December 21, 1780, from Flushing that the Roes were helping whaleboat captain Caleb Brewster carry messages across Long Island Sound for the Culper Ring. "I have found out where Brewster holds a correspondence of intelligence and who supplied him with goods," Marks wrote. "I got my information from one that has a commission in the rebel's service." Marks said that Brewster was relying on "Nathaniel Roe for intelligence and Phillip Roe at Round [Drowned] Meadow [then the name of what would become Port Jefferson] for goods....These are the villain that assist Brewster."[448]

The historical marker out front notes that the house owned by the Village of Port Jefferson was relocated and restored from 2000 to 2010. It is opened

A hand-hewn ceiling beam in the Phillips Roe House in Port Jefferson. *Photo by Audrey C. Tiernan, copyright 2020.*

usually on Culper Spy Day in mid-September and a few weekends before Christmas. There is parking behind the building. For details, see https://portjeff.com.

TERRELL-HAVENS-TERRY-KETCHAM INN
81 Main Street, Center Moriches

Samuel Terrell, a blacksmith, constructed a timber-frame one-room structure on the site in 1693. Subsequent additions brought the building up to fifteen rooms, and it was used as an inn, tavern, public house and stagecoach stop by the Havens, Terry and Ketcham families.

Benjamin Havens ran the inn during the Revolutionary War. He is believed to have been a member of the Culper Spy Ring because he had strong connections to the network. He was married to Abigail Strong of Setauket, sister of Patriot leader Selah Strong and related to Culper chief spy Abraham Woodhull through her mother, Suzanna Thompson.

In 1791, Thomas Jefferson and James Madison stayed there on their way to visit William Floyd at his estate in Mastic. Samuel Terry and his son Nelson bought what was then known as the Moriches Inn around 1800. In 1851, Andrew Ketcham bought the farm and inn. His sons Townsend Valentine Ketcham and Andrew Watson Webb Ketcham ran the Ketcham Hotel until 1912.

The Terrill-Havens-Terry-Ketcham Inn in Center Moriches. *Photo by Audrey C. Tiernan, copyright 2020.*

Subsequent owners used the structure as a teahouse, residence, restaurant and boardinghouse. In 1989, the structure, after years of neglected maintenance, was damaged by a dining room fire. That same year, the Ketcham Inn Foundation was formed and bought the property. It undertook a full restoration of the structure to bring it back to its historic colonial appearance. On March 9, 1992, the Terrell-Havens-Terry-Ketcham Inn was listed on the National Register of Historic Places.

Ketcham Inn is open for special events. See www.ketchaminnfoundation.org

THREE VILLAGE HISTORICAL SOCIETY HISTORY CENTER, ORIGINALLY THE HAWKINS-BAYLES-SWEZEY HOUSE
93 North Country Road, Setauket

Although it has no direct connection to the Culper Spy Ring or the American Revolution, the circa 1800 home that serves as headquarters for the Three Village Historical Society has permanent exhibits on the espionage network and the war. It is open Sunday afternoons. The society also offers walking tours.[449]

GRAVE OF AUSTIN ROE
80 Jenning Avenue, Patchogue

The chief courier for the Culper Spy Ring is buried in Cedar Grove Cemetery in Patchogue.

OYSTER BAY TOWN

RAYNHAM HALL MUSEUM
20 West Main Street, Oyster Bay

Samuel Townsend's house, best known as the home of his Culper spy son Robert, was named Raynham Hall during the Victorian era. It was occupied for most of the war by a succession of British and Loyalist commanders from five different regiments.

Robert Townsend's grave is nearby with other family members in the Fort Hill Cemetery in the woods at the end Simcoe Street, named for Lieutenant Colonel John Graves Simcoe, commander of the Queen's Rangers, who was billeted at the Townsend home.

Twenty-one-year-old Samuel Townsend purchased waterfront property that encompassed most of modern downtown Oyster Bay in 1738. His move from his father's house in Jericho to Oyster Bay benefited his growing shipping business. The house was a four-room frame structure that Samuel expanded with a four-room lean-to addition on the north side, creating a saltbox-style home. He called the property "The Homestead." Samuel lived

Raynham Hall, the Oyster Bay home of Culper spy ring member Robert Townsend and now a museum. *Photo by Audrey C. Tiernan, copyright 2019.*

there with his wife, Sarah Stoddard Townsend, their eight children and at least nineteen enslaved people.

In 1851, Solomon Townsend II, grandson of Samuel and Sarah, purchased the property from his uncle Dr. Ebenezer Seely. He remodeled and enlarged the colonial dwelling in Gothic Revival style, raising the number of rooms to twenty-two with the addition of a large rear wing and a tower. Family letters and other writings indicate Solomon II was teased about having taken a modestly sized house and enlarged it into a huge structure, saying he had built a "little Raynham Hall."

That was a reference to the huge ancestral estate of an unrelated Townshend family in England. Solomon II began to call the house Raynham Hall, initially as a joke.

By 1912, the house had been inherited by Solomon II's grandson Edward Nicoll Townsend Jr. Two years later, he sold it to a cousin, Julia Weekes Coles, who owned it until 1933. She never lived there, but she and her sister Sarah Townsend Coles Halstead operated a tearoom. Julia sold the house for ten dollars to the Oyster Bay chapter of the Daughters of the American Revolution.

The organization donated the property to the Town of Oyster Bay in 1947. In the early 1950s, the town removed the tower and rebuilt the façade to resemble its appearance in the 1700s. The museum is operated by the nonprofit Friends of Raynham Hall. For information, go to http://raynhamhallmuseum.org.[450]

OTHER SITES WITH TIES
TO THE REVOLUTION

BABYLON TOWN

CAPTAIN JOEL COOK MONUMENT
Argyle Park, Route 27A, Babylon

Captain Joel Cook, a native of Wallingford, Connecticut, tried to enlist at age sixteen in an infantry company when the war began. The Connecticut unit said the boy was not fit for combat but allowed him to sign up as a waiter. A year later, he enlisted as a soldier and fought for the rest of the war. He later served in the War of 1812 after raising a company of soldiers in New Haven, Connecticut, where he lived. Afterward he lived in Ohio, Yonkers and then Babylon, where he died on November 8, 1851. The monument was dedicated in 1907 at Babylon High School but was moved to Argyle Park in 1957.[451]

GRAVE OF SOLDIER DAVID SMITH
Babylon Cemetery, 392 Deer Park Avenue, Babylon

American Revolution veteran David Smith lived in a house at 527 Deer Park Avenue in Babylon that was demolished in 2017. He served for almost the entire war but because of poor health he spent some of the conflict making and repairing clothing for other soldiers.[452]

ZEBULON KETCHAM HOUSE
178 South Bayview Avenue, Amityville

Zebulon Ketcham was a Patriot during the Revolution who was visited by President George Washington during his 1790 tour of Long Island. The house was originally located near Deauville Boulevard in Copiague but was moved to its current location sometime before 1950. It is now a private home.[453]

BROOKHAVEN TOWN

BREWSTER HOUSE
18 Runs Road, East Setauket

Built circa 1665, the Brewster House was home to six generations of the family. Considered the oldest home in the town of Brookhaven, it is listed on the National Register of Historic Places.

During the Revolution, Joseph Brewster, who was also a tailor, operated the wood-shingled saltbox-style structure as a tavern, ordinary or inn and general store patronized by occupying troops. Although he was a second

Brewster House in East Setauket, built circa 1665, is considered the oldest house in the Town of Brookhaven. During the Revolution, Joseph Brewster operated it as a tavern, inn and general store patronized by British occupying troops. *Photo by Audrey C. Tiernan, copyright 2020.*

cousin of Culper Spy Ring member Caleb Brewster, Joseph Brewster has no known connection to the spy network. Local historian Beverly Tyler believes he probably was more aligned with the Loyalists. In 1777, Brewster was elected head of the town government after many Patriots fled to Connecticut after the Battle of Long Island.

Philanthropist Ward Melville bought the house in 1948, and it was later restored to its appearance in a landscape painting by nineteenth-century artist William Sidney Mount.

The house was built with pegged tenon-and-mortise joinery. "It was not on this site until after the Continental period and the Revolutionary War based on the results of an archaeological dig at the current site," Tyler said. The structure was expanded on the southern end after the war.

The Ward Melville Heritage Organization owns and operates the property. The Brewster House is open for tours by appointment. Call 631-751-2244.[454]

CAROLINE CHURCH OF BROOKHAVEN
1 Dyke Road, Setauket

Originally an Anglican church, the 1729 white-shingled timber-frame structure by the Village Green was transformed after the war. Because no one wanted to be associated with anything British, all Anglican churches in the United States became independent Episcopal institutions.

British soldiers quartered in Setauket probably attended the church, according to historian Beverly Tyler's research. A musket ball was discovered lodged in a beam in the tower in 1936 when philanthropist Ward Melville restored the church. He had it displayed in the vestibule. During the Battle of Setauket on August 22, 1777, raiders from Connecticut gathered down the hill at Patriot's Rock and fired toward the fort occupied by Loyalists near

A musket ball found in the Caroline Church of Brookhaven in Setauket in 1936 was probably fired by Patriot raiders from Connecticut during the Battle of Setauket on August 22, 1777. *Photo by Audrey C. Tiernan, copyright 2020.*

The Caroline Church of Brookhaven in Setauket was built in 1729, and occupying British soldiers are believed to have attended services during the Revolution. *Photo by Audrey C. Tiernan, copyright 2020.*

the church. "I think some of them were shooting at the bell to ring it and one of the musket balls got stuck in the beams up there," Tyler said.

The historical marker in front of the church reads: "Caroline Church of Brookhaven, 1729. Second oldest Episcopal Church in constant use in America." (Bruton Parish in Williamsburg, Virginia, was the first.) The graveyard contains the remains of seven Patriot soldiers.[455]

COUNTRY HOUSE RESTAURANT
1175 North Country Road, Stony Brook

Originally a farmhouse built circa 1710, it was occupied by the British during the Revolution when Annette Williamson lived there with her younger siblings. When the British left, the townspeople murdered her, believing she was a Loyalist. (She is said to haunt the building.) The structure is little changed from colonial days. The restaurant is owned by the Ward Melville Heritage Organization and is open Tuesday through Sunday. Call 631-751-3332.

DAVIS TOWN MEETING HOUSE
263 Middle Country Road, Coram.

The original owner of the structure, Elijah Davis, born in 1727, used it as a tavern and inn. The property was the site for the Revolutionary War incident known as "The Burning of the Hay" on November 23, 1870, after the Patriot attack on Fort St. George in Mastic. (See the following section on Fort St. George.)

When Elijah Davis died in 1802, his son, Goldsmith Davis (1756–1825), inherited the property. At the outset of the Revolutionary War, Goldsmith enlisted in the local militia. After the company disbanded, twenty-year-old Goldsmith enlisted in the Continental Army in March 1776 and served until June 1780.

According to tradition, sometime after Davis returned home, he was confronted by British soldiers who knew he was a Patriot. When he would not divulge military information, the soldiers hung him upside down by his ankles in the well. Davis was rescued when his wife, Elizabeth, ran a half mile to a neighbor for help. The father of four operated a general store out of the house and was appointed Coram's first postmaster in 1794.

"Since the Davis family knew all the players, I believe they were involved with the Culper Spy Ring and hid it to protect their family," said Maryanne Douglas, president of the Davis Town Meeting House Society Inc.[456]

Davis Town Meeting House in Coram, where Patriot whaleboat raiders burned three hundred tons of hay in 1780. *Photo by Audrey C. Tiernan, copyright 2020.*

Interior of the Davis Town Meeting House under restoration. *Photo by Audrey C. Tiernan, copyright 2020.*

Right: Staircase in the Davis Town Meeting House. *Photo by Audrey C. Tiernan, copyright 2020.*

Below: The Davis family cemetery in Coram with original and modern headstones for Revolutionary War soldier Goldsmith Davis. *Photo by Audrey C. Tiernan, copyright 2020.*

In 1790, Brookhaven Town leaders moved the site of government from Setauket to more central Coram with annual town meetings held in April at the Davis house until 1884.[457]

Two wings were added to the house. The first was constructed about 1860. Lester H. Davis III, the seventh generation of the family to own the house, sold it and three-quarters of an acre to the town in 1999. The town later purchased the family cemetery behind the house. The Davis Town Meeting House Society is currently renovating the house.[458]

FORT ST. GEORGE SITE
William Floyd Parkway, Shirley

The fort was located on the Manor of St. George at Smith Point. The manor, a huge tract that encompassed more than a third of current-day Brookhaven Town, was acquired in the late 1600s by Colonel William "Tangier" Smith.

When Major Benjamin Tallmadge initially recommended to George Washington that he be allowed to attack the fort, the general denied the request. But the commander changed his mind after receiving a letter written on November 6, 1780, by Culper Spy Ring member Caleb Brewster to Tallmadge noting that three hundred tons of hay was being stored in Coram before it was transported to Manhattan to feed British army horses. Tallmadge forwarded Brewster's letter to headquarters with his own recommendation that the hay be destroyed. In a November 11 letter, Washington told Tallmadge to cross to Long Island and burn the hay and also capture the fort if it could be done "without frustrating the other design, or running a great hazard."[459]

General Henry Clinton had ordered Captain Thomas Hazard to establish the fort. Fifty Loyalist troops from Rhode Island constructed a triangular stockade with walls 200 to 250 feet long of sharpened logs anchored by the manor house, another plantation structure and a blockhouse earlier that year. The enclosure encompassed several acres with a redoubt in the center. It was further protected by a deep ditch and two cannons. The Rhode Island men had remained to garrison the fort, which also became the home of Loyalist refugees in September 1780 after the British evacuated Newport, Rhode Island.

On November 21, 1780, Tallmadge, a twenty-six-year-old officer in the Second Light Dragoons, left Fairfield, Connecticut, with eighty men in whaleboats. Five hours later, they landed at Old Mans (now Mt. Sinai). After hiding the boats in the woods, the soldiers marched five miles until they were engulfed by a storm and retreated to the beach to spend the rest of the night under their craft. When the weather cleared the following afternoon, they marched across Long Island. They halted two miles from the fort at 4:00 a.m. on November 23. Tallmadge ordered the attack to be launched simultaneously on the three sides of the palisade when the officers heard the signal: a cry of "Washington and glory!" To ensure no premature gunfire would ruin their surprise, the assault was to be made with unloaded muskets, relying on bayonets. But as the Americans neared the fort, a Loyalist guard fired an alarm shot. The sentry was bayoneted, and Tallmadge ordered his "pioneer," or engineering, troops to use their axes to cut through the main gate. Once inside the palisade, the Americans captured most of the fort within ten minutes.

But many Loyalists remained in the two houses. Tallmadge wrote in a memoir that

> *while we were standing, elated with victory, in the center of the fort, a volley of musketry was discharged from the windows of one of the large houses, which induced me to order my whole detachment to load and return the fire. I soon found it necessary to lead the column directly to the house, which, being strongly barricaded, required the aid of the pioneers with their axes. As soon as the troops could enter, the confusion and conflict were great. A considerable portion of those who had fired after the fort was taken, and the colors had been struck, were thrown headlong from the windows of the second story to the ground. Having forfeited their lives by the usages of war, all would have been killed had I not ordered the slaughter to cease.*[460]

When all resistance had been suppressed, seven Loyalists were dead or wounded and fifty-three officers and men captured in the Battle of Fort St. George. Tallmadge's loss was just one man wounded.

Observing that ships at the dock were preparing to escape with their cargo, Tallmadge had his men fire on them with the fort's cannons, burning and sinking them. Then the Americans turned their attention to destroying the fort, which was accomplished by 8:00 a.m. The prisoners were led out of the fort and made to carry captured supplies back across the width of the island to the whaleboats by the beach.

Tallmadge, meanwhile, led a dozen men, including whaleboat captain and Culper Spy Ring member Caleb Brewster, on horses liberated from the Loyalists to destroy the hay. His party reached Coram in an hour and a half, overwhelmed the guards and set fire to the hay before reuniting with the rest of his force in the middle of the island and then reaching at the shore at 4:00 p.m. By midnight, they were back in Fairfield, Connecticut.

The site of Fort St. George was acquired by the Town of Brookhaven in 1974 and is preserved as a park. The manor house now on the property was built after the war and is now the privately operated Museum Manor of St. George, which is open seasonally. The only remaining element from the fort is the outline of the central redoubt in the grass.[461]

General Nathaniel Woodhull Grave
Neighborhood Road and Lakeview Drive, Mastic Beach

Nathaniel Woodhull was a martyr to the Patriot cause. As detailed in chapter 1, as the Battle of Long Island was looming in August 1776, Woodhull was ordered to take militiamen to herd cattle spread across Long Island east to keep them out of British hands. During a severe thunderstorm, the general took refuge in a tavern east of Jamaica and a British cavalry patrol surrounded it. Woodhull was captured and mortally wounded. The general died on September 20, 1776, at age fifty-four and was buried at his Mastic home, which has been replaced by suburban houses surrounding the graveyard.

Left: Grave of Patriot General Nathaniel Woodhull at the family cemetery in Mastic. *Photo by Audrey C. Tiernan, copyright 2020.*

Above: Historical marker for General Nathaniel Woodhull's grave in Mastic. *Photo by Audrey C. Tiernan, copyright 2020.*

The grave is in a small private family cemetery in Mastic Beach. Located on Neighborhood Road between Lakeview and Whittier Drives, the cemetery, maintained by the Town of Brookhaven, is open to the public. The epitaph on his headstone reads that his death was "regretted by all who knew how to value his many private virtues, and that pure zeal for the rights of his Country to which he perished a victim." The headstone was repaired by residents in 2014 after it was found broken into four pieces.[462]

NORTH COUNTRY ROAD REMNANT
Near Stony Brook Road, Stony Brook

A historical marker denotes a partially paved section several hundred yards long of the original North Country Road that ran through Stony Brook during the Revolutionary War. The remnant connects with Dogwood Drive, which is off Stony Brook Road. The marker notes it was in use until 1873 and adds, "President George Washington and his entourage passed near here on April 23, 1790, following his visit with spy ring member Captain Austin Roe at the Roe Tavern in Setauket."

Historian Beverly Tyler stands by a historical marker commemorating a remnant of the original North Country Road that ran through Stony Brook during the Revolutionary War. President George Washington traveled on the road on April 23, 1790, during his visit to Long Island. *Photo by Audrey C. Tiernan, copyright 2020.*

PATRIOT'S ROCK
Main Street, Setauket

A plaque on the huge boulder marks the site of the Battle of Setauket, August 22, 1777 (although it incorrectly lists the date as August 24.). Patriots under the command of General Samuel Parsons crossed Long Island Sound from Black Rock, Connecticut, in whaleboats backed by a sloop. Various records give the number of soldiers as anywhere from 150 to 500, but local historian Beverly Tyler believes the lower number is more accurate. They landed on Crane Neck and headed for Setauket to attack the fortified Presbyterian church about three miles away. Earthen walls six feet high had been erected around the church and topped with logs rising another six feet. Swivel guns were mounted in the upper windows. Depending on the account, Loyalist Lieutenant Colonel Richard Hewlett commanded 50 to 250 defenders; Tyler subscribes to the lowest figure.

When the Patriots reached what is now named Patriot's Rock, whaleboat captain and Culper Spy Ring member Caleb Brewster positioned a six-

Patriot's Rock in Setauket where whaleboat raiders from Connecticut began the August 22, 1777, Battle of Setauket. *Photo by Audrey C. Tiernan, copyright 2020.*

Plaque on Patriots' Rock commemorating the Battle of Setauket on August 22, 1777. *Photo by Audrey C. Tiernan, copyright 2020.*

pound cannon and a demand to surrender was carried to the fort. When Hewlett refused, both sides began firing. The Loyalists had seen the Patriots coming and sent a rider for reinforcements. The fighting lasted for several hours until the rebels learned the British were sending warships to cut the raiders off from returning to Connecticut. The attackers withdrew and made a hasty retreat back across the Sound. The Patriots' only accomplishment was destroying some military supplies.[463]

SETAUKET PRESBYTERIAN CHURCH
Caroline Avenue, Setauket

During the Battle of Setauket on August 22, 1777, Patriots attacked the Presbyterian church, which was erected in 1714 and had been fortified by the British. That church was demolished or burned down some time before the current church was built in 1812.

During the war, local historian Beverly Tyler said, the British used the church as a stable and fortified it because "they had no appreciation for anything aside from Anglican churches."[464]

The Presbyterian Churchyard was originally the town cemetery unaffiliated with a church. Many members of locally famous families, including Woodhulls, are buried there. The most prominent grave is that of farmer and chief Culper spy Abraham Woodhull, who died on January 23, 1826. Bricks from the foundation of the Woodhull homestead on Little Bay, which was destroyed by fire in 1931, were used in his memorial.[465]

Sherwood-Jayne House
Old Post Road, East Setauket

The structure owned by Preservation Long Island was the home of William Jayne, a prominent Revolutionary War Tory. During the conflict, Jayne, known colloquially as Big Bill the Tory, was captured by the rebels but eventually freed through a prisoner exchange. Despite the hostility to Loyalists on Long Island, Jayne returned to Setauket after the Revolution and by the 1790s managed to become the town commissioner of highways.

The house was built in 1730 by William's father, Mathias, as a modest one-and-a-half-story dwelling. William inherited it before the war. His first wife died in 1785, and by 1790 Big Bill had remarried and greatly enlarged the home into a full two-story structure with an east wing.

In 1908, the property was acquired by Howard C. Sherwood, founder of the Society for the Preservation of Long Island Antiquities, the original name of Preservation Long Island, and restored. The house museum is open periodically.[466]

Thompson House
91 North Country Road, East Setauket

Built circa 1709 by Samuel Thompson, it was home to his son, Jonathan, and Jonathan's son, Dr. Samuel Thompson, during the Revolution.

"Lieutenant Colonel Richard Hewlett, the commander of the Loyalists who fortified the area around the Setauket Presbyterian Church, during or after the Battle of Setauket on August 22, 1777, wrote a letter to New York Royal Governor William Tryon in New York City," local historian Beverly Tyler said. "He wrote that Jonathan and Samuel Thompson, father and son who were Patriots and part of the militia posing as Loyalists until they were outed by Hewlett, had been directing the Patriot forces to where his wounded men were hospitalized, and that the hospital was near the Thompson House."

"Hewlett mentioned that they and Selah Strong were giving information to the Patriots on the activities of the British army," Tyler continued. "I think it led to the immediate departure of the Thompsons to Connecticut, although there is no record of when they went."[467]

After he received the letter, as noted previously in the Smith-Strong House section, Tryon had Selah Strong confined in the Sugar House prison

Left: Sherwood-Jayne House in East Setauket was the home of William Jayne, a prominent Revolutionary War Tory. *Photo courtesy of Preservation Long Island.*

Below: The Thompson House in East Setauket was the home of Patriots Samuel Thompson and his son Doctor Samuel Thompson. *Photo by Audrey C. Tiernan, copyright 2020.*

in Manhattan. There is no evidence that the Thompsons were active with the spy ring.

But Samuel's brother Isaac Thompson, who lived in Bay Shore at Sagtikos Manor, remained on Long Island during the war and is believed to have engaged in espionage for General Washington.

The Thompson House, which is listed on the National Register of Historic Places, was purchased in 1953 by philanthropist Ward Melville. The Ward Melville Heritage Organization now owns the property and opens it for tours by appointment. Call 631-751-2244.[468]

TIMOTHY SMITH HOUSE
55 Main Street, Setauket

The circa 1695 structure was the seat of government in the Town of Brookhaven from 1738 to 1778 and was the site of several incidents between Patriots and British and Loyalist soldiers.[469]

TYLER-JAYNE TAVERN
2 Tavern Way (off Main Street)

During the Revolution, British soldiers came to the circa 1750 structure looking for deserters and ended up shooting a young Patriot from the Smith family. The tavern was originally located on Main Street, and Edward Acker moved it after buying it in the 1930s or 1940s.[470]

WILLIAM FLOYD ESTATE
Park Drive, Mastic Beach

This site, owned by the National Park Service and part of Fire Island National Seashore, was the home of a signer of the Declaration of Independence and other members of his family for eight generations over more than 250 years.

In 1724, Nicoll Floyd bought 4,400 acres with a six-room residence known as Old Mastic House. Thirty years later, his son William Floyd, born in 1734, was forced to assume management of the estate and care of his eight siblings after Nicoll and William's mother, Tabitha Smith, died in an epidemic when he was twenty.

Cattle, sheep, grain, flax and wood for export to New York City were all produced on the estate by fourteen enslaved adults as well as indentured servants, making Floyd one of Long Island's largest slaveholders.

Floyd served as a colonel in the Suffolk County militia before the Revolution. As discussed in chapter 2, during the war Floyd's family became refugees in Middletown, Connecticut, while he served with the Continental Congress in Philadelphia. With a one-year break when he was a member of the New York State Senate in 1778, Floyd was a member of Congress from 1774 to 1783 and signed the Declaration of Independence in 1776.

After the British evacuated New York in 1783, Floyd returned to Mastic and the family shifted from farming to business and politics with the estate used for recreation.

Floyd's wife, Hannah, died in 1781. Three years later, he married Joanna Strong, a cousin of Anna Smith Strong of the Culper Spy Ring. He served in the first U.S. Congress from 1789 to 1790 but failed to win reelection. In 1787, New York State honored him for his role in the Revolution by giving him ten thousand acres along the Mohawk River. Throughout the 1790s, he cleared and developed the property during summer visits. He was also promoted to major general in the state militia.

In 1803, when he was sixty-nine, he deeded his Long Island estate to his son, Nicoll, and moved with Joanna, their two daughters, a niece and some of the enslaved people to the property upstate. He built a home similar to Old Mastic House near Utica in what is now Westernville, where he died in 1821 at age eighty-six. It is now a private home. Floyd is buried in the Westernville Presbyterian Church Cemetery with Joanna.

Floyd's descendants expanded Old Mastic House to twenty-five rooms. By the 1970s, all but 613 acres had been sold. In 1976, William Floyd's great-great-granddaughter Cornelia Floyd Nichols and her children donated the house to the National Park Service. They retained rights for family members to be buried on the grounds.

Of the four New Yorkers who signed the Declaration of Independence, Floyd's is the only house still standing and open to the public. The estate is open from Memorial Day to Veterans Day. Visitors can tour the historic house museum on weekends and holidays and explore some of the dozen outbuildings, forest fields, the marshland along the Great South Bay as well as a cemetery that includes graves of many members of the family and their enslaved people.[471]

East Hampton Town

Culloden Point
West end of Soundview Drive, Montauk

On January 24, 1781, the seventy-four-gun HMS *Culloden* was in Block Island Sound on blockade duty when a nor'easter blew in. The third-rate ship of the line and two other similar men-of-war tried to clear Montauk Point to ride out the storm in the Atlantic. Captain George Balfour was following the lights of HMS *Bedford* when around 12:30 a.m. that ship reversed course. Balfour, however, continued on. At 4:00 a.m. *Culloden* went aground on

HMS *Culloden* ran aground on the north side of Montauk in a 1771 winter storm and was burned by the crew to keep the vessel out of American hands. The remains of the wreck lie off what is now called Culloden Point. *Courtesy of the Dan Berg Wreck Valley Collection.*

Culloden Monument in Montauk. *Photo by Ben Roberts.*

the northern shore of Montauk, west of today's inlet. When the weather cleared, Balfour tried unsuccessfully to refloat his vessel and then ordered everything of value transferred ashore. *Culloden* was set afire and burned to the waterline.

Today, the wreckage—listed on the National Register of Historic Places and protected by New York State law—lies mostly covered by sand in twenty feet of water. It is a popular scuba diving site with access from a 14.3-acre park jointly owned by the Town of East Hampton and Suffolk County. A monument commemorating the sinking is located on the west side of Flamingo Road inland from the beach.[472]

Umbrella House
89A Division Street, Sag Harbor

This private house was occupied by British soldiers in 1777 and later served as an arsenal.[473]

Hempstead Town

Battle of Hempstead Swamp site
Tanglewood Preserve, 1400 Tanglewood Road, Lakeview

A skirmish took place in the swamp before the signing of the Declaration of Independence. Patriot leaders dispatched men to arrest Tories suspected of plotting to poison George Washington with tainted peas. The Tories fled into the woods and swamps above Smith Pond, and the two sides skirmished before six of the Tories were arrested and one of them, George Smith, was wounded in the shoulder. It is believed to have been the first blood of the Revolution spilled on Long Island. In 2019, Town of Hempstead officials dedicated a historical marker inside the preserve, which is owned by Nassau County.[474]

Hewlett House
86 East Rockaway Road, Hewlett

This was the home of Lieutenant Colonel Richard Hewlett, a prominent Loyalist officer. It was built circa 1740 by descendants of George Hewlett, the first member of his distinguished family to settle on Long Island. The home remains on its original site and includes many Dutch Colonial architectural features. It is one of only about a dozen surviving Dutch-style houses on Long Island.

Richard Hewlett was born on November 1, 1729, in what is now Merrick. In 1753, he married Mary Townsend, and over the next twenty years they would have eleven children.

During the French and Indian War, he served as captain in a New York regiment of provincial troops and fought in Canada. When the war ended in 1763, Hewlett returned to Hempstead, where he became a community leader and served as lieutenant colonel of the Queens County Militia. When the Revolution erupted, Hewlett remained a Loyalist, as did most residents of Queens County, which included what would become Nassau County.

After British General William Howe's army landed in Brooklyn in August 1776 and routed George Washington's forces in the Battle of Long Island, Hewlett became a lieutenant colonel in the Third Battalion of DeLancey's Brigade, raised by Brigadier General Oliver DeLancey, Hewlett's commander in the French and Indian War.

Hewlett and his men were stationed at a primitive fort in Setauket during a Patriot raid in August 1777 given the overly grand name of the Battle of Setauket. For the rest of the war, Hewlett's battalion garrisoned different posts on Long Island, including Fort Hill on Lloyd Neck, overlooking the entrance to Oyster Bay and Cold Spring Harbor, which was the largest British fortification on Long Island.

When the war ended, Hewlett's last duty was commanding all the Loyalist regiments heading to exile in Nova Scotia in September 1783. Hewlett settled on a grant of land on the Saint John River and died there in 1789. He is buried at St. Stephen's Anglican Church in Queenstown, New Brunswick, but his wife, who returned to Long Island, is buried at Saint George's Church Cemetery in Hempstead, where a marker also commemorates Richard Hewlett.

His former house, listed on the National Register of Historic Places, was bequeathed by the late Cerecies Hewlett to the Hewlett-Woodmere School District, which took possession in 1984 upon her death.[475] It remained empty and deteriorated badly until after the district sold it to Nassau County in 1998, according to Geri Barish, executive director of 1 in 9, the not-for-profit breast cancer awareness and support group that uses the house as a community learning resource center.

Hewlett House in Hewlett, former home of Loyalist officer Lieutenant Colonel Richard Hewlett and now owned by Nassau County and used as the offices of 1 in 9, a not-for-profit breast cancer support group. *Photo by Audrey C. Tiernan, copyright 2019.*

The interior is little changed from the days of the Revolution. "The wood floors are original," Barish, who worked with the contractor hired by the county to handle the restoration, explained during a private tour. "It's all the original stained glass. I left areas open in the different rooms so you can see how this house was built" with plaster applied as the interior finish.

Barish said an archaeological dig in the outhouse, which still exists, provided a trove of artifacts, including a letter, a pair of glasses, pewter plates and pottery fragments. "Upstairs, there was a hidden room," she continued. "And when we were working in that area, a wall fell down, and behind that wall was the most magnificent chest of drawers. There was a sword that must've belonged to Lieutenant Colonel Hewlett. There were handmade handkerchiefs. There was lead crystal glassware." A large family Bible was also found in the house.[476]

Tours of the house are available by advance request (http://www.hewlett-house.org). A faded historical marker outside erected in 1936 provides some history of the structure.[477]

ROCK HALL MUSEUM
199 Broadway, Lawrence

Rock Hall was built in 1767 for Josiah Martin, who was born and raised on Antigua in the West Indies, where he owned a large sugar plantation. His Georgian-style home is one of the finest pre–Revolutionary War homes on Long Island.

In part because of fear of slave uprisings, Martin decided to retire from active management of his plantation at age sixty-eight. He decided to live near the Atlantic Ocean and New York City, so he purchased six hundred acres and built Rock Hall while a manager continued to oversee the plantation in Antigua.

As discussed in chapter 2, after the beginning of the American Revolution, Martin, a prominent Loyalist, and his family had to endure having their home occupied by Patriot soldiers in the early months of 1776. The Battle of Long Island in August that resulted in British control of the area ended any predation against the family for the rest of the war.

Josiah's eldest son, Dr. Samuel Martin, who was imprisoned briefly in Philadelphia for Loyalist views, inherited Rock Hall after Josiah's death in 1778 at the age of seventy-nine.

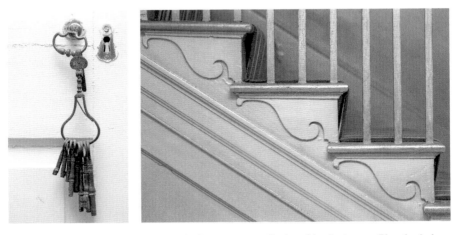

Left: The original keys for Rock Hall in Lawrence are displayed in the house. *Photo by Audrey C. Tiernan, copyright 2020.*

Right: A detail of the staircase at Rock Hall in Lawrence. *Photo by Audrey C. Tiernan, copyright 2020.*

When the estate declined, Thomas Hewlett acquired Rock Hall and 125 acres from Samuel's heirs in 1824. The family owned it until 1948, using it as a farm home, a boardinghouse beginning around 1830 and finally as a summer home for the family. By the 1930s, the house was vacant.

The Hewlett family donated the property to the Town of Hempstead in 1948. It opened as a house museum in 1953 after extensive restoration. Besides tours of the house, visitors can see a display of eighteenth- and nineteenth-century artifacts uncovered during archaeological excavations.[478]

ST. GEORGE'S EPISCOPAL CHURCH GRAVEYARD
319 Front Street, Hempstead

The current Episcopal church was constructed in 1822, but the cemetery contains graves of Revolutionary War soldiers. During the conflict, the earlier church served as headquarters and a place to worship for occupying soldiers. Folklore has it that the original rooster weathervane, still in the possession of the church, was used for target practice, leaving it with sixteen bullet holes.[479]

Grave of Revolutionary War soldier John Carman in St. George's Cemetery in Hempstead. *Photo by Audrey C. Tiernan, copyright 2019.*

HUNTINGTON TOWN

FORT GOLGOTHA SITE
Route 25A east of Route 110, Huntington.

The British built Fort Golgotha atop Huntington's hilltop burial ground in November 1782—more than a year after the decisive Battle of Yorktown in Virginia had ensured American victory. The British desecrated more than one hundred tombstones, felled trees and ripped apart a church and meetinghouse for their boards. All that remains is a clearing on top of the hill. A historical marker identifies the location.[480]

NATHAN HALE MEMORIALS

There are two memorials to the ill-fated spy in the Huntington area. The Nathan Hale Rock with three brass explanatory plaques is at the corner of New York Avenue and Mill Dam Road in Halesite. Developer George Taylor placed the 145-ton boulder by the beach at the end of Vineyard Road, north of its current location, and named the area Halesite because that's where historians believe Hale originally landed to begin his mission. In 1976, the boulder was moved inland to its current location and later donated to the Town of Huntington.[481] There is also a granite column commemorating Hale in front of the Soldiers & Sailors Memorial Building at 228 Main Street.[482]

TARGET ROCK
Off the eastern shore of Lloyd Neck

The captains of British warships patrolling Long Island Sound used a large glacial "erratic" boulder protruding from the sandy bluff on the west side of Huntington Bay for target practice by their gun crews. Their name for the New England boulder dragged to Long Island by a glacier has been handed down through the centuries. Over the years, the bluff has eroded, leaving the boulder out in the bay.[483]

THE ARSENAL
Park Avenue by the Village Green, Huntington

The colonial home of weaver Job Sammis from 1775 to 1776 also served as the arsenal for the Suffolk County Militia, which conducted regular drills on

Above: A vintage postcard of Target Rock, the glacial boulder used by British warships for target practice during the American Revolution. *Author's collection.*

Left: Interior of the Arsenal in Huntington. *Photo by Audrey C. Tiernan, copyright 2020.*

The Arsenal in Huntington was the home of weaver Job Sammis in 1775–76 and also served as the arsenal for the Suffolk County Militia. It is now a museum. *Photo by Audrey C. Tiernan, copyright 2020.*

the adjacent Village Green prior to the British occupation of Long Island in 1776. It is owned today by the Town of Huntington and is a restored house museum and headquarters for the reenactors of the Ancient and Honorable Huntington Militia.[484]

Islip Town

Sagtikos Manor
677 Montauk Highway, West Bay Shore

General Henry Clinton, the British commander in North America, is said to have stayed in the second-floor master bedroom facing south toward the bay during the war.

"We don't have any dates," Christine Gottsch, president of the Sagtikos Manor Historical Society, said during a private tour of the house. But the society is conducting research.

The British requisitioned supplies from Sagtikos Manor, and a receipt they gave to Thompson is on display at the house. "He did get paid back for what they took from his property," Gottsch said.

The tract was purchased from the Secatogue band of Native Americans in 1692 by Stephanus Van Cortlandt, who in 1697 had the original section of the house constructed. The property was owned by the Thompson-Gardiner family from 1758 until it was purchased by Suffolk County in 2002.

Judge Isaac Thompson, who owned the house during the American Revolution, expanded it. Gottsch believes Thompson was a member of the Culper Spy Ring. "We just have to find proof," she said. Thompson was related to Abraham Woodhull, chief Culper spy, as his mother, Mary, was Woodhull's aunt.

Above: Sagtikos Manor in West Bay Shore, where British commander Sir Henry Clinton stayed during the war. *Photo by Audrey C. Tiernan, copyright 2019.*

Left: Gravestone of Isaac Thompson, owner of Sagtikos Manor during the Revolutionary War, located on the property in West Bay Shore. *Photo by Audrey C. Tiernan, copyright 2019.*

After the colonies won their independence, George Washington visited during his tour of Long Island on April 21, 1790. The president wrote about his overnight stay in his journal. "The story is that they offered him the master bedroom, which is where General Clinton had stayed, and he didn't want to stay where Clinton stayed so he stayed in the adjoining bedroom," Gottsch said. "He did pay for it, according to his diary."

In 1902, there was another addition to the house for owner Frederick Diodati Thompson by the well-known local architect Isaac Green.

For more information about tours with costumed docents, go to www. sagtikosmanor.org or call 631-854-0939.

Samuel Greene House
93 West Main Street, West Sayville

On his 1790 tour of Long Island, President George Washington "halted a while" on April 21 at the home of Samuel Greene, sometimes spelled without the *e*. It is now is used as office space. A historical marker commemorates Washington's stop.

North Hempstead Town

Monfort Cemetery
250 feet east of the intersection of Port Washington Boulevard and Main Street, Port Washington

The cemetery owned by the Town of North Hempstead contains the grave sites of five Patriots, including Adrian and Petrus Onderdonck, Thomas Dodge and Martin Schenck, who signed a declaration of independence from Loyalist Hempstead nine months before the nation's Declaration of Independence. This led to the division of the town after the war, separating North Hempstead Town from today's Town of Hempstead. Adrian Onderdonck became the first town supervisor.[485]

Sands-Willets House
336 Port Washington Boulevard, Flower Hill

The Sands family of merchants and farmers built and lived in the original west wing of the house starting about 1735. Seven brothers served in the

Headstone of Revolutionary War Patriot Adrian Onderdonck in Monfort Cemetery in Port Washington. *Photo by Howard Kroplick.*

The Sands-Willets House in Flower Hill, which was expanded extensively after the Revolution. Seven brothers from the Sands family fought in the war. *Photo by Audrey C. Tiernan, copyright 2020.*

American Revolution, including Colonel John Sands IV (1737–1811), a militia leader who fought with the Continental Army at the Battle of Brooklyn. The Cow Neck Peninsula Historical Society operates the house as a museum.[486]

MANHASSET QUAKER MEETING HOUSE
1421 Northern Boulevard at Shelter Rock Road

The meetinghouse was constructed in 1760. When Hessian cavalrymen occupied it in 1782, the Friends protested to the English governor-general, who ordered the soldiers to vacate and restore the building. The following year, it was again occupied by soldiers who used it as a guardhouse. They caused considerable damage to the seats and fence, which had to be repaired by the members of the meeting after the British and Hessians evacuated Long Island at the end of the war.[487]

SMITHTOWN TOWN

FORT SLONGO SITE
Route 25A, Fort Salonga

The Battle of Fort Slongo on October 3, 1781, was one of the last engagements of the war on Long Island. The British outpost on Long Island Sound was likely named for George Slongo, the contractor who built it, probably between 1778 and 1779. It was a hollow square about fifty feet on each side with a wooden palisade about seven feet tall erected on a berm. A blockhouse was constructed in the center.

The remains of the earthen mounds that supported the wooden palisade at Fort Slongo are visible in a Fort Salonga backyard. *Courtesy of Richard F. Welch.*

The fort was attacked by one hundred soldiers dispatched by spymaster Benjamin Tallmadge from Norwalk, Connecticut. The Patriots killed four of the defenders, wounded two and took twenty-one prisoners. The fort was burned and cannons captured or rendered inoperable. Only one of the raiders was seriously wounded. The earthworks from the fort can still be seen in the backyard of a private home overlooking the Sound. A historical marker on Route 25A commemorates the battle.[488]

SOUTHAMPTON TOWN

BRIDGEHAMPTON PRESBYTERIAN CHURCH SITE
66 Sagaponack Road, Bridgehampton

A stone marker on the north side of Sagaponack Road just east of Ocean Road denotes the site where the church stood from 1737 until 1842. After a July 2, 1775, sermon, Colonel John Hulbert gathered the men of the congregation at the church door and enlisted twenty-one of them for one of the first Patriot militia companies in the area.[489]

BRITISH GARRISON SITE/OLD BURYING GROUND
Union Street opposite Church Street, Sag Harbor

This is the location of a British fort captured during the Meigs Raid or Battle of Sag Harbor early on May 24, 1777. A monument is situated just west of the Old Whalers Church on Union Street north of the Old Burying Ground.[490]

COOK HOMESTEAD
439 Hayground Road, Bridgehampton

Built circa 1760, the house was occupied by Hessian troops, who destroyed the family's personal property.[491]

GENERAL WILLIAM ERSKINE HEADQUARTERS SITE
17 North Main Street, Southampton

A historical marker denotes the site of the headquarters for the commander of British troops on Long Island in 1777–78.[492]

John Howell's Inn Site
45 Main Street, Sag Harbor

The inn was located on the current site of the American Hotel. During the Meigs Raid or Battle of Sag Harbor early on May 24, 1777, Patriots from Connecticut captured Sag Harbor and took British soldiers sleeping in the inn prisoner.[493]

Lemuel Pierson House
473 Sagg Main Street, Sagaponack

Hessian and British troops occupied this house and left carved graffiti on walls.[494]

Meigs Raid Landing Site
Noyack Road and Noyack-Long Beach Road, Noyack

A historical marker at the intersection denotes the site where Patriot raiders from Connecticut under the command of Lieutenant Colonel Return Jonathan Meigs landed late on May 23, 1777, before successfully attacking the British garrison in Sag Harbor in the Battle of Sag Harbor at 2:00 a.m. the following morning.

Southold Town

Meigs Raid Landing Site
Town Beach, Sound Avenue

A historical marker west of the entrance to the town beach marks the spot where Patriot raiders from Connecticut under the command of Lieutenant Colonel Return Jonathan Meigs made their first landfall on May 23, 1777, on their way to attack the British garrison in Sag Harbor in what became known as the Meigs Raid or Battle of Sag Harbor.

The Old House
Route 25, Cutchogue

The structure built in the late 1600s was occupied by three generations of the politically powerful Wickham family. After the Revolution, the house

Monument in the Old Burying Ground in Sag Harbor at the site of the British fort captured during the Meigs Raid on May 24, 1777. *Photo by Audrey C. Tiernan, copyright 2020.*

The Old House in Cutchogue was built in the late 1600s and occupied by three generations of the politically powerful Wickham family. After the Revolution, the house and 240 acres were confiscated on the pretense that Parker Wickham was a Loyalist. *Photo by Audrey C. Tiernan, copyright 2020.*

and 240 acres were confiscated in 1784 on the pretense that owner Parker Wickham was a Loyalist. Wickham moved to Waterford, Connecticut, where he died in 1785. The oldest English medieval-style house in New York State, it was restored in 1940 and opened as a museum house. It was designated a National Historic Landmark in 1962.[495]

NOTES

Introduction

1. Kilmeade and Yaeger, *George Washington's Secret Six*, xviii .

Chapter 1. The Battle of Long Island

2. Schecter, *Battle for New York*, 95, 99.
3. Ibid., 100–101.
4. Ibid.; Welch, *General Washington's Commando*, 11.
5. Schecter, *Battle for New York*, 116; Flint, *Long Island Before*, 372.
6. Schecter, *Battle for New York*, 116.
7. De Wan, "Patriots' First"; Welch, *General Washington's Commando*, 11.
8. Schecter, *Battle for New York*, 118–19; Luke and Venables, *Long Island*, 19–21; De Wan, "Patriots' First."
9. Schecter, *Battle for New York*, 123; Luke and Venables, *Long Island*, 23.
10. Daigler, *Spies*, 94.
11. Ibid.
12. Rose, *Washington's Spies*, 84–85.
13. Ibid.
14. De Wan, "Hero's Last Words"; Rose, *Washington's Spies*, 84–86.
15. De Wan, "Hero's Last Words"; Rose, *Washington's Spies*, 84–86.
16. Schecter, *Battle for New York*, 123, 126–27.

17. Ibid., 135.
18. Ibid., 132, 141–43, 146; Luke and Venables, *Long Island*, 21, 23.
19. Schecter, *Battle for New York*, 136–37.
20. Ibid., 138–39.
21. Ibid., 147; Luke and Venables, *Long Island*, 25.
22. Schecter, *Battle for New York*, 148; De Wan, "Days of Defeat."
23. Schecter, *Battle for New York*, 149–50; Luke and Venables, *Long Island*, 25–26; Gallagher, *Battle of Brooklyn*, 129–30.
24. Schecter, *Battle for New York*, 152–53; Luke and Venables, *Long Island*, 25–26.
25. Schecter, *Battle for New York*, 153; Luke and Venables, *Long Island*, 27.
26. Schecter, *Battle for New York*, 154, 156.
27. Ibid., 154, 156; Tallmadge, *Memoir*, 10; De Wan, "Leading the Charge."
28. Schecter, *Battle for New York*, 156–57.
29. Ibid., 158; Luke and Venables, *Long Island*, 26.
30. Schecter, *Battle for New York*, 159; Johnson, *Campaign of 1776*, 218.
31. Schecter, *Battle for New York*, 162.
32. Welch, *General Washington's Commando*, 14–15.
33. De Wan, "Risking His Life."
34. Schecter, *Battle for New York*, 166–67; Gallagher, *Battle of Brooklyn*, 153; Welch, *General Washington's Commando*, 14–15.
35. Luke and Venables, *Long Island*, 27; De Wan, "Patriots' First"; Daigler, *Spies*, 95.
36. Daigler, *Spies*, 95.

Chapter 2. The British Occupation

37. Naylor, *Women in Long Island's Past*, 42.
38. Hanc, "Hidden History."
39. Welch, *General Washington's Commando*, 37; Rose, *Washington's Spies*, 163–64; interview with Raynham Hall historian Claire Bellerjeau.
40. Naylor, *Women in Long Island's Past*, 33, 35, 38–39; Tiedemann and Fingerhut, *Other New York*, 2, 43, 47, 64.
41. Tiedemann and Fingerhut, *Other New York*, 48.
42. Naylor, *Women in Long Island's Past*, 35–37.
43. Luke and Venables, *Long Island*, 32–33; Gallagher, *Battle of Brooklyn*, 165.
44. Gallagher, *Battle of Brooklyn*, 165.
45. Luke and Venables, *Long Island*, 34–36.

46. De Wan, "Long Island's 7-Year Hitch," 128; Luke and Venables, *Long Island*, 35–36; Bleyer, *Long Island*, 103; Bellerjeau, interviews.

47. Beverly Tyler, interviews.

48. Griffin, *Lost British Forts*, 14–15.

49. De Wan, "They Signed."

50. Welch, *General Washington's Commando*, 37; Bleyer, *Long Island*, 95; De Wan, "They Signed."

51. Welch, *General Washington's Commando*, 46–47; Rose, *Washington's Spies*, 83.

52. Welch, *General Washington's Commando*, 53–54, 91–96; Naylor, *Women in Long Island's Past*, 38.

53. Welch, *General Washington's Commando*, 48.

54. Staudt, "State of Wretchedness."

55. Bleyer, *Long Island*, 73–74; Bellerjeau, interviews.

56. Bellerjeau, interview.

57. Ibid.

58. Ibid.

59. Onderdonk, *Documents and Letters*, 133.

60. Tiedemann and Fingerhut, *Other New York*, 67–68; Luke and Venables, *Long Island*, 39–40; Welch, *General Washington's Commando*, 37.

61. Luke and Venables, *Long Island*, 32–33.

62. Gallagher, *Battle of Brooklyn*, 153; Welch, *General Washington's Commando*, 48, 51.

63. Luke and Venables, *Long Island*, 53–54; De Wan, "Long Island's 7-Year Hitch," 128.

64. De Wan, "Long Island's 7-Year Hitch," 128; Luke and Venables, *Long Island*, 42, 53–54; interviews with Beverly Tyler, Claire Bellerjeau and Mary Cascone.

65. Tiedemann and Fingerhut, *Other New York*, 50–52.

66. Staudt, "State of Wretchedness," 122–23.

67. Ibid.; Staudt, "From Wretchedness to Independence," 135; Naylor, *Women in Long Island's Past*, 40–41; Bellerjeau, interviews.

68. Luke and Venables, *Long Island*, 32.

69. De Wan, "Long Island's 7-Year Hitch," 128.

70. Beverly Tyler, interview, April 19, 2020.

71. Tiedemann and Fingerhut, *Other New York*, 71; Luke and Venables, *Long Island*, 44.

72. Tiedemann and Fingerhut, *Other New York*, 67–68; Luke and Venables, *Long Island*, 39–40; Grasso, *American Revolution*, 114.

Chapter 3. Nathan Hale and Washington's
Early Intelligence Operations

73. Daigler, *Spies*, 13–14.

74. Allen, *George Washington*, 146; Daigler, *Spies*, 1.

75. Daigler, *Spies*, 95–96.

76. Ibid.

77. Ibid.

78. Ibid.

79. Ibid., 99.

80. Ibid., 99–100, 105, 107.

81. Phelps, *Nathan Hale*, 143–44.

82. Daigler, *Spies*, 102.

83. Ibid., 99–100, 105, 107; Allen, *George Washington*, 40–42; Phelps, *Nathan Hale*, 141; Rose, *Washington's Spies*, 17.

84. Rose, *Washington's Spies*, 17.

85. Daigler, *Spies*, 99–102; Pennypacker, *General Washington's Spies*, 24–29; Allen, *George Washington*, 40–42; Phelps, *Nathan Hale*, 166; Rose, *Washington's Spies*, 17.

86. Daigler, *Spies*, 100, 105–6.; Phelps, *Nathan Hale*, 156–58, 160; Rose, *Washington's Spies*, 18, 27.

87. Phelps, *Nathan Hale*, 157–58.

88. Ibid.

89. Daigler, *Spies*, 100, 105–6; Rose, *Washington's Spies*, 18, 29.

90. Daigler, *Spies*, 100, 105–7; Rose, *Washington's Spies*, 29–30.

91. Phelps, *Nathan Hale*, 172; Anderson, *Martyr*, 142.

92. Anderson, *Martyr*, 142.

93. Phelps, *Nathan Hale*, 172–74, 182.

94. Daigler, *Spies*, 107; Phelps, *Nathan Hale*, 187; Rose, *Washington's Spies*, 30.

95. Daigler, *Spies*, 107; Allen, *George Washington*, 40–42; Phelps, *Nathan Hale*, 188, 190; Rose, *Washington's Spies*, 31.

96. Daigler, *Spies*, 107; Allen, *George Washington*, 40–42; Phelps, *Nathan Hale*, 188, 190–93; Kilmeade and Yaeger, *George Washington's Secret Six*, 1.

97. Daigler, *Spies*, 107.

98. Ibid., 108.

99. Ibid., 107; Allen, *George Washington*, 40–42; De Wan, "Hale's Travels," 135; Phelps, *Nathan Hale*, 188, 190–93; Rose, *Washington's Spies*, 31–32.

100. Pennypacker, *General Washington's Spies*, 19–20; Daigler, *Spies*, 107–8; Rose, *Washington's Spies*, 32–33.

101. Rose, *Washington's Spies*, 34.

Chapter 4. Creation of the Spy Ring

102. Rose, *Washington's Spies*, 43.
103. Welch, *General Washington's Commando*, 34.
104. Rose, *Washington's Spies*, 43.
105. Ibid., 44.
106. Ibid., 43–45.
107. Ibid., 46–47; Daigler, *Spies*, 183.
108. Bellerjeau, interview.
109. Daigler, *Spies*, 183; Pennypacker, *General Washington's Spies*, 11, 16.
110. University of Michigan, William L. Clements Library, Sir Henry Clinton Papers, volume 23, item 31.
111. Tyler, interviews.
112. Ibid.
113. Rose, *Washington's Spies*, 50–51.
114. Ibid.
115. Ibid.
116. Ibid., 47–48.
117. Ibid., 70.
118. Ibid., 71.
119. Ibid., 48, 71; Daigler, *Spies*, 174; Welch, *General Washington's Commando*, 35.
120. Bellerjeau, interview, May 2020.
121. Rose, *Washington's Spies*, 72–74.
122. Ibid., 74–75.
123. Ibid., 75, 84.
124. Ibid., 75, 84.
125. Ibid., 75.
126. Ibid., 78, 87; Daigler, *Spies*, 178–79; Welch, *General Washington's Commando*, 41–42; Tyler and Bellerjeau, interviews, May 18, 2020.
127. Rose, *Washington's Spies*, 87.
128. Ibid.
129. Ibid., 75–77.
130. Ibid., 78.
131. Ibid., 79.
132. Ibid., 48, 71, 75–76; Pennypacker, *General Washington's Spies*, 31; Charles River Editors, *Culper Ring*, 14–15; Daigler, *Spies*, 174; Meltzer and Mensch, *First Conspiracy*, 352.
133. Welch, *General Washington's Commando*, 35.

134. Ibid., 34.

135. Daigler, *Spies*, 178–79; Welch, *General Washington's Commando*, 41–42.

136. Rose, *Washington's Spies*, 90; Tyler and Bellerjeau, interviews, May 20, 2020.

137. Rose, *Washington's Spies*, 133–34.

138. Kilmeade and Yaeger, *George Washington's Secret Six*, 71–72.

139. Bellerjeau, interview, June 12, 2020.

140. Rose, *Washington's Spies*, 150.

141. Ibid.

142. Ibid., 151.

143. Ibid., 90; Pennypacker, *General Washington's Spies*, 7–8.

144. Pennypacker, *General Washington's Spies*, 34.

145. Ibid., 50.

146. Bellerjeau and Tyler, interviews.

147. Pennypacker, *General Washington's Spies*, 44.

148. Rose, *Washington's Spies*, 132; Bellerjeau, interviews.

149. Rose, *Washington's Spies*, 171.

150. Daigler, *Spies*, 179.

151. Welch, *General Washington's Commando*, 41–42; Bellerjeau, interview, June 16, 2020.

Chapter 5. Operation of the Espionage Network

152. Bellerjeau, interview, June 22, 2020.

153. Pennypacker, *General Washington's Spies*, 60, 209–10; Rose, *Washington's Spies*, 114, 120.

154. Daigler, *Spies*, 182; Rose, *Washington's Spies*, 114, 120–22.

155. Daigler, *Spies*, 182; Rose, *Washington's Spies*, 114, 120–22.

156. Rose, *Washington's Spies*, 122–23.

157. Ibid., 123–24.

158. Daigler, *Spies*, 182.

159. Rose, *Washington's Spies*, 106–7.

160. Ibid., 110.

161. Ibid.

162. Ibid., 108; George Washington, letter to James Jay, April 9, 1780, National Archives, Founders Online.

163. Rose, *Washington's Spies*, 108.

164. Pennypacker, *General Washington's Spies*, 52.

165. Ibid., 51–52; Allen, *George Washington*, 68–70.

166. Pennypacker, *General Washington's Spies*, 61.
167. Bellerjeau, interview, June 22, 2020.
168. Rose, *Washington's Spies*, 110.
169. Ibid., 88.
170. Daigler, *Spies*, 184; Rose, *Washington's Spies*, 132.
171. Bellerjeau, interviews.
172. Strong, "In Defense."
173. Kilmeade and Yaeger, *George Washington's Secret Six*, 93.
174. Bellerjeau, interview, April 19, 2020.
175. Tyler, interview, April 20, 2020.
176. Bellerjeau, interview.
177. Tyler, interview, April 20, 2020.
178. Pennypacker, *General Washington's Spies*, 246.
179. Luke and Venables, *Long Island*, 52–53.
180. Rose, *Washington's Spies*, 129.
181. Melton and Wallace, *Spy Sites, 6–7;* Rose, *Washington's Spies*, 151.
182. Kilmeade and Yaeger, *George Washington's Secret Six*, 84.
183. Pennypacker, *General Washington's Spies*, 13; *Rose, Washington's Spies*, 151.
184. Pennypacker, *General Washington's Spies*, 13; *Rose, Washington's Spies*, 151.
185. Kilmeade and Yaeger, *George Washington's Secret Six*, 106–7.
186. Ibid., 107–8.
187. Bellerjeau, interviews.
188. Ibid.
189. Kilmeade and Yaeger, *George Washington's Secret Six*, 106–7.
190. Bellerjeau, interviews.
191. Ibid.
192. Pennypacker, *General Washington's Spies*, 252.
193. Rose, *Washington's Spies*, 173.
194. Kilmeade and Yaeger, *George Washington's Secret Six*, xviii.
195. Ibid., 84.
196. Ibid., 93–94.
197. Ibid., 149.
198. Ibid., 178, 213.
199. *Daigler, Spies, 189.*
200. Tyler, interview, May 2, 2020.
201. Bellerjeau, interview, May 2, 2020.
202. Ibid.
203. "Hercules Mulligan (1740–1825)," Fenian Graves, http://feniangraves.net/Mulligan,%20H/Mulligan,%20%20H..htm; "Hercules Mulligan,"

American Battlefield Trust, https://www.battlefields.org/learn/biographies/hercules-mulligan; Rose, *Washington's Spies*, 225.

204. Rose, *Washington's Spies*, 225.

205. Ibid.

206. Ibid.

207. Pennypacker, *General Washington's Spies*, 252.

208. Rose, *Washington's Spies*, 226.

209. Daigler, *Spies*, 188; Bellerjeau, interview.

210. "Hercules Mulligan (1740–1825)," Fenian Graves; "Hercules Mulligan," American Battlefield Trust.

Chapter 6. The Culper Letters, 1778–1779

211. Bellerjeau, interviews.

212. Bellerjeau, interview, July 2, 2020.

213. Rose, *Washington's Spies*, 92.

214. Ibid.

215. Ibid.

216. Ibid.

217. Ibid.

218. Pennypacker, *General Washington's Spies*, 35.

219. Rose, *Washington's Spies*, 93.

220. Ibid., 95.

221. Pennypacker, *General Washington's Spies*, 37–38.

222. Ibid., 35.

223. Ibid., 36.

224. Ibid.

225. Ibid.

226. Rose, *Washington's Spies*, 95.

227. Ibid., 102.

228. Ibid.

229. Ibid., 102–3.

230. Ibid.

231. Ibid., 126.

232. Pennypacker, *General Washington's Spies*, 38.

233. Ibid., 38–39.

234. Ibid., 39.

235. Ibid., 40–41.

236. Ibid., 41.
237. Ibid., 41–43; Rose, *Washington's Spies*, 127–28.
238. Pennypacker, *General Washington's Spies*, 42.
239. Ibid., 43.
240. Rose, *Washington's Spies*, 128.
241. Ibid., 131.
242. Ibid., 129.
243. Ibid., 131.
244. Pennypacker, *General Washington's Spies*, 43.
245. Rose, *Washington's Spies*, 131.
246. Ibid., 111.
247. Ibid., 112.
248. Ibid.
249. Ibid.
250. Pennypacker, *General Washington's Spies*, 44–45; Tyler, interview, May 4, 2020; Rose, *Washington's Spies*, 132.
251. Rose, *Washington's Spies*, 165.
252. Ibid., 166.
253. Ibid., 166–67.
254. Ibid., 169–70.
255. Pennypacker, *General Washington's Spies*, 47–48.
256. Ibid., 51–52.
257. Rose, *Washington's Spies*, 170.
258. Pennypacker, *General Washington's Spies*, 252.
259. Ibid., 55.
260. Ibid., 57.
261. Ibid.
262. Rose, *Washington's Spies*, 172.
263. Pennypacker, *General Washington's Spies*, 58.
264. Ibid.
265. Rose, *Washington's Spies*, 176.
266. Pennypacker, *General Washington's Spies*, 62–63.
267. Rose, *Washington's Spies*, 173.
268. Ibid., 173–74.
269. Ibid., 178–79.
270. Pennypacker, *General Washington's Spies*, 49–50.
271. Ibid., 65.
272. Ibid., 66.
273. Ibid., 66–68.

274. Rose, *Washington's Spies*, 174.
275. Ibid., 174–75.
276. Pennypacker, *General Washington's Spies*, 69.
277. Ibid.
278. Ibid., 70–71.
279. Ibid., 71.
280. Rose, *Washington's Spies*, 180.
281. Ibid., 183.
282. Ibid., 183–84.
283. Pennypacker, *General Washington's Spies*, 72.

Chapter 7. The Culper Letters, 1780

284. Ibid., 72–73.
285. Ibid., 74.
286. Ibid.
287. Ibid., 75–77; Daigler, *Spies*, 185; Rose, *Washington's Spies*, 185–86.
288. Rose, *Washington's Spies*, 187.
289. Ibid.
290. Pennypacker, *General Washington's Spies*, 77–78.
291. Rose, *Washington's Spies*, 188.
292. Pennypacker, *General Washington's Spies*, 78.
293. Ibid., 79.
294. Ibid., 80.
295. Ibid., 81.
296. Ibid.
297. McBurney, "Culper Spy Ring"; Rose, *Washington's Spies*, 190.
298. Pennypacker, *General Washington's Spies*, 82.
299. Ibid., 43–44; Rose, *Washington's Spies*, 129–30.
300. Tyler, interview, May 14, 2020.
301. Rose, *Washington's Spies*, 130.
302. Bellerjeau, interview, May 13, 2020.
303. Pennypacker, *General Washington's Spies*, 82–84; Bellerjeau, interview, May 14, 2020; Rose, *Washington's Spies*, 190; McBurney, "Culper Spy Ring."
304. Pennypacker, *General Washington's Spies*, 82–84.
305. McBurney, "Culper Spy Ring."
306. Pennypacker, *General Washington's Spies*, 87.
307. Ibid.

308. Rose, *Washington's Spies*, 192–93.
309. Pennypacker, *General Washington's Spies*, 100.
310. Ibid., 88, 94.
311. Ibid., 89.
312. Ibid., 90–91.
313. Ibid., 92.
314. Ibid.
315. Pennypacker, *General Washington's Spies*, 96.
316. Ibid.
317. Rose, *Washington's Spies*, 213–14, 224.
318. Pennypacker, *General Washington's Spies*, 185.
319. Ibid.
320. Rose, *Washington's Spies*, 215.
321. Pennypacker, *General Washington's Spies*, 186–87.
322. Ibid., 187–88.
323. Ibid., 189.
324. Rose, *Washington's Spies*, 224, 226.
325. Pennypacker, *General Washington's Spies*, 191.

Chapter 8. The Culper Letters, 1781–1783

326. Rose, *Washington's Spies*, 251.
327. Ibid.
328. Ibid.
329. Pennypacker, *General Washington's Spies*, 198.
330. Rose, *Washington's Spies*, 252.
331. Pennypacker, *General Washington's Spies*, 200.
332. Ibid.
333. Ibid.
334. Charles River Editors, *Culper Ring*, 27; Rose, *Washington's Spies*, 256.
335. Rose, *Washington's Spies*, 256.
336. Pennypacker, *General Washington's Spies*, 201.
337. Rose, *Washington's Spies*, 255.
338. Ibid., 258.
339. Ibid., 258–59; Bellerjeau, interview, July 10, 2020.
340. Pennypacker, *General Washington's Spies*, 203–4.
341. Rose, *Washington's Spies*, 259.
342. Ibid.

343. Ibid., 259–60.
344. Charles River Editors, *Culper Ring*, 28–29.
345. Pennypacker, *General Washington's Spies*, 206–7; Charles River Editors, *Culper Ring*, 28–29.
346. Pennypacker, *General Washington's Spies*, 207.
347. Charles River Editors, *Culper Ring*, 29.
348. Ibid.
349. Rose, *Washington's Spies*, 261.
350. Pennypacker, *General Washington's Spies*, 207.
351. Ibid.
352. "Why a Pound Today Is Worth Only 0.7% of a Pound in 1783," CPI Inflation Calculator, https://www.in2013dollars.com/uk/inflation/1783.
353. Rose, *Washington's Spies*, 264–65.
354. Ibid., 265.
355. Welch, *General Washington's Commando*, 131.
356. Charles River Editors, *Culper Ring*, 30.
357. Ibid.
358. Rose, *Washington's Spies*, 266.
359. Tyler, interview, July 2, 2020.
360. Bellerjeau, interview, July 3, 2020.
361. Rose, *Washington's Spies*, 265.
362. Ibid., 266.
363. Charles River Editors, *Culper Ring*, 30–31.
364. Rose, *Washington's Spies*, 266.

Chapter 9. The End of the War

365. Tyler, interviews.
366. Ibid.
367. Luke and Venables, *Long Island*, 55–56.
368. Onderdonk, *Documents and Letters*, 253.
369. Luke and Venables, *Long Island*, 55–56; De Wan, "America Celebrates."
370. De Wan, "Washington's Says"; De Wan, "Dec. 4: LI's Liberation Day."
371. Rose, *Washington's Spies*, 267.
372. Bleyer, *Long Island*, 104; Tiedemann and Fingerhut, *Other New York*, 54–55; Rose, *Washington's Spies*, 268.
373. Luke and Venables, *Long Island*, 55–56.
374. Bleyer, *Long Island*, 104–5; De Wan, "Long Island."
375. De Wan, "Long Island's 7-Year Hitch," 128.

Chapter 10. Impact of the Intelligence

376. Pennypacker, *General Washington's Spies*, 31–32.
377. Ibid.
378. Ibid.
379. Pennypacker, *General Washington's Spies*, 200.
380. Charles River Editors, *Culper Ring*, 30.
381. Bleyer, "Inspired by the Story."
382. Daigler, *Spies*, 241.
383. Ibid., 191.
384. Rose, *Washington's Spies*, 266.
385. McBurney, "Culper Spy Ring."
386. Bellerjeau, interview.
387. Tyler, interview, May 13, 2020.
388. DeWan, "A Ruse."
389. Daigler, *Spies*, 191.
390. Ibid., 192–93.
391. Charles River Editors, *Culper Ring*, 37.

Chapter 11. After the Revolution

392. Pennypacker, *General Washington's Spies*, 208.
393. Ibid., 31.
394. De Wan, "Leading the Charge"; Charles River Editors, *Culper Ring*, 16, 32; Rose, *Washington's Spies*, 278.
395. Thompson, *History of Long Island*, 288.
396. Tyler, interview, April 19, 2020.
397. Charles River Editors, *Culper Ring*, 32; De Wan, "After Their Revolution," 138; Rose, *Washington's Spies*, 278.
398. Bellerjeau, interview, September 3, 2020.
399. Bellerjeau, interview, 2020.
400. Rose, *Washington's Spies*, 132.
401. De Wan, "Mystery of Agent 355," 139; Pennypacker, *General Washington's Spies*, 4, 103, 204, 232; Charles River Editors, *Culper Ring*, 32; Macy, "Robert Townsend Jr."; Bellerjeau, interview, April 19, 2020.
402. Robert Townsend Account Books, East Hampton Library, http://easthamptonlibrary.org/long-island-history/robert-townsend-account-books/robert-townsend-papers-project/; Pennypacker, *General Washington's*

Spies, 4, 103, 204; Charles River Editors, *Culper Ring*, 32; De Wan, "Passionate About."

403. Pennypacker, *General Washington's Spies*, 232.

404. Bellerjeau, interviews; Rose, *Washington's Spies*, 273.

405. Tyler, interviews.

406. Charles River Editors, *Culper Ring*, 32; De Wan, "After Their Revolution," 138; Rose, *Washington's Spies*, 273, 278.

407. Charles River Editors, *Culper Ring*, 32; De Wan, "After Their Revolution," 138; Stryker-Rodda, "George Washington," 17–18; Rose, *Washington's Spies*, 277; "Capt Austin Roe," Find a Grave, https://www.findagrave.com/memorial/47954832/austin-roe.

408. Charles River Editors, *Culper Ring*, 32; Tyler, interviews.

409. Charles River Editors, *Culper Ring*, 32; Richard F. Welch, interview, April 23, 2020.

Chapter 12. President Washington's 1790 Tour

410. *George Washington's Diary*.

411. De Wan, "An LI Victory," 158–60.

412. Ibid.; Lossing, *Diary of George Washington*, 125.

413. De Wan, "An LI Victory," 158–60; Lossing, *Diary of George Washington*, 125; Naylor, "George Washington," 54.

414. Naylor, "George Washington," 54.

415. Lossing, *Diary of George Washington*, 122.

416. Ibid., 123.

417. "President Washington in Copiague," Town of Babylon Historian, April 20, 2020, https://tobhistorian.blogspot.com/2020/04/president-washington-in-copiague.html.

418. Ibid.; information from Babylon Town historian Mary Cascone; Grasso, *George Washington's 1790*, 45.

419. De Wan, "An LI Victory," 158–60; *George Washington's Diary*.

420. Sayville Library, https://www.sayvillelibrary.org.

421. De Wan, "An LI Victory"; Stryker-Rodda, "George Washington," 17.

422. Lossing, *Diary of George Washington*, 124.

423. Stryker-Rodda, "George Washington," 17–18.

424. Tyler, interview.

425. De Wan, "An LI Victory"; Pennypacker, *General Washington's Spies*, 60.

426. Welch, interview, April 22, 2020.

427. Tyler, interview, April 24, 2020.

428. Welch, interview, April 24, 2020.

429. Lossing, *Diary of George Washington*, 125; "Old Huntington Green Incorporated"; Huntington town historian Robert Hughes, interview, September 4, 2020.

430. Tyler, interview.

431. Bellerjeau, interview; De Wan, "An LI Victory"; Hammond and Roosevelt, *Cove Neck*, 36–38.

432. John Hammond, interview, April 18, 2020.

433. Hammond and Roosevelt, *Cove Neck*, 37–38.

434. Bellerjeau, interview.

435. Bellerjeau, interview, April 23, 2020.

436. De Wan, "An LI Victory," 158–60; Grasso, *George Washington's 1790*, 71, 73; Roslyn Landmarks Society president Howard Kroplick, interview, April 23, 2020.

437. De Wan, "An LI Victory," 158–60.

438. Tyler, interview, April 18, 2020.

Chapter 13. *New York State's George Washington Spy Trail*

439. Gloria Rocchio, interview, July 23, 2020.

440. Olson, "Washington Spy Trail."

441. Rocchio, interview, July 23, 2020.

Chapter 14. *Spy Ring Sites Today*

442. Information from Beverly Tyler.

443. Ibid.

444. Ibid.

445. Ibid.

446. Information from Beverly Tyler and the Long Island Museum.

447. Tyler, interview, July 19, 2020.

448. William L. Clements Library, University of Michigan, Clinton Papers, Volume 134:26.

449. Three Village Historical Society, https://www.tvhs.org/visit.

450. Raynham Hall Museum, https://raynhamhallmuseum.org; Bellerjeau, interview, July 7, 2020.

Chapter 15. Other Sites with Ties to the Revolution

451. Information from Babylon town historian Mary Cascone.

452. Ibid.

453. Ibid; "President Washington in Copiague."

454. Ward Melville Heritage Organization and Beverly Tyler interviews.

455. Tyler, interviews.

456. Maryanne Douglas, interview, 2020.

457. Davis Town Meeting House Society, http://www.davistownmeetinghouse. org; Zimmermann, "Burning of the Hay," 2.

458. Davis Town Meeting House Society.

459. Ibid.; Zimmermann, "Burning of the Hay," 2; Rose, *Washington's Spies*, 238.

460. Tallmadge, *Memoir*, 42.

461. Bleyer, *Long Island*, 99–101; Davis Town Meeting House Society; Zimmermann, "Burning of the Hay," 2; Tallmadge, *Memoir*, 42.

462. De Wan, "Hero's Last Words"; "Gen Nathaniel Woodhull," Find a Grave, https://www.findagrave.com/memorial/21423702/nathaniel-woodhull; Barrios, "Tombstone of Revolutionary War Hero."

463. Tyler, interviews; Luke and Venables, *Long Island*, 47–48.

464. Tyler, interview.

465. Ibid.

466. Information from Preservation Long Island.

467. Tyler, interview, 2020.

468. Information from Ward Melville Heritage Organization and Beverly Tyler.

469. Information from Beverly Tyler.

470. Ibid.

471. *General William Floy*d; "William Floyd Estate," NPS, https://www.nps. gov/fiis/planyourvisit/williamfloydestate.htm.

472. Bleyer, *Long Island*, 103–4.

473. Information from Southampton town historian Julie Greene.

474. Asbury, "Hempstead Town"; information from the Town of Hempstead.

475. Morris, "Hewlett House."

476. Geri Barbash, of One-in-Nine, interviews.

477. "Col Richard Hewlett," Find a Grave, https://www.findagrave. com/memorial/75375336/richard-hewlett; "Hewlett House," Town of Hempstead, https://hempsteadny.gov/landmarks-preservation/hewlett-house; "Lieutenant Colonel Richard Hewlett: The Loyal-est Loyalist," Turn to a Historian, https://spycurious.wordpress.com/2015/04/27/lieutenant-colonel-richard-hewlett-the-loyal-est-loyalist.

478. Rock Hall Museum—Town of Hempstead, https://www.friendsofrockhall.org/rock-hall.

479. St. George's Episcopal Church, https://stgeorges-hempstead.org.

480. Hanc, "Hidden History"; information from Huntington town historian Robert Hughes.

481. De Wan, "Nathan Hale Monument," 135.

482. Hughes, "Nathan Hale Memorials."

483. Bleyer, *Long Island*, 104.

484. Order of the Ancient and Honorable Huntington Militia, www.huntingtonmilitia.com.

485. Information from Howard Kroplick; Historic Marker Monfort Cemetery, William G. Pomeroy Foundation, https://www.wgpfoundation.org/historic-markers/monfort-cemetery.

486. Sands-Willets House, Cow Neck Peninsula Historical Society, https://www.cowneck.org/sands-willets-house.

487. "Histoy," Manhasset Meeting, https://nyym.org/manhasset/history.html.

488. Bleyer, *Long Island*, 101.

489. Information from Southampton town historian Julie Greene.

490. Ibid.

491. Ibid.

492. Ibid.

493. Ibid.

494. Ibid.

495. Cutchogue–New Suffolk Historial Council, https://www.cutchoguenewsuffolkhistory.org; Old House, The (Cutchogue)," National Historic Landmarks Programs, https://web.archive.org/web/20110606002852/http://tps.cr.nps.gov/nhl/detail.cfm?ResourceId=415&ResourceType=Building.

BIBLIOGRAPHY

Allen, Thomas B. *George Washington, Spymaster: How the Americans Outspied the British and Won the Revolutionary War.* Washington, D.C.: National Geographic Society, 2004.

Anderson, Virginia DeJohn. *The Martyr and the Traitor.* New York: Oxford University Press, 2007.

Asbury, John. "Hempstead Town Marks First Bloodshed on LI during Revolutionary War." *Newsday*, July 2, 2019. https://www.newsday.com/long-island/nassau/revolutionary-war-hempstead-1.33091794.

Barrios, Jennifer. "Tombstone of Revolutionary War Hero Repaired in Mastic Cemetery." *Newsday*, May 26, 2014. https://www.newsday.com/long-island/history/tombstone-of-revolutionary-war-hero-repaired-in-mastic-cemetery-1.81803172014.

Bleyer, Bill. "Hot on George Washington's Trail: 50-Mile Route Marks Visit of First President." *Newsday*, February 16, 1996.

———. "Inspired by the Story of LI's Spies." *Newsday*, January 20, 2014.

———. *Long Island and the Sea: A Maritime History.* Charleston, SC: The History Press, 2019.

———. "Taking Liberties in a Series about Fighting for Liberty." *Newsday*, April 2, 2014.

Charles River Editors. *The Culper Ring: The History and Legacy of the Revolutionary War's Most Famous Spy Ring.* Lexington, KY: 2017.

Daigler, Kenneth A. *Spies, Patriots, and Traitors: American Intelligence in the Revolutionary War.* Washington, D.C.: Georgetown University Press, 2014.

De Wan, George. "After Their Revolution Was Won." In *Long Island: Our Story*, 138. Melville, NY: Newsday, 1998.

———. "Alive to Fight Another Day." In *Long Island: Our Story*, 124.

———. "America Celebrates Its New Freedom." In *Long Island: Our Story*, 153.

———. "An LI Victory Tour." In *Long Island: Our Story*, 158–60.

———. "Days of Defeat." In *Long Island: Our Story*, 121.

———. "Dec. 4: LI's Liberation Day." In *Long Island: Our Story*, 152.

———. "Hale's Travels." In *Long Island: Our Story*, 135.

———. "A Hero's Last Words." In *Long Island: Our Story*, 125.

———. "Leading the Charge." In *Long Island: Our Story*, 141.

———. "A Long Island Exodus." In *Long Island: Our Story*, 152.

———. "Long Island's 7-Year Hitch." In *Long Island: Our Story*, 126–28.

———. "The Mystery of Agent 355." In *Long Island: Our Story*, 139.

———. "Nathan Hale: Failed Spy, Superb Patriot." In *Long Island: Our Story*, 134–35.

———. "Nathan Hale Monument." In *Long Island: Our Story*, 135.

———. "Passionate About the Past." In *Long Island: Our Story*, 140.

———. "The Patriots' First Big Test." In *Long Island: Our Story*, 120.

———. "A Ruse Saves the French Fleet." In *Long Island: Our Story*, 136.

———. "Risking His Life for His Horse." In *Long Island: Our Story*, 141.

———. "They Signed for Independence." In *Long Island: Our Story*, 150.

———. "Washington Says Thanks." In *Long Island: Our Story*, 154.

Flanagan, James W. "Decisive Victory Let Go." *Great Battles*, September 1993.

Flint, Martha B. *Long Island Before the Revolution: A Continental Story*. Port Washington, NY: Ira J. Friedman, 1967.

Ford, Corey. *A Peculiar Service*. Boston: Little, Brown & Company, 1986.

Gallagher, John J. *The Battle of Brooklyn, 1776*. Edison, NJ: Castle Books, 1995.

General William Floyd, Signer of the Declaration of Independence. Patchogue, NY: Fire Island National Seashore, n.d.

George Washington's Diary Entries Describing His 1790 Tour of Long Island. Bay Shore, NY: Sagtikos Manor Historical Society, 2017.

Grasso, Joanne S. *The American Revolution on Long Island*. Charleston, SC: The History Press, 2016.

———. *George Washington's 1790 Grand Tour of Long Island*. Charleston, SC: The History Press, 2016.

Griffin, David. *Lost British Forts of Long Island*. Charleston, SC: The History Press, 2017.

Hammond, John E., and Elizabeth E. Roosevelt. *Cove Neck: Oyster Bay's Historic Enclave*. Charleston, SC: The History Press, 2019.

Hanc, John. "Hidden History." *Newsday*, January 27, 2019.

————. "A Nest of Spies." *New York Times*. March 15, 2019, F12.

Hughes, Robert C. "Nathan Hale Memorials." Huntington History, June 6, 2013. https://huntingtonhistory.com/2013/06/06/nathan-hale-memorials-2/.

Johnson, Henry Phelps. *The Campaign of 1776 Around New York and Brooklyn*. Brooklyn, NY: Brooklyn Historical Society, 1878 and 1971.

Kilmeade, Brian, and Don Yaeger. *George Washington's Secret Six: The Spy Ring That Saved the American Revolution*. New York: Sentinel, 2013.

Lossing, Benson J. *The Diary of George Washington from 1789–1791: Embracing the Opening of the First Congress and His Tours through New England, Long Island, and the Southern States Together with His Journal of a Tour of the Ohio in 1753*. Richmond, VA: Press of the Historical Society, 1861.

Lowenthal, Larry. *William Floyd—Long Island Patriot*. Cold Spring Harbor, NY: Society for the Preservation of Long Island Antiquities, 2013.

Luke, Myron H., and Robert W. Venables. *Long Island in the American Revolution*. Albany: New York State American Revolution Bicentennial Commission, 1976.

Macy, Harry, Jr. "Robert Townsend, Jr. of New York City." *New York Genealogical and Biographical Record* 126 (January 1995): 25–34.

Manhoffer, Barbara. *Eyewitness 1776*. Hicksville, NY: Long Island Lighting Company, 1982.

Marks, Nehemiah. Letter to British Major General Oliver DeLancey, December 21, 1780. William L. Clements Library, University of Michigan, Clinton Papers. Vol. 134:26.

McBurney, Christian M. "The Culper Spy Ring Was Not the First to Warn the French at Newport." *Journal of the America Revolution*, December 9, 2014. https://allthingsliberty.com/2014/12/the-culper-spy-ring-was-not-the-first-to-warn-the-french-at-newport.

————. *Spies in Revolutionary Rhode Island*. Charleston, SC: History Press, 2014.

Melton, H. Keith, and Robert Wallace. *Spy Sites of New York City: A Guide to the Region's Secret History*. Washington, D.C.: Georgetown University Press, 2020.

Meltzer, Brad, and Josh Mensch. *The First Conspiracy: The Secret Plot to Kill George Washington*. New York: Flatiron Books, 2018.

Morris, Joel J. "The Hewlett House 1749–1984: A Family History." *Nassau County Historical Society Journal* 51 (1996): 12–18.

Naylor, Natalie A., ed. "George Washington, 'Tour of Long Island, 1790.'" In *Journeys on Old Long Island: Travelers' Accounts, Contemporary Descriptions, and Residents' Reminisiscences, 1744–1893*, 53–62. Interlaken, NY: Empire State Books/Hofstra University, 2002.

———. *Women in Long Island's Past: A History of Eminent Ladies and Everyday Lives.* Charleston, SC: The History Press, 2012.

Old Huntington Green Incorporated: A History of Preservation. Town of Huntington, Historian's Office, n.d.

Olson, David. "Washington Spy Trail, Along Rte. 25A, Could Get Historic Status." Newsday.com. July 29, 2017.

Onderdonk, Henry, Jr. *Documents and Letters Intended to Illustrate the Revolutionary Incidents of Queens County.* Port Washington, NY: Kennikat Press, 1970.

Pennypacker, Morton. *General Washington's Spies on Long Island and in New York.* Brooklyn: Long Island Historical Society, 1939.

Phelps, M. William. *Nathan Hale.* New York: Thomas Dunne Books, 2008.

Rose, Alexander. *Washington's Spies: The Story of America's First Spy Ring.* New York: Bantam Books. 2006.

Schecter, Barnet. *The Battle for New York: The City at the Heart of the American Revolution.* New York: Walker & Company, 2002.

Simcoe, John Graves. *A Journal of the Operations of the Queen's Rangers from the End of 1777 Until the Conclusion of the Revolutionary War.* Exeter, 1787, reprinted in New York in 1844.

Simon, Darran. "Visitors Tour Restored Historic Farmhouse and Tavern where Jefferson and Madison Lodged." Newsday.com. July 4, 2015.

Staudt, John. "From Wretchedness to Independence: Suffolk County in the American Revolution." *Long Island Historical Journal* 20 (Fall 2007/Spring 2008): 135.

———. "A State of Wretchedness: A Social History of Suffolk County, New York in the American Revolution." PhD diss., George Washington University, 2005.

Strong, Kate Wheeler. "In Defense of Nancy's Clothesline." *True Tales from the Early Days of Long Island.* (Reprinted from the Long Island Forum, Amityville, NY), 1969.

Stryker-Rodda, Kenn. "George Washington on Long Island." *Journal of Long Island History* 1 (1961): 17.

Tallmadge, Benjamin. *Memoir of Colonel Tallmadge.* New York: Sons of the Revolution, 1904.

Thompson, Benjamin F. *History of Long Island: From Its Discovery and Settlement to the Present Time.* New York: E. French, 1839.

Tiedemann, Joseph S., and Eugene R. Fingerhut. *The Other New York: The American Revolution beyond New York City, 1763–1787.* Albany: State University of New York Press, 2005.

Welch, Richard F. *General Washington's Commando: Benjamin Tallmadge in the Revolutionary War*. Jefferson, NC: McFarland & Co. Inc., 2014.

Wood, Silas. *A Sketch of the First Settlement of the Several Towns on Long Island*. Brooklyn, NY: Alden Spooner, 1828.

Zimmermann, Mildred. "The Burning of the Hay in Coram." *Davis Town Meeting House Society Newsletter* 3, no. 4 (Fall 2018): 2.

INDEX

T

W

Y

ABOUT THE AUTHOR

Photo by Audrey C. Tiernan, copyright 2016.

Bill Bleyer was a prize-winning staff writer for *Newsday*, the Long Island daily newspaper, for thirty-three years before retiring in 2014 to write books and freelance for the newspaper and magazines.

He is coauthor, with Harrison Hunt, of *Long Island and the Civil War* (The History Press, 2015). He is the author of *Sagamore Hill: Theodore Roosevelt's Summer White House* (The History Press, 2016), *Fire Island Lighthouse: Long Island's Welcoming Beacon* (The History Press, 2017) and *Long Island and the Sea: A Maritime History* (The History Press, 2019).

He contributed a chapter to the anthology *Harbor Voices: New York Harbor Tugs, Ferries, People, Places & More*, published in 2008. And he was a contributor and editor of the Bayville history book published by Arcadia in 2009.

The Long Island native has written extensively about history for newspapers and magazines. In 1997–98, he was one of four *Newsday* staff writers assigned full time to "Long Island: Our Story," a year-long daily history of Long Island that resulted in three books and filled hundreds of pages in the newspaper.

His work has been published in *Civil War News*, *America's Civil War*, *Naval History*, *Sea History*, *Lighthouse Digest* and numerous other magazines and in the *New York Times*, *Chicago Sun-Times*, *Toronto Star* and other newspapers.

Prior to joining *Newsday*, Bleyer worked for six years at the *Courier-News* in Bridgewater, New Jersey, as an editor and reporter. He began his career as editor of the *Oyster Bay Guardian* for a year.

Bleyer graduated Phi Beta Kappa with highest honors in economics from Hofstra University, where he has been an adjunct professor teaching journalism and economics. He has also been an adjunct professor teaching Long Island maritime history at Webb Institute, the naval architecture college in Glen Cove, New York. He earned a master's degree in urban studies at Queens College of the City University of New York.

He lives in Bayville, Long Island.